**Regional
Dimensions of
Industrial Policy**

Regional Dimensions of Industrial Policy

Edited by
Michael E. Bell
U.S. Department of Commerce
Paul S. Lande
Data Resources, Inc.

LexingtonBooks
D.C. Heath and Company
Lexington, Massachusetts
Toronto

Library of Congress Cataloging in Publication Data
Main entry under title:

Regional dimensions of industrial policy.

Includes index.
1. United States—Economic policy—1971-   —Addresses, essays,
lectures. 2. Industry and state—United States—Addresses, essays, lectures.
3. Regional planning—United States—Addresses, essays, lectures. I. Bell,
Michael E. II. Lande, Paul S.
HC106.7.R345   338.973   80-8994
ISBN 0-669-04491-1   AACR2

Published simultaneously in Canada

Printed in the United States of America

International Standard Book Number: 0-669-04491-1

Library of Congress Catalog Card Number: 80-8994

*To our families—Vianne, Derek, and
Aaron Bell and Nancy, Dana, and
Joel Lande*

Contents

Acknowledgments

We would like to express our appreciation to the Department of Commerce for providing an environment that encourages the interchange and development of new ideas and perspectives. Specifically, we would like to thank Lucy Falcone, Jeff Mayer, Victor Hausner, and Leo Penne of the Department of Commerce for their support and encouragement. Also, in crystalizing our thoughts and developing the idea for this book, we benefited greatly from discussions with Robert D. Ebel, John King, Hugh Knox, Ronald Kramer, Catherine Kweit, Jean McFarland, Peter Morici, Nonna Noto, Alan Olson, Andrew Reamer, Donald Reeb, and Morton Schnabel.

Regional
Dimensions of
Industrial Policy

1

Industrial and Regional Development Policies: An Overview

Michael E. Bell and
Paul S. Lande

In comparison to historical standards, the U.S. economy performed very poorly during the 1970s. Although the causes of this poor performance are many, supply-side factors have been unusually important. In particular, the poor performances of major sectors, such as the steel and auto industries, have led many policymakers to conclude that federal industrial policies may be necessary as a means of addressing certain supply-side problems to improve the performance of the economy in the 1980s. The purpose of this book is to present the principal components of industrial policies and to derive the implications of these policies for regional economies.

After the essential elements of traditional macroeconomic goals and policies are outlined and the recent performance of the U.S. Economy is reviewed, this chapter will provide a brief summary of the characteristics of what is generally considered to be industrial policy and discuss some reasons such a policy has been advocated by many for the United States at this time. The summary of characteristics and the rationale establish a foundation for further analysis of the importance of the linkage between national, industrial, and regional economic problems. It is this critical linkage which has been neglected during the recent industrial policy debate to the detriment of both industrial and regional development policies.

Traditional View and Performance of the National Economy

Since the Full Employment Act of 1946, the federal government has accepted an increasing responsibility for managing the national economy. In carrying out that responsibility, the federal government has relied on the traditional macroeconomic tools that have been extended and refined over twenty-five years of experience. These policy levers are intended to affect the magnitude of a variety of aggregate economic variables—for example, prices, unemployment rates, aggregate investment—by influencing the level of overall spending, that is, aggregate demand. Traditional policy tools used to achieve macroeconomic goals include public expenditures, taxes, and the control of credit.

Traditional monetary and fiscal policies, however, have had little success in ameliorating the problems that plagued the U.S. economy throughout the 1970s.

1

As indicated in table 1-1, the aberrant behavior of the economy in the 1970s was characterized by high rates of unemployment, high rates of inflation, lagging real growth, and falling productivity contributing to the rising cost of production and the declining competitiveness of U.S. producers in international markets.

It is generally asserted that the poor performance of the U.S. economy during the 1970s was a consequence of staggering increases in energy costs, low rates of investment, excessive government regulations, and substantial federal budget deficits exacerbated by unfair foreign competition from subsidized producers and the growing economic interdependence of western countries. Consequently, the U.S. economy confronts declining productivity, shortages of factor inputs, aging capital stock, and an increasing reliance on imports, particularly nonrenewable resources. Thus, there seems to be a growing consensus that a new industrial policy initiative which focuses on supply-side problems is needed to complement the traditional demand-oriented policies, if the problems that plagued the economy during most of the 1970s are to be eradicated in the 1980s.

Characteristics of and Rationale for an Industrial Policy

Unfortunately, the concept of an explicit industrial policy is unfamiliar to policymakers in the United States and generally lacks specific substantive content. In fact, a recent report by the Trilateral Commission highlights the diversity of industrial policies actually in operation in European and other countries and concludes that it is difficult to think in terms of *an* industrial policy.[1] The notion of an industrial policy must be adapted to the unique problems and circumstances in each country. This section provides a synthesis of the generally accepted broad characteristics of an industrial policy and discusses the arguments presented by many for why such a new policy initiative might be appropriate in the United States at this time.

Industrial policy, itself, can be viewed broadly or narrowly. In the broadest sense, it would include all government programs and practices that significantly affect industrial performance. By intent or by default, federal taxing, spending, and regulating activities constitute an industrial policy, albeit unintended for the most part. The choice is not whether government actions should affect the competitive position of various industries; that is already the case. The question is whether the effort should be undertaken in a focused, conscious, comprehensive, and systematic manner.

If the answer is yes, than a more narrow and operational definition of an industrial policy would be limited to those government programs and practices

Table 1-1
U.S. Economic Indicators for the Postwar Period

Period	Average Unemployment Rate	Annual Average Inflation Rate	Annual Average Rate of Growth of Real GNP	Annual Average Rate of Growth of Real Output[a] Per Hour	Imports as a Percent of GNP	Exports as a Percent of GNP
1950–1959	4.5	2.3	3.9	3.2	3.0	3.8
1960–1969	4.7	2.5	4.1	3.0	3.3	3.9
1970–1979	6.2	7.4	3.0	1.4	6.9	6.2
1980	7.2	13.4	-0.6	-0.8	11.9	12.1

Source: Bureau of Labor Statistics: U.S. Department of Labor. Washington, D.C. Bureau of Economic Analysis: U.S. Department of Commerce. Washington, D.C.

[a]Growth of real Gross Domestic Product (GDP) in the private-business sector.

whose explicit purpose is to promote domestic and/or international competitiveness of individual firms or industries. The goals, objectives, and means of implementation affect an industrial policy, which may be:[2]

> Defensive—protecting the existing level of employment and production of a particular industry from all threats, whether they are the result of fair or unfair competition from abroad, unpredictable events at home, or changing comparative advantages. An example would be quotas on the importation of automobiles or electronics from Japan.

> Stabilizing—providing for an orderly adjustment to excess industrial capacity by partially protecting the home market so that production and employment will be stabilized. Full adjustment is thus delayed but not prevented. An example is the trigger-price mechanism used by the United States to ensure that imports of steel do not fall below a minimum price.

> Positive—providing assistance to facilitate the flow of resources to more viable uses, including the replacement of declining or inefficient activities with new high-technology activities that will strengthen the economy. An example is tax incentives for research and development or new investment by growing and profitable firms.

In any of these cases, it is generally agreed that the policies should work *with* market forces in order to increase the long-term improvement of the efficiency and productivity of the economy. This is most difficult to achieve in the case of defensive industrial policies which usually involve older, capital-intensive industries. Ordinarily, mere protection of an industry from competition would not be in the long-term interest of the economy and is a policy that tends to fail. The purpose of a federal industrial policy would be to assist natural market forces by overcoming barriers to adjustment and facilitating the movement of resources to their most productive use.

The declining health of several major industries in this country is well known and publicized. However, the substance of a supply-side response and the rationale for a new major industrial policy initiative are not well developed. It is appropriate, therefore, to reflect on the general rationale for an industrial policy.

Generally, there is no explicit discussion of the qualitative differences between traditional macroeconomic policies—taxes, expenditures, monetary policy—and an industrial policy designed to address new problems that have come to popularly represent incentives to stimulate private investment. In fact, some have argued that the problems and solutions being considered now are the same as those discussed during the 1950s and 1960s and are only being discussed under the new rubric of supply-side or industrial policy. However, the current policy emphasis on supply-side solutions to recent economic problems implicitly assumes that traditional demand-oriented policies are no longer adequate to meet the challenges of the 1980s. This assumption may seem reasonable if it can be shown that:

structural changes in the U.S. economy during the 1970s reduced the efficacy of traditional demand-oriented policies in addressing the problems of inflation and unemployment;

recent government policies tend to impede the flow of resources between competing uses in response to changing economic signals; or

new problems confront the U.S. economy for which demand-oriented policies are inappropriate and ineffectual.

It is difficult, without a comprehensive framework of analysis, to actually test these various hypotheses and assess the relative importance of these or other factors in contributing to current economic problems. However, it is likely that all of these factors have contributed to current economic problems to some extent.

Structural Changes

Substantial increases in energy costs have caused some structural changes to occur. Other developments during the 1970s also indicate that the 1980s will be a period of substantial structural adjustment. For example, potentially severe structural adjustment problems may result not only from shifts away from the production and consumption of energy-intensive goods, but also from:

the increased importance of exporting industries and the increased competition facing import-competing industries;

the increased international competition for factor inputs, particularly non-renewable resources. For example, the United States is heavily dependent on foreign countries for the importation of bauxite, chromium, cobalt, manganese, nickel, platinum, tin, tungsten, and zinc and faces decreasing domestic production of a number of other critical metals including copper, iron, lead, potassium, silver, and sulfur;

demographic factors which will influence the demand for a variety of durable and nondurable goods as well as the supply of labor;

the increase in two-worker families which may inhibit job mobility and geographic relocation;

changes in relative prices for factor inputs which in the 1970s caused labor to be relatively more attractive than capital; and the effect of inflationary expectations on the spending-and-savings decisions of corporations and individuals.

It appears, at least on the surface, that traditional macroeconomic policies may not address adequately some of the new adjustment problems confronting the economy during the 1980s.

Government Policies

A number of government policies enacted over the last decade designed to ameliorate the effects of a stagnant or declining economy and to meet other social objectives may also reduce the efficacy of traditional demand-oriented policies. For example, structural change may be impeded by:

the growth of a variety of safety-net measures designed to protect particular sectors or groups from the consequences of economic change, for example, indexing social security and other transfer-payment programs to eliminate the impact of inflation on the recipients or providing loan guarantees for Chrysler, Lockheed, synfuel firms, and other large corporations; and

social regulations that increase the uncertainty of the expected rate of return on investment, for example, environmental and job safety regulations which generally result in capital-intensive investments but which are subject to frequent challenge, redefinition, and/or reform.

New Problems

As a direct result of the dynamic nature of the market economy, new problems will arise as economic actors adjust to government intervention, changing comparative advantages, and other market forces. These new problems may or may not be adequately addressed by traditional macroeconomic policies. For example, Klien, who popularized the concern with supply-side issues, argued that a whole new set of economic issues will be raised in the future. These new issues include the "development of new, greater energy supplies, protection of the environment, controlling the exhaustion of resources, enhancing agricultural supplies, balancing population development, and others of like nature. . . . Juggling public budgets, setting tax rates and giving a tone to money market conditions are not going to deal effectively with this new class of problems."[3]

Regardless of the relative importance of any of these or other developments in contributing to current economic problems, the efficacy of traditional demand-oriented macroeconomic policies to meet these challenges has been seriously questioned. Therefore, consideration of a new industrial policy initiative may be timely for a variety of reasons, including:

current ad hoc industrial policies, which are now implemented in a piece-meal fashion and could potentially work at cross purposes, may not be cost effective and should be reviewed in light of these new concerns;

the frictions of adjustment that exist even in a well-functioning market system may, in the current political and economic environment, actually hinder adjustment and promote inefficiencies associated with defensive industrial policies; and

other countries, with which we compete in world markets, have established industrial policies that could have adverse effects on domestic industries in the United States.

Current Ad Hoc Policies

As the concern with facilitating structural adjustment to improve economic efficiency becomes a major issue in the 1980s, it will become increasingly necessary to review and analyze current ad hoc federal industrial policies. For example, the U.S. Department of Housing and Urban Development provided $52.5 billion in new loan guarantees in fiscal year (FY) 1979 (over half of all new federal loan guarantees), with nearly 90 percent of these guarantees being dispensed through the Federal Housing Administration (FHA) and the Government National Mortgage Association (GNMA) programs designed to stimulate the housing industry. In addition, in FY 1979, the U.S. Department of Agriculture provided nearly $21 billion in direct loans to farmers to help finance the planting, cultivation, and marketing of a variety of agricultural products. Also, in FY 1979, the general investment tax credit provided nearly $14 billion of tax relief to profitable capital-intensive industries (like steel) for new plants and equipment.

Operating in isolation, these myopic ad hoc policies may generate other adjustment problems and/or frustrate the efforts of other federal agencies to pursue their individual program objectives. Government tax and expenditure decisions result in differential impacts on various groups of economic actors, often resulting in other government programs designed to aid particular industries—sometimes on a massive scale. For example, programs designed to make reasonably priced housing available to all citizens respond to a laudable social objective. However, to the extent that these programs encourage the suburbanization of the population, they create other social problems in urban areas. Similarly, price-support programs designed to remove some of the uncertainty in farmer's planting and investment decisions contribute to inflationary pressures, thereby increasing the cost of indexed federal assistance programs. Unfortunately, the United States does not have any institutional means of identifying—much less resolving—conflicts between existing ad hoc industrial policy programs. This is one potential area of benefit from an explicit industrial policy.

Frictions of Adjustment

A dynamic market system, through the use of prices, is supposed to insure that all resources tend to attain their highest and best uses over time. In this manner, resources are efficiently allocated. However, because of a variety of market failures, these theoretical results are not easily attained. Thus, one might argue that government's role in economic development should be to identify, define, and correct these market failures so that the system works more efficiently. Some of the important market failures include, but are not limited to:

imperfect information about costs and benefits of competing investment and consumption opportunities, job availability, and so on;

externalities that prevent prices from accurately reflecting true benefits and costs;

transaction costs that are large fixed costs and prohibit individuals and/or firms from making decisions at the margin; and

natural monopolies that drive a wedge between prices and costs.

The case for an industrial policy, whether general or specific, rests essentially on the contribution it could make to improving social welfare by removing barriers to adjustment and increasing economic efficiency. However, in a period of relative economic stagnation, such as the United States experienced during the 1970s, political pressures tend to cause ad hoc industrial policies to protect and preserve existing jobs rather than stimulate the economy in general (or in selected nonassisted sectors) and encourage the development of new permanent private-sector jobs. These ad hoc defensive measures, which represent short-term politically expedient solutions, may simply divert profits, capital, and managerial skill from more- to less-dynamic sectors of the economy and ultimately may result in less investment, lower productivity, larger government subsidies and taxes, and more inflation.

Other Countries and Their Industrial Policies

As indicated in table 1-1, imports and exports are becoming much more important to the U.S. economy. In part, this reflects the results of efforts during the 1970s to enhance international trade, for example, the realignment of international currencies, multilateral trade negotiations, and so on, as well as to change comparative advantages. In an effort to enhance their international competitive position, a number of nations have responded by increasing their assistance to industries hurt by international competition (France's redundant labor program) or industries competing for new international markets. Therefore, it could be argued that in order to successfully compete in world markets in the 1980s, the United States should seriously consider program initiatives that would act as countervailing powers to similar foreign industrial policies which might give foreign firms an artificial competitive advantage.

Regional Dimension of Macroeconomic and Industrial Policies

An industrial policy may be necessary to complement traditional demand-oriented macroeconomic policies and resolve the problems that plagued the U.S. economy in the 1970s. However, for the most part, industrial policy has been discussed without reference to the geographic distribution of economic activity. Thus, this section of the chapter discusses the regional dimension of the national economy and develops some of the implications for designing a comprehensive industrial policy.

Macroeconomic concepts are devoid of any spatial content. So that a spatial dimension can be inserted into national economic discussions, a regional economic perspective must be developed. For many policy purposes, then, it may be useful to regard most national economic variables as being merely the sum total of regional variables measuring the disparate levels of regional activity. This recognition has led to the formulation of a new generation of regional econometric models which are characterized as being bottom-up models in contrast to the traditional top-down models which merely take national totals and allocate them to each region rather than looking initially at the level of activity at the regional level in order to generate national totals.

The impetus for the formulation of subnational economic development policies and programs has traditionally derived from the existence of significant disparities in economic well-being among regions and/or the potential for contributing to national economic growth. The relative level of economic well-being and performance of any given local or regional economy and disparities among regions are ordinarily measured by several economic indicators of the level of income of the residents, the rate of growth of income, the unemployment rate and number of unemployed, the stability of employment, and rate of growth of employment. The performance of these indicators is dependent on the underlying structure of the regional economy, including such productive factors as the educational level of the labor force, the size of the labor force, the age and type of capital, the endowment of natural resources, the public infrastructure, and the industrial structure of the regional economy.

The selected regional economic indicators shown in table 1-2 illustrate the kinds of disparities that have led to remedial government actions. Specifically:

annual per capita income varied by $2,400 from the high to low region in 1978;

the unemployment rate in the same year differed by more than a factor of two among regions; and

employment growth between 1970 and 1978 was as low as 5 percent of the national growth in one region and as high as 262 percent in another.

These statistical measures indicate substantial variation among regions; however, the actual policy implications may not be as clear. For example, Alonso has argued:

that too often we assume that decline means that times are getting worse when in fact they may be getting better. . . . To summarize, the demographically defined problems of size, growth, or decline are not problems in themselves. They are statistical descriptions, and as such neutral. There may be, sometimes or always, grave problems associated with them, and balanced growth policies should address these. But it is misleading to formulate policies as if we were after particular population distributions and growth rates for their own sake. Balanced growth must refer to socially desired conditions for real people.[4]

In designing a regional policy, one must remember there are a variety of economic factors that interact to determine the relative desirability of any specific region for any individual firm. Important economic factors that vary across regions, but interact to uniquely determine the region's comparative advantage and resulting sectoral composition include:

the quality and quantity of the available public and private capital stock;

the characteristics of the local labor market, including the demand for labor, labor-force participation rates, wage rates, and productivity;

the level and composition of investments in housing, and plant and equipment in industries serving local markets;

the sectoral composition of the regional economy which influences what types of industries would be attracted to the area;

the differential impact of federal regulations, especially environmental regulations;

the area's endowment of natural resources; and

the markets that have developed in response to both regional and national requirements.

Table 1-2
Selected Regional Economic Indicators

Region	Per Capita Income 1978	Percent of U.S. Per Capita Income 1978 U.S. = 100	Per Capita Income Growth 1970–1978 U.S. = 100	Unemployment Rate 1978	Percent of Employment in Manufacturing 1978	Employment Growth 1970–1978 U.S. = 100
New England	$7,967	102	87	5.8%	23.3%	69
Mid-Atlantic	8,206	105	86	7.3	25.1	5
East North Central	8,167	105	101	5.9	30.2	69
West North Central	7,632	98	108	3.7	20.8	114
South Atlantic	7,260	93	103	5.7	21.9	140
East South Central	6,326	81	115	6.0	27.8	155
West South Central	7,259	93	118	5.2	18.4	196
Mountain	7,443	95	109	4.9	12.4	262
Pacific	8,730	112	101	7.7	19.6	164
United States	7,810	100	100	6.0	24.9	100

Source: Bureau of Economic Analysis, U.S. Department of Commerce, Washington, D.C. Bureau of Labor Statistics, U.S. Department of Labor, Washington, D.C.

Regional comparative advantages are dynamic and change through time as a result of:

changing demands at the local, national, and international level;

changes in relative prices that affect factor costs; and

changes in technology that make certain production processes obsolete in favor of other production processes that may combine factor inputs in different proportions and therefore be more suited to alternative regional locations.

In this dynamic context, then, the regional variation in the pattern of economic indicators is produced in part by the influence of competitive market forces on each region's productive factors. These differential patterns of economic growth are affected by the movement of human and physical resources (including capital) among regions. Regional reallocation of resources is, in part, a response to differences in economic opportunities across regions, and, in principle, is an equilibrating process reducing regional disparities. In practice, however, this process is slowed and made less complete because the market mechanism is costly, time consuming, and imperfect. Government intervention is often required when regional disparities are not reduced sufficiently by market forces.

Because of the importance of the relationship between the level of regional and national economic activity, a comprehensive regional policy should have *two* primary dimensions. First, as alluded to previously, such a policy should address large interregional disparities in indices of growth and welfare. These regional inequities, however, would exist in a national economy simply because the market works and reflects the fact that some regions are better endowed with natural resources and, in a dynamic economy where price changes induce resources to move from low-profitability to high-profitability uses, local economies experience some adjustment problems as the level *and* composition of economic activity change. However, although this equity dimension of regional policy has provided the major focus for past federal regional development efforts, it may receive relatively less emphasis in the 1980s.

The second, and increasingly important, dimension of a comprehensive regional policy is the focus on promoting efficiency and growth in the national economy. Such a policy would be designed to make the most efficient use of existing resources by facilitating the flow of resources to their highest and best use. It would identify market failures resulting from factor immobilities, lack of competition, and so on, which inhibit regional and national growth, and design program initiatives to overcome these obstacles. The result of such a policy would be not only to improve regional growth, but also to promote national growth and improve productivity.

The dual efficiency and equity objectives of a comprehensive regional policy were first articulated by Isard twenty years ago when he observed that:

> An analyst is perplexed with many problems when he looks at a region. One problem may be to identify specific industries which can individually or in groups operate efficiently and with profit in the region. Another related problem may be to improve the welfare of the people of the region, that is, to raise per capita incomes and perhaps achieve a more equitable distribution of income. . . . Still another problem may be to avoid an industrial mix which is too sensitive to the ups and downs of national and world business, and which is composed too heavily of old, slow growing, or declining industries.[5]

Isard's primary focus is clearly on the efficiency dimension of regional development policy. Similarly, Senator Paul Douglas's original proposal for the Area Redevelopment Administration focused on the efficiency concern of correcting structural problems in specific local areas that were not benefiting from the national growth of the 1960s. However, the need for broad political support resulted in a slow shift of the emphasis of federal regional development policies toward addressing the equity questions without much concern for the efficiency implications of various programs.[6] The pendulum may now be swinging back toward a greater concern with efficiency issues.

A regional policy that successfully promotes regional *and* national objectives must be sensitive to the unique sectoral composition of each region's economic base. Although the appropriate definition of a region may vary from situation to situation, one must recognize that the behavior of an industry at the national level is not necessarily an accurate barometer of the industry behavior at the local level because:

regional supply and demand conditions for any one industry will differ across regions;

the industrial composition of regional economies will differ to reflect differences in comparative advantages of each region; and

the characteristics of individual firms will vary from region to region, reflecting the differences in appropriate production technologies and each region's comparative advantage.

In the final analysis, then, a successful regional policy must be designed and implemented with sufficient flexibility so that it can respond adequately to the unique needs of each region. That is, the myopic concentration on the goal of reducing interregional disparities in selective indices of social welfare through policies that generally attempt to stimulate demand through programs providing welfare payments to individuals in lagging regions or subsidizing a large but noncompetitive local industry, is no longer adequate to deal with the problems of regions adjusting to changing economic realities. What is required is the tailoring of regional development policies to meet the needs of individual firms in their efforts to fully exploit the unemployed and underutilized resources in a specific region.

Some policymakers argue that there is a basic conflict between the goals of traditional regional development policies and a regional policy that addresses sectoral concerns. They argue that traditional regional policies have been designed to ameliorate the spatially concentrated consequences of a well-functioning market system. Regional policies intervene in the market system to encourage capital not to move to its highest and best use, but rather to move to distressed areas. This is in direct conflict, they argue, with a regional policy that stresses the goal of economic efficiency.

In part, these arguments are correct. Economists have long argued about the appropriate trade-offs between equity and efficiency concerns. There is no reason to suspect that regional development issues would be spared this concern —especially given the pluralistic environment in which political decisions regarding the scope and design of regional development policies are made. Even Isard recognized that regional issues dealt with both dimensions. However, a regional development policy that recognizes that there are strong externalities associated with the process of adjustment to changing economic realities and that there are certain market failures that inhibit adjustment, need not apologize for its concern with economic efficiency. This is merely a dimension of regional policy that has been neglected in the past and is likely to become more important in the near future.

As pointed out earlier, statistical measures of disparate levels of economic activity do not provide sufficient information to design a meaningful regional development strategy. One needs to look beyond the statistics and try to understand why there are disparate levels of economic activity among regions and how they change over time. Given the dramatic changes that are taking place in the U.S. economy, it may be necessary for the primary emphasis of regional development policies in the 1980s to shift toward overcoming barriers to adjustment and promoting economic efficiency and growth.

The refocusing of attention on this long-neglected dimension of regional policy provides an opportunity to design new national industrial policy initiatives in a manner beneficial to distressed regions. A successful national industrial policy designed to improve productivity and employment must focus on the sectoral concerns of individual regions. A simplistic approach that concentrates on industries at the national level cannot be successful and may actually exacerbate current regional problems. This point can be illustrated at an aggregate level in terms of the distribution and performance of manufacturing across census regions and in a specific industry, textiles.

An analysis of the data for the manufacturing sector (table 1-3) reveals that:

the Mid-Atlantic and East North Central regions contained nearly 50 percent of 1970 manufacturing value-added (that is, production) and employment;

manufacturing in the Mid-Atlantic region was about as efficient (value-added per worker, 1970) as the average for the U.S. economy. Manufacturing in the East North Central region was 6 percent more efficient than the U.S. average;

manufacturing output grew (1970-1977) in the Mid-Atlantic region at less (63 percent) than the rate for the U.S. economy, with the East North Central region growing at about the national rate. It is interesting to note, however, that in the East North Central region, growth in value-added per worker (growth in labor productivity) was 2 percent above the national rate;

the East South Central region experienced growth in manufacturing value-added and employment above the national rate, but labor productivity growth was less than the national rate.

Thus, in one region (East North Central) output is not growing above national rates but productivity is; in a second region (East South Central) output and employment are growing but productivity growth is lagging; and in a third region (Mid-Atlantic) output, employment, and productivity growth are all lagging. This diversity of manufacturing performance across regions is more than just interesting. It implies that the outcome to be expected from the implementation of an industrial policy will depend on, among other things, the regional and locational characteristics of the industry in question, the supplying industries, the labor force, the credit markets, and the markets for its products.

Similarly, the ability and willingness of firms to respond to federal economic incentives will be affected by these and other regional and local factors. The design of the policy and the incentive mechanisms should take account of the importance of regional factors for industries that are the object of the policy if the type, magnitude, and pace of desired national outcomes are to be achieved.

The point can be seen more clearly in the case of a single manufacturing industry—textiles (table 1-4). During the period 1958-1977, the textile industry in the South grew significantly, while at the national level the industry declined. Despite the national decline, it is a growing, productive, and efficient industry in certain regions of the country. Investments are being made in the South and are not being made in the Northeast. The factors that have brought this about include the economic characteristics of the regional economies. It is reasonable

Table 1-3
Manufacturing Growth in Census Regions

Region	Percent of U.S. Manufacturing Value Added 1970	Percent of U.S. Manufacturing Employment 1970	Growth in Value Added 1970–1977 U.S. = 100	Growth in Manufacturing Employment 1970–1977	Value Added per Worker 1970 U.S. = 100	Growth in Value Added per Worker 1970–1977 U.S. = 100
New England	6.8%	7.7%	66	−4.5%	90	77
Mid-Atlantic	21.5	21.8	63	−12.2	99	91
East North Central	27.5	25.9	98	0.2	106	102
West North Central	6.5	6.2	108	8.8	105	95
South Atlantic	11.9	13.5	124	8.3	88	112
East South Central	5.8	6.1	112	12.8	94	93
West South Central	6.8	6.1	161	22.2	110	118
Mountain	2.0	1.8	140	31.3	106	86
Pacific	11.0	10.3	120	14.3	107	97
Unites States	100.0	100.0	100	2.5	100	100

Source: 1970 Annual Survey of Manufactures and 1977 Census of Manufactures, Bureau of Economic Analysis, U.S. Department of Commerce

Table 1-4
Growth of the Textiles Industry, 1957-1977
(*percents*)

Region	Growth of Real Value Added	Growth of Employment	Growth of Number of Establishments
Northeast	-16.7	-45.8	-34.6
South	94.7	9.8	42.6
United States	49.2	-11.4	-7.4

Source: 1958 Census of Manufactures and 1977 Census of Manufactures, Bureau of Economic Analysis, U.S. Department of Commerce.

to conclude that greater or lesser investment would have taken place if the characteristics of the regional economy of the South had been more or less attractive to textile producers. That is, had other regions of the country had economic characteristics important to textiles similar to those of the Northeast, the decline of the industry at the national level would have been far greater. It is obvious, therefore, that the behavior of this industry at the national level is, in part, a result of differential regional economic conditions that influence local investment decisions.

Some of the implications for industrial policy are clear. Certain industries that are national "losers" may be regional "winners." Both national and selected regional economies may be weakened if the strength of these industries is reduced directly or indirectly by actions taken to benefit national winners. And, in turn, efforts to improve the position of the national winners in all regions will be less than optimally effective if they do not take into account the regional influences on the industry's current condition and future possibilities. Thus, improvements in national growth and productivity may be achieved through the selection of industries in certain regions, some of which may be national losers. This will have to be balanced with regional economic growth and stability objectives.

Conclusion

This chapter has sketched a conceptual overview of the goals and components of a regional economic development and an industrial policy. One can argue that the forces that led to the recent concern over establishing an explicit industrial policy and improving industrial competitiveness at the national level are mirrored at the regional level as well. As a result of this overlap, there may be real potential benefits to be derived from coordinating industrial policy initiatives with regional development efforts.

Political and institutional impediments to joint policy development and implementation may hinder a coordinated government effort to promote regional industrial growth and diversification. However, the emphasis in regional economic development policy will shift in the next decade from its previous preoccupation with equity issues toward a greater concern with questions of economic efficiency. The goal is to strike a better balance between the equity/efficiency trade-off. The following chapters provide theoretical and empirical support and qualifications to the conceptual arguments discussed in this chapter.

Chapter 2 analyzes the political dimensions of the national policy-formulation process. By identifying the positions and roles of various public-interest groups affected by regional and industrial policies, Friedman illustrates the complexities involved in formulating and implementing national policies in a pluralistic decision-making framework. Given these institutional impediments, Friedman argues that the likelihood of coordinating the development and implementation of regional and industrial policies at a national level is, at best, remote.

Chapter 3 like chapter 2, investigates the potential overlap between regional economic development and industrial policies. Unlike Friedman, who examines the political forces underlying the formulation and implementation of these seemingly disparate policies, Garn and Ledebur provide an empirical analysis of the target populations of successful regional economic development and industrial policies. Although an analysis of the two policies on an aggregate level appears to be consistent with Friedman's skepticism, a microlevel analysis emphasizing economic efficiency rather than traditional equity issues provides a more optimistic prognosis of the potential benefits to be accrued by the coordinated implementation of regional and industrial policies.

Chapter 4 starts with the recognition that traditional equity-concerned regional development policies are too frequently indiscriminate with respect to the types of industrial/commercial development that take place. Lande argues that the rate of growth of the regional economy is not independent of the industrial structure of the region. Thus, an informed discussion of the relative merits of a national industrial policy and regional development and stabilization policies requires a clear understanding of the relationship of the industrial structure to both growth and stability of regional economies. Lande then develops a portfolio-analytic approach to study the problems of regional economic instability and growth and the implications of changing industrial structure on the stability/growth trade-off. This microlevel analysis supports the observation that national industrial policies designed to stimulate certain sectors of the economy will have significant differential regional impacts that will affect each region's stability/growth trade-off.

Chapter 5 compares the sectoral composition of the economies of less-developed countries (LDCs) and developed countries (DCs). From this perspective, Richardson then analyzes the differences in regional and industrial policy objectives both between LDCs and DCs and among LDCs. After reviewing some examples of regional dispersion and industrial policies in LDCs, Richardson develops an integrated policy approach for LDCs that minimizes the efficiency/ equity trade-offs associated with the simultaneous pursuit of regional and industrial development objectives.

Chapter 6 explores some of the regional consequences of federal industrial policies that encourage western coal production. Specifically, Kroll focuses on the local distributional impacts of regional economic development that result from national policies designed to stimulate energy development. A research methodology is developed to identify and measure the differential impacts of energy development experienced by specific population groups in the region. This methodology is then applied to a substate energy-rich region in Wyoming. The analysis supports the conclusion that the traditional economic base model of regional growth may not be applicable to regions experiencing rapid economic growth because of the distributional impacts of the benefits of energy development. In fact, long-time residents may actually incur additional economic hardships as a result of energy development—hardships that Kroll argues should be addressed by federal policies.

Finally, chapter 7 evaluates the usefulness of existing analytical tools available for regional policy analysis and the increasing attention to regional industrial structure. Bolton provides a critical review of the field of multiregional modeling and explores some of the recent research in the field. He then speculates on future innovations necessary in the development of tools capable of analyzing the congruence of industrial and regional development policies.

Notes

1. John Pinder, Takoshi Hosomi, and William Diebold, *Industrial Policy and the International Economy* (Trilateral Commission, 1979).

2. Ibid., pp. 42–48.

3. L.R. Klien, "The Supply Side," *American Economic Review,* March 1978.

4. William Alonso, "The Purposes of Balanced Growth," in *White House Conference on Balanced Growth,* vol. 6 (January 1978), pp. 629–667.

5. Walter Isard, *Methods of Regional Analysis* (New York, 1960), p. 413.

6. Charlotte Breckenridge, "Federal Regional Policy: Federal Programs to Promote Economic Development," in *Selected Essays on Patterns of Regional Change* (Committee on Appropriations, U.S. Senate, October 1977).

The Political Question: Can We Have a National Industrial Policy or a National Regional Policy?

Miles Friedman

Industrial Policy and Regional Policy: Taking the Political Center Stage

The presidential campaign of 1980 picked up on and highlighted the growing concern over the state of American industry. The overwhelming message in the waning days of the Carter presidency was that the national economy was in trouble, largely owing to the myriad woes that have beset our industrial sector. Thus, one of the last major proposals by the Carter administration was a national economic recovery program, and a central theme of both major party candidates for the White House became the need for a national industrial policy.

Jimmy Carter and Ronald Regan were both forced to react to the powerful impact of consistently bad economic news. Likewise, politicians throughout the country were forced to express concern over the increasingly alarming trends concerning our industrial base. They were faced not only with immediate problems such as high unemployment, failing companies, and soaring inflation, but also with long-term, underlying factors that were even more disturbing. It had been suggested by various measures that American industry was experiencing: declining productivity; declining rate of innovation; declining birth rate of new firms; declining proportional expenditures on research and development; declining investment in productive capacity; and declining competitiveness with other countries.

The question that Carter and Reagan, along with other presidential hopefuls, tried to grapple with was just what role government should play in the revitalization of American industry. Pointing out (as economists have for some time) that we already had a relationship between government and business, the candidates seemed to agree that Washington needed to help bring about a reindustrialization of America. The traditional feeling that government and business do not mix had, after all, become a sham already. We actually had a de facto industrial policy, embodied in the numerous regulations, legislation, and tax codes that substantially influence private-sector decisions, often providing disincentives to investment.

In this light, diverse proposals were offered for scrapping the fragmented, often contradictory, instances of government intervention in the economy for a more rational overall approach to industrial policy. Although the political campaign of 1980 provided only the most general kinds of suggestions for

21

reindustrialization policy, the thought of government playing a positive role in economic growth became more and more fashionable. This brought to the fore the many individuals and groups that were aching to see the national government emulate some of our European and Asian trading partners by adopting a clear-cut policy toward industry. The national press examined the issue of whether it was time for the federal government to: develop a rationale for economic intervention; set goals and formulate strategies; adopt a conscious, comprehensive national industrial-policy-targeting aid to key sectors; and promote a more efficient U.S. economy.

Ironically, the intense concern over national economic recovery was a major shift in the domestic agenda for the Carter administration. The first three years of Jimmy Carter's presidency were largely committed to the economic revitalization of lagging urban and rural areas through regional policy initiatives. Early Carter priorities had included a national urban policy, a national rural policy, a conference on balanced growth, and community conservation guidelines. But the woes of American industry, highlighted by the Chrysler Corporation emergency, the failure to control inflation, and our declining position in international trade, caused a change in priorities—to get American industry moving was now the major goal.

The need for national economic recovery was also of concern to distressed areas. After all, national economic ills are often felt most severely in distressed communities, as reflected in Detroit Mayor Coleman Young's now famous observation that a national economic sneeze meant that his city caught pneumonia. This represented the competition for national political attention between national industrial policy and regional policy.

The traditional approach to bolstering distressed areas has been that of pursuing regional policy. This concept embodies national concern over the disparities of employment and income among geographic areas. One can trace back to the 1960s the federal government's concern over unemployment, low per-capita incomes, and weak economic bases in declining inner cities and under-developed rural areas. In pursuit of a successful regional policy, national programs have tried to ameliorate these economic disparities and to use public funds to direct the flow of private resources. Regional policy carries the connotation of improving the quality of life and restoring the economic vitality in lagging communities.

Thus far, however, regional initiatives have met with only limited success because they generally run counter to the forces of the private market. Efforts to foster more balanced growth and alleviate economic disparities have not been totally satisfying, and even after twenty years of programs we are still confronted with urban decline and rural poverty. Nevertheless, we could argue persuasively that national government programs have helped make life tolerable for millions of Americans and have sparked resurgence and economic growth in many distressed communities. This could lead to a strong debate (and in fact it has) over whether the problem is not the failure of regional policy principles, but rather the quality and quantity of the effort.

Now we are confronted with identifying the effects this new preoccupation with industrial revitalization will have on lagging regions. In other words, will there be any chance for congruence between national industrial policy goals and regional policy goals? The potential area of congruence may be limited, since regional policy seeks to succor the victims of the private marketplace, whereas industrial policy is generally construed to mean reinforcement of the private market. Specifically, industrial policy implies the encouragement of growing industries, whereas regional policy implies support for the industries found in declining areas. This conflict of basic ideologies can be analyzed by looking at policymaking as the selection of winners and losers and by examining the conflicting criteria (efficiency versus equity) that underlie industry and regional policy.

Government, through the execution of its routine responsibilities, notably taxing and spending, allocates and reallocates scarce resources among segments of the population. In adopting industrial or regional policies to guide their actions, public decision makers must (intentionally or unintentionally) pick winners and losers. This makes the guiding philosophies of these policies vital because they provide the criteria for selecting winners and losers. In the case of industrial and regional policies, those criteria—efficiency as opposed to equity—may lead to the selection of different target populations.

Industrial Policy and Regional Policy: Conflicting Goals

The pursuit of a national industry policy is a legitimate search for a public-policy framework that will allow government to revitalize the American industrial machine. Given that government involvement with industry is an accomplished fact by virtue of the taxing, regulatory, and spending policies that already influence private-business activity,[1] there is logic in adopting a more intentional and consistent government policy that is consciously designed to enhance, rather than restrain, productivity. In other words, let a government currently making random selections of winners and losers in the private sector begin to make *efficient* allocations of resources so as to improve the national economy.

Regional policy, on the other hand, is based on equity rather than efficiency. In general, the idea of regional policy in this country has evolved from a perceived need for public-sector intervention in economically deprived areas.[2] The notion here is that the government bears collective responsibility for those regions with lagging private-sector activity. One merely has to scan the federal initiatives through the 1960s and early 1970s for legislation such as the Area Redevelopment Act, the Public Works and Economic Development Act, the Rural Development Act, and the Comprehensive Employment and Training Act, to see examples of our national efforts to equalize the distribution of employment and income across regions.

Regional policy is a concept that stems from the belief that public policy can intervene so as to bring about a more equitable geographic distribution of jobs and income. This has been reflected by individual programs that attempt to use public dollars to leverage private investment, jobs, and economic activity in areas that meet some criterion for distress. The adoption of a national regional policy would attempt to draw together the piecemeal threads of economic development assistance so as to bring about consistency and reduce overlap. In other words, a regional policy would create a comprehensive framework for picking winners and losers geographically. The guiding criterion would be some definition of regional equity.

The politics involved in setting national industrial policy must utilize efficiency as a primary criterion for allocating resources. Whether picking winners and losers between specific industries or between classes of industries (sectors), political decision makers must look at factors that will determine productivity, growth, and trade potential with an eye toward expanding the national economy. Gail Garfield Schwartz and Pat Choate, in their fine work on national sectoral policies, explain that "the goals are to increase efficiency, expand production, and secure markets."[3]

These objectives, all so necessary to the improvement of the national economy, will probably dictate choices that are inconsistent with regional policy objectives. After extensive empirical analysis Garn and Ledebur conclude in the next chapter: "It is important to recognize that the primary objectives of 'regional policy' and 'national industrial policy' are quite different." Examining the efficiency versus equity criteria behind the two policies, Garn and Ledebur apply these tests to alternative actions in regard to the national performance of manufacturing industries, the performance of small firms, and the start and closure of firms. Their analysis suggests that at the national level the selection of any one policy option may satisfy one, but not both, sets of criteria simultaneously. The findings are that there are "harsh tradeoffs between the objectives of national industrial policy and regional policy." Even the currently exalted perception of small-business stimulation as a means of blunting the conflicts by serving both industrial and regional policy goals is found wanting. Ledebur and Garn call for coordination in the pursuit of these policies, but state in so many words that "the two sets of objectives cannot be met simultaneously at the national level."

This leads us to believe that public policymakers, in selecting winners and losers, may have to opt for different choices, depending on which long-range objective they seek to satisfy. In itself, this is a worrisome conclusion, for it implies that the economic "facts of life" will dictate different policy and program decisions and thus the need to choose which course the government wishes to pursue: adoption of an efficient industry policy or adoption of an equitable regional policy.

National Policies: Political Fact and Fiction

The political makeup of American government simply does not lend itself to the formulation and implementation of broad national policies. Although many rave about the effective regional and industrial policies in European nations and the enlightened industrial policies of Japan and some of our other trading partners, no one can be certain that these concepts could be grafted onto the American political system. To an unparalleled degree, ours is a fragmented network of government, with numerous decision centers and independent fiefdoms. This creates maximum dispersion of power within government and generates incredible demands for attention from outside of government. Ours is a system wherein components of the government and elements from without compete and play off of one another. This either preserves and/or paralyzes our democracy, depending on your point of view.

In a pluralistic system like ours, which allows for numerous points of decision making and access at those points to a large number of groups, policy-making can become a complex, lengthy, and often difficult exercise. What some proudly point to as "democracy at work" and others disdainfully criticize as "interest-group government" can be seen as the ongoing business of government deciding between the competing interests of various population segments.

There are those who applaud this multiplicity of interests within and outside of government. In the *Federalist Papers*, written to encourage the adoption of our constitution, James Madison lauded "factionalism" as the greatest safeguard against single-minded, and thereby potentially tyrannical, government.[4] Nearly two hundred years later in *The Governmental Process*, David Truman portrayed interest-group government as the essence of practical democracy.[5] And yet the potential excesses of interest-group government were decried by Theodore Lowi in *The End of Liberalism* as a mockery of the democratic process,[6] and in 1978 President Jimmy Carter blamed the influence of self-serving interest groups for failures in the adoption of his national policies.[7]

Love them or hate them, organized and unorganized segments of the populace will fight to protect their interests in our society, and a government like ours must constantly act as a mediator between them. This makes the adoption, even of single-purpose policies, a task of weighing alternatives and building fragile coalitions. It probably means that the adoption of comprehensive policies, which by their nature affect broad segments of the population in multiple applications, would be a monumental task.

The federal government, which would have to adopt national regional or industrial policies, has separation of powers between the executive and legislative branches of government, which is reinforced by the checks and balances written into the Constitution by the founding fathers. Many other nations have no such clearly defined separation of legislative and executive power. This often competitive relationship is further complicated by the dispersion of power *within* each branch. Each of the two houses of Congress conducts its business through numerous semiautonomous domains known as committees. The executive branch is characterized by a distance, and sometimes estrangement, between the White House leadership and the largely independent bureaucracy. It is often an amazing feat to get the administration or Congress alone to reach internal accord on a program, no less to find the two branches in agreement.

The executive branch is not a monolith, despite the appearance of being less divided than a legislature. The *administration,* in the strictest sense, constitutes primarily the elected president and his handpicked assistants. Even within the chosen presidential deputies there are conflicts over turf: for example, who will make policy?—the cabinet or White House advisers?; who will run urban development programs?—the Department of Housing and Urban Development (HUD) or the Department of Commerce? There is also a dichotomy within the agencies between the secretarial-level appointees loyal to the president and the career civil servants with their own loyalties to the agencies or various constitutent groups. Then there is the Office of Management and Budget (OMB) which, since the Nixon presidency, has wielded enormous policymaking power through its preparation and control over administration budget proposals. Although headed by a presidential appointee, the OMB will generally act as a guardian of the public treasury, concerned more with economy than programs. This will often set the OMB against various agencies in the development of program proposals.

Congress is made up of 435 representatives and 100 senators with their own minds and independent power bases. The potential divisions between houses are exacerbated by the different kinds of constituencies represented by House and Senate members. Whereas individual senators represent entire states with fairly diverse interests, each representative is elected by a substate district that may have a set of very clearly defined interests. This, plus a natural rivalry between the two houses can create enough tensions, but sometimes we have the added factor of different parties controlling the two houses. Even the old standbys of seniority and party discipline are declining as means of molding the decision process.

Each house is divided into committees and subcommittees. This system allows for specialization and is the working backbone of Congress. Nonetheless, it also creates numerous independent power bases for individual members (and their staffs) and promotes rivalries for jurisdiction on overlapping legislation. These committees also develop an affinity for the agencies and programs they oversee, creating further incentives for pursuing alternative courses of action. This simply adds to the myriad economic and political interest groups that members of Congress must respond to. For example, when legislation intended to provide financial assistance to small businesses is introduced, it can conceivably be referred to congressional committees on small business, banking and urban affairs, and economic development. The competition for authority on

Capitol Hill may be intensified by the competition for the program among the constituent agencies of those committees, namely: the Small Business Administration; the Department of Housing and Urban Development; and the Economic Development Administration. If rural as well as urban firms are to be eligible, then add the agriculture committees on the Hill and the Farmers Home Administration to the equation.

It is necessary to understand this incredible fragmentation of political power and the complexity of coping with it, if we are to ponder national policymaking. The argument here is that the U.S. political system is sufficiently diffuse that it is difficult to build coalitions to formulate, no less implement, national industrial policy *or* national regional policy.

We spent much of the 1960s and 1970s seeking ways to support and revitalize our nation's cities with fiscal aid, housing and welfare assistance, and economic development assistance. Yet a litany of other federal programs that contributed to urban economic decline may well have constituted a de facto "anti-urban policy." Federal programs helped people buy homes in the suburbs and built highways for them to commute back to work in the cities. Powerful urban interests such as mayors, national urban groups, and spokesmen for the poor lobbied for aid to the cities, while the automakers, homebuilders, and construction industry pushed for the programs that promoted suburban growth. Furthermore, rural groups pushed for development programs that put infrastructure in their areas, drawing economic activity out of the cities. Perhaps these programs were more successful than anyone counted on.

These factors were compounded by tax incentives (investment tax credits) that favored new construction over older or rehabilitated facilities and depreciation allowances that hastened the move to modern facilities, often in outlying areas. In researching the problems of distressed cities, President Carter's Urban and Regional Policy Group identified the federal government itself as a major contributor to urban decline. This aspect of the problem in part led to the strong statement of support for urban America that became central to Carter's *New Partnership to Conserve America's Communities.*[8]

The mere statement of the federal government's intention to cease doing harm to the cities constituted a major breakthrough. This statement of prourban intentions in March 1978 was buttressed later in the Carter presidency by the "Community Conservation Guidelines." The guidelines contained in the document were meant to curtail federal actions that operated at cross purposes to each other in regard to leveraging private investment. Of particular concern was the elimination of federal financial support for fringe development that detracted from center-city commercial activity.[9] This constituted a directive to stop giving with one hand and taking away with the other.

Clearly, we cannot overlook the possibility that the concept of an urban policy or any comprehensive regional policy is just too broad. There may just be too many players in the formulation process to develop a meaningful compromise. Any policy would have to satisfy the competing demands of a host of public- and private-interest groups. Both the White House and Congress may be destined to fail in their attempts to appeal to mayors, city councilmen, governors, state legislators, county and regional officials, urban-development officials, academic experts, minority groups, small businesses, large businesses, developers, bankers, labor unions, and so on. Further splintering occurs because of regional battles between the sun belt and snow belt; between the east and west; between the north and south; and between urban, suburban, and rural interests. Those trying to bring about a consensus on industrial policy have had just as much to cope with. Here the conflicts between the employed and unemployed; lenders and borrowers; management and labor; producers and consumers; and free traders and protectionists come to the fore.

Once again, inconsistent government programs may well have contributed to the ills of American industry. Federal tax and regulatory policies, paperwork requirements, and trade impediments have been cited as potential culprits in holding back American industrial development.[10] In light of these factors, it may be incautious to suggest that it is now possible for the government to become the arbiter between competing private interests.

It must be remembered that our government is further decentralized by nature of being a federal system. The fifty states, with a constitutional status of their own, maintain a tradition of political and cultural independence that allows for tremendous diversity and often leads them far afield of the national government. The states are jealous of their sovereignty and reserve the right to maintain some control over their own destiny. Frequently, state governments and the one in Washington are uneasy partners in the federal system. The total success of both industrial and regional policies depends on the cooperation of state governments; more easily said than done.

In fact, many states already have their own, often conflicting, policies. State governments have been involved in the pursuit of industrial investment with a fervor that often leads to bitter rivalries. Development officials have prospected declining regions, neighboring areas, and even foreign countries for firms with the potential to invest in their states. In addition, more and more states have adopted business-retention programs, often employing circuit-rider specialists (often former businessmen) to monitor the needs of existing companies. Often, states have used capital improvements, financing, or technical assistance to help promote industrial retention and expansion. More and more, states have developed formal or informal industrial policies designed to target classes of existing or new industries for their states.

Some state programs (like those in California) may target growth industries, whereas others prioritize firms by need or by current role in the state's economy. Nevertheless, the problem of reconciling varying state policies into a national model is compounded by the refusal of many states to target at all. This can be exacerbated by the variations in attitude toward foreign firms. Whereas some states spend millions courting overseas investors, others actually shun investment of foreign dollars. Those which do seek such firms see them as crucial to the generation of jobs and taxes, but this itself runs counter to the official federal posture of neutrality toward foreign investment. The critical issue is that state activities in the area of industrial development (described further in a later section) are aggressive, diverse, and often at odds with the national government's agenda.

Similarly, state actions concerning regional policy have been varied, and often at odds with Washington. States frequently have been characterized as being neglectful of urban areas, because their legislatures are often dominated by rural legislators that considered nonurban development a priority. The very neglect of big-city problems common to so many state governments in the 1960s drove the national government to form a direct partnership with urban areas. The proliferation of federal housing and community-development programs in the 1960s administered by a special cabinet-level department (HUD) reflected the intense national preoccupation with cities and the growing acceptance of the diminishing responsibility of states for their urban communities.

The antagonism between states and cities and between states and the federal government continues to be a problem today. The ultimate exclusion of state governments from a major role in the Carter urban policy (described later) illustrated an ongoing mistrust and perhaps helped doom the urban policy. To add to the confusion, many states recently have taken considerable interest in the economic development of their communities. Some, like North Carolina, have adopted balanced-growth strategies, whereas others, like Michigan, actually have state urban policies.

For the most part, state efforts to influence local development have been informal. Techniques including targeted financial aid, special technical assistance, and packaging of federal programs have all been used to enhance economic development at the local level. Yet once again, the degree, style, and objectives of state aid in this area vary widely. Thus, some states continue to pursue development solely on a statewide scale, whereas others vigorously promote the development of revitalization of specified communities.

Regardless of their posture on local development, states do not like to be directed by Washington to behave in a particular manner. Federal efforts to encourage states to direct more foreign investors to distressed cities have thus far been relatively unsuccessful. It is unlikely that federal directives about modifying regional imbalances within states will in themselves render massive results. Such activities generally are most enthusiastically pursued by states when initiated on their own. Needless to say, federal policies that attempt to allocate resources among states are not well received by those on the losing end.

These difficulties are compounded by the vital role states must play in the implementation of industrial and regional policies. This role (examined later on) is crucial since states have the greatest degree of contact with private industry and local governments. Some have working groups (like the South Carolina Economic Development Allies) that bring states, communities, and the private sector together to discuss economic-development issues on a regular basis. The case is strong, therefore, for utilizing the state as the administering unit of government for industrial and regional policies, and the current administration in Washington appears to be headed in this direction. Such an approach may have the best prospects for success, though it says little for the prospects of national industrial or regional policies.

Diverse Approaches to National Industrial Policy

Those who would have the federal government make rational choices that encourage growth sectors of the economy must reckon with the political nature of these choices. The notion of an industrial policy has different meanings for the many players in the game of national policymaking. For many in the private sector and for those who represent them in Congress, an industrial policy would call for the bolstering of sagging American companies that are adversely affected by foreign competition. This argument hinges on the need to maintain a domestic industrial base, even at the cost of some protectionism. Such an argument has particular appeal for manufacturing concerns such as those in the steel, automobile, and footwear industries and for those in Congress who represent them.

Thus far, the federal government has looked sympathetically at such cases and has tried to bolster these companies with Trade Adjustment Assistance, special loan-guarantee programs, and grants and loans from the Economic Development Administration. This technique has been questioned, however, by those who now propose a single national financing authority to meet the special needs of such firms. If we believe that foreign manufacturers subsidized by their own governments or aided by unfair "dumping" tactics are winning because of unfair advantages, then such subsidies make sense. On the other hand, if U.S. firms are failing because of poor management decisions or inevitable market forces, then our policies may not have met the efficiency standard.

Whereas many northeastern and midwestern areas may like to see support for lagging firms, other regions of the country would prefer to see support for growing sectors, such as the electronics and computer industries. The American southwest and west coast have prospered by becoming havens for high-technology companies as they have developed the labor force and incentives to attract such firms. California is currently engaged in an all-out effort to promote the attraction and expansion of high-technology firms and its success to date has sparked similar programs in other states. In fact, several northeastern states are trying to regain their industrial prominence by starting venture capital programs to foster the growth and development of high-risk, innovative firms.

These trends may suggest that a national industrial policy should concentrate on stimulating growth sectors of the economy—precisely what many competitor nations do. This approach has been endorsed by a number of economists and the business press (discussed in more detail later in this chapter). Those industries with bright prospects and regions of the country that harbor such firms might welcome concentrated government support. After all, the Japanese have generously subsidized their growing electronics industry and have even protected fledgling high-technology firms from outside competition until they were ready to fly. Yet only recently, Republican governors from some midwestern states met with the president to urge import quotas, not to protect fledgling companies but to protect our declining auto industry.

The dilemma of selecting sectors of the economy for government benefits is compounded by the dilemma of selecting an approach for building a positive relationship between government and business. The Reagan administration, avowedly probusiness, is faced with some tough choices. Specifically, the administration (and Congress) may have to decide whether less government or more government is the way to stimulate industry. One argument opts for less government—deregulating business, eliminating tax disincentives, easing export barriers, and reducing red tape. Such concepts would be embodied in proposals that would ease environmental regulations, reduce federal wage requirements, loosen antitrust restrictions, lower corporate income taxes, eliminate government-mandated paperwork, and so forth. Even distressed-area revitalization would be approached from this point of view, as symbolized by the enterprise-zone legislation which would ease tax (and perhaps regulatory) burdens for businesses in distressed areas.

This school of thought is countered by those who would like to see more government programs to aid business. Proponents of such an approach call for more government loan-guarantee programs, greater depreciation allowances and tax credits to stimulate investment, expansion of federal assistance to small businesses, import quotas, and promotion of export opportunities. Naturally, the two approaches—less government versus more government—are not mutually exclusive. Yet, can we have a national industrial policy without a consistent government posture toward business?

Underlying the confrontation between these alternative government actions are a myriad of fragmented public and private interests. To a large extent, the larger, more successful companies favor less government, since government only interferes with their natural marketplace advantages. On the other hand, where do we classify a firm like General Motors, which purportedly wants less government restrictions concerning passenger safety and air quality, but favors more government intervention in the form of import quotas? Likewise, politicians from auto-industry-dominated states want import quotas to protect their home firms, but express concern over retaliatory quotas by our trading partners that would restrict exports of U.S. goods. Workers in trade-impacted industries might support import restrictions, but those in export industries such as agriculture and farm equipment might suffer from constriction of the trade flow.

The banking industry is also filled with mixed feelings over the proper role of government. Although government guarantees and subsidies may improve the quantity of attractive loans available, government restrictions limit usury rates and branch banking. The larger banks have long lobbied for decontrol to allow for interstate branching, yet many small bankers fear the resulting competition in their states from giant banks in New York, Chicago, and Los Angeles. As American bankers lobby for federal decontrol of domestic banking, they also push for restrictions on foreign-bank operations in the United States. Thus, Carter administration recommendations on bank deregulation got bogged down in deliberation. Fear of foreign-bank takeovers led to an official moratorium on this activity—but no long-term policy has yet been articulated. The process of bringing together the "snow belters" and the "sun belters," the laissez-faire economists and the progovernment experts, and the diverse factions within business, labor, and banking, may provide an insurmountable challenge to national industrial policy.

The difficulty in determining criteria for public selection of winners and losers comes to the fore in the continuing debate over the fate of the Chrysler Corporation. The most frustrating aspect of the Chrysler debate in Washington was not the interminable delays nor the less than anticipated impact of the loan guarantees. The worst part of the Chrysler mess is that the debate left us with no guidelines for making future decisions on the fate of Chrysler or any other companies. Those who hope for a national industrial policy that picks winners and losers based on efficiency might argue that such a policy would avoid Chrysler-type controversies. But we still do not know whether these situations call for public policy based on equity or efficiency. A national policy that emphasizes economic efficiency might have precluded the Chrysler bail out; yet a national regional policy that emphasizes equity concerns might have demanded it. To date, there is no clear framework to establish just how we would make such decisions in the future.

Although labor groups and most congressmen from the impacted region argued the inefficiency of letting Chrysler employees go on the welfare rolls, others called for retraining of these workers by the government. Industry analysts bemoaned the Chrysler losses traceable to government-induced problems created by safety, environmental, and gas-mileage standards that were costly to meet. Thus, some argued, government assistance would merely counterbalance government interference. The question of how a comprehensive government policy toward industry would address such issues remains unanswered.

Perhaps the process itself is the problem. We have made no decision whether economists, industrialists, or politicians should set national economic policy. Certainly all three must have a role—but how will the players interact? The long-term inconsistency of federal policy as set by the president and Congress has long confounded attempts at rationality and has brought to the fore a new wave of proposals. Some recent suggestions have, in fact, come from those outside government.

It is interesting to note that the press, as well as the academic community, has become a central player in the game. None other than *Business Week* proclaimed the need for a reindustrialization of America. In a special June 30, 1980 issue, the editors presented a detailed plan for rebuilding our industrial machine. The goal was to boost the U.S. economy through adoption of a plan that would rationalize the relationship between government and business in this country so as to increase efficiency. Among other things, the plan "requires an industrial policy that chooses which industries, sectors, and product lines should be encouraged because they have a good chance in international competition and which should be abandoned as likely failures." The editors of *Business Week* were quick to point out that such an approach to promoting economic growth would have massive scope. In the introduction to their plan, they proclaimed that "reindustrialization will require sweeping changes in basic institutions, in the framework for economic policymaking, and in the way the major actors on the economic scene—business, labor, government, and minorities—think about what they put into the economy and what they get out of it."[11]

In 1980, perhaps the most comprehensive framework for rebuilding the economy and regaining economic health appeared in a book entitled *Being Number One: Rebuilding the U.S. Economy* by Gail Garfield Schwartz and Pat Choate. Schwartz and Choate pointed out the need for a sectoral policy that would revitalize the economy, and also a framework for partnership between business, labor, and government in the rebuilding process. They explain why efficiency and productivity must be the goals of government policy in the selection and stimulation of growth sectors.[12]

These works symbolize the way in which those currently removed from the exigencies of day-to-day politics can define efficient criteria by which government may approach business assistance. It may be that Jimmy Carter, recognizing the need for such policy input, sought in the waning days of his presidency to change the process by which national industrial policy is formulated. His was an attempt to provide national politicians with some private-sector input on these matters. Searching for a means to stimulate private innovation and investment and create jobs in late 1980, Carter recognized the need for special expertise in this area. He proposed the establishment of a new Economic Revitalization Board to help shape national industrial policy. The board was to emphasize business and labor participation and was to be headed by DuPont Chairman Irving Shapiro and AFL–CIO President Lane Kirkland.[13]

Of course, this would have added to the list of players. There are no guarantees that this board's recommendations would have been heeded with any more regularity than those made by numerous presidential panels of experts before it.

The Carter Urban Policy and Pursuit of Regional Equity

Just as Chrysler may epitomize our national dilemma over industrial policy, New York City may be the bellwether of regional policy. One could point to the federal intervention on behalf of New York City as a decision made on equity grounds. Yet others, fearing a collapse of the municipal-bond market if New York City defaulted, might see federal aid as having been highly efficient. What we see may be described somewhat indelicately as a national schizophrenia over how to pick winners and losers. We want growth and economic power, but we also worry over distressed people and places. The federal government stepped in once to forestall New York's bankruptcy—but why, or whether it would do so again, remain open questions.

The equity versus efficiency dilemma and the agony over regional versus industrial policy within our political system are nowhere better exemplified than by the Carter presidency. The same president who committed himself to rebuilding the South Bronx, and issued a national urban policy, a national rural policy, and community conservation guidelines, all committed to the economic health of depressed areas, ultimately concluded his tenure with talk of reindustrialization, national industrial policy, and balancing the budget. Although the Carter administration opened with an emphasis on saving, rebuilding, and strengthening declining urban areas and neighborhoods, it closed with an emphasis on controlling inflation and stimulating productivity. In essence, then, the predominant theme of domestic policy in the early years of the Carter White House was achieving regional equity, which gave way without a fully satisfactory resolution to the steamroller issue of the early 1980s: bolstering industrial efficiency.

The most recent national flirtation with regional policy can be traced back to before the Carter presidency. Congress initiated legislation in 1976 that directed President Ford to convene a White House Conference on Balanced National Growth and Economic Development involving persons "broadly representative of American Society." In doing so, the Congress noted that, while in the aggregate the nation appears to have achieved levels of production and technological advancement unparalleled in the world, there have evolved neither satisfactory levels of employment nor distribution of economic growth among the nation and its citizens.

In keeping with the congressional mandate, the White House convened such a conference in January and February 1978 with some five hundred public and private officials from around the country. The Conference on Balanced National Growth and Economic Development identified some important regional policy goals, including: an emphasis on the private sector; the need for creative public-private partnership; a stress on economic development; the concept of bringing jobs to people; an end to regional conflict; and targeting aid to distressed areas. But the conference may have doomed its own goals to oblivion. Although meeting to address the need for a national growth policy process, the group included in its recommendations "decentralizing decision-making in the federal system" and "increasing State responsibilities" for local problems.[14] Unfortunately, we never found out how to integrate these ideas into a national policy process.

This inability to pin down a national growth policy or even initiate the process was merely a prelude to the frustration experienced by the Carter administration in trying to formulate and implement a national urban policy. This effort, the most comprehensive attempt at a national regional policy to date, shows the federal system at its level best (or worst), depending on one's point of view.

The effort by President Carter to develop and implement a national urban policy provides the classic example of how such comprehensive undertakings can go awry in a pluralistic political system. The president had declared from the streets of the South Bronx during the campaign and from the Oval Office of the White House after the election that support for the nation's cities was to be a major priority of his administration. In March 1977, a formal process was initiated with the creation of a task force called the Urban and Regional Policy Group (URPG). The six departments involved (Commerce; HUD; Labor; Health, Education, and Welfare; Treasury; and Transportation) were asked to provide the framework for a national urban policy. Chaired by HUD Secretary Patricia Harris, the group was to report by fall 1977. The now famous document, "Cities and People in Distress," delivered in December of that year was rejected by President Carter with complaints that it did not present a clear assessment of past programs nor a focused blueprint for new ones. The failure of this six-agency task force to produce a "decision document" should have come as no surprise, for the report basically contained the aggregate collection of old and new programs that each agency wanted to preserve or add to its authority. One internal critic characterized the paper as an agency "wish list" that proposed new programs but failed to eliminate old ones. It was unlikely that any of the agencies would have offered to sacrifice program authority.

The hoped-for January 1978 urban-policy announcement was forced to slide, and the President's Domestic Policy Staff, particularly Stuart Eizenstat, took a hand in the revised effort. By early January, Eizenstat and URPG chairperson Harris had a memorandum for the president with some general goals for the urban policy, including a retreat from the distressed-area theme and a call for private-sector, state, and neighborhood involvement in urban development. The process of broadening the program to address diverse constituencies had begun. The memorandum set general goals of stabilizing and strengthening urban economic bases, to be pursued through an urban-development bank, a state incentive program, and improvement or expansion of existing programs. More specific agency recommendations were turned in by February and the president finally got to make his announcement in March 1978. The president and his top advisers were still writing and rewriting the final pieces of the policy forty-eight hours before the formal announcement was made.

Along with a host of other issues, two major factors had disrupted the effort to finalize the urban-policy proposal. One involved the relative role that states were to play, the other involved agency authority over the proposed development bank. The administration had been wrestling with the issue of how to deal with the states throughout the year-long discussions. According to some sources, there were administration insiders who favored a strong role for states, essentially a reemergence of the state as a partner in the federal system. Advocates of this point of view had called for massive federal block grants to states, to be used for the economic development of their communities. Others within the White House had argued that states should be omitted entirely, based on poor past performance in the area of urban development. Ultimately, the "new partnership" continued the trend toward direct federal-local cooperation and included a mere $200 million for unspecified incentives to states with acceptable urban-development plans. Despite the pleadings of governors, state legislators, and their constituent organizations, the administration had relegated the states to a minor role, pleasing instead the mayors and urban groups that wanted direct federal assistance.

The fight over who would administer the bank was a beauty, and ultimately may have doomed the proposal forever. Although there was widespread agreement over the need for a capital-financing program directed at distressed areas, there was disagreement over how it should work. The concept of a national bank was broadened to satisfy rural interests, particularly those in Congress, from the early notion of an urban-development bank or Urbank to that of a national-development bank for urban and rural distressed areas. The bank would assist firms investing in such areas with the financing of fixed-asset capital. But agreement was tough to reach on whether the bank should be located within Commerce, HUD, Treasury, or stand as an independent agency. Interests within Commerce and HUD fought to protect the funding and prestige that the bank would carry with it. Private business and many in the public sector that worked with the private sector were generally more accustomed to dealing with the Department of Commerce and largely supported that department's position. The urban constituency of HUD supported that agency as the repository for the bank, with the general backing of congressional committees on Banking and Urban Affairs which held jurisdiction over HUD. The Public Works committees hoped to see the bank go to Commerce's Economic Development Administration (EDA) where they would gain jurisdiction. Interestingly enough, the Treasury department, which developed the bank concept, showed little interest in administering it.

As the debate raged on, the issue of the bank intensified the developing rivalry between HUD and Commerce over who was to be lead agency for economic development. Some felt that the business-oriented Department of

Commerce held the best claim because of its experience in public-private development projects, whereas others favored HUD, with its experience in dealing with communities and their development problems. It is reported that a tentative decision to install the bank at Commerce was checked by an anxious HUD Secretary Harris who was able to win a compromise decision. The bank, as finally announced, would be ruled by a three-agency triumvarite—HUD, Commerce, and Treasury—with the chair rotating. This decision split congressional jurisdiction over the bank in both houses, helping to set the stage for a fierce battle on Capitol Hill over this, the centerpiece of the entire urban policy.

A year had been spent deciding what the basic problems of distressed cities were. The Carter team identified a broad range of issues, including technological change, shifting population, rising costs, declining tax bases, and even federal-government interference (through incentives that drew people and businesses out of cities). Basically, the findings indicated a need to make public-sector activities more consistent and more sensitive to private-sector needs. Ten general goals were included in the national policy that was ultimately announced:

Coordination of federal programs

Partnership with the states

Development of local capabilities

Involvement of neighborhood groups and the private sector

Improvement of local economic bases

Provision of fiscal relief

Increasing the attractiveness of central cities

Assistance with growth management

Special attention to minority needs

Employment and training for the unemployed

Exciting new programs were outlined to pursue these goals, including the national-development bank, targeted fiscal assistance, a labor-intensive public-works program, investment and employment tax credits, the state incentive program, and some neighborhood-oriented development initiatives.[15] A policy was outlined and some programs were described by March, but their translation into legislative initiatives was to be slow and painful.

Congress, proceeding with its spring 1978 work, was marching through the various stages for authorization and appropriation legislation mandated by the congressional budget process. Deadlines for authorizing committees to report bills came and went and little or no legislation came from the White House. Meanwhile, the process of appropriating money for programs new and old was largely brought to a standstill as Congress waited for the authorizing committees that give the programs life to complete their work. The operation of Congress is cumbersome at best—but a House and Senate without urban-policy legislation could not authorize or appropriate on schedule. As time passed, appropriations committees got tired of waiting for authorizing legislation and authorizing committees became concerned about having insufficient time to consider the new proposals. Schedules got crowded with legislative business that could no longer wait and the chances of new programs being in place by the start of the fiscal year on October 1 dwindled.

What happened? Why was urban-policy legislation slow, late, and piecemeal in moving from one end of Pennsylvania Avenue to the other? The administration was finding that those same terrible issues which had plagued it during the previous year were still tough to resolve. Should we have mostly all-new programs or try to build on or refocus existing ones? Should we emphasize business investment and economic-base building, or direct assistance to people in need of immediate relief? Which agency should dominate the new policy, if any? Should we spend lots of additional money in the hope of making cities more self-sufficient, or should we hold down spending? Should we target programs to regions most in need, or provide broad coverage to prevent deterioration of healthy areas? Should the states have a large or small role in urban development? All of these were tempered by the question: what can we hope to get through Congress?

While the administration tried to convert broad program objectives into specific legislative proposals, various interests continued to push their own points of view. Recipients of funds from HUD and EDA largely pushed for expansion of existing programs. A score of congressional committees urged that legislation be written so as to wind up under their jurisdiction. Committees concerned with banking and urban affairs, taxing and finance, intergovernmental relations, public-works and economic development, small business, and employment jockeyed for position over the bank, tax credits, state incentives, EDA expansion, neighborhood programs, special revenue-sharing aid, and jobs programs. In some cases, two or three committees in each house could lay claim to a single bill if it were written just so.

The private sector, in the form of individual businesses and national trade associations, pushed for an emphasis on investment leveraging and economic-base building, whereas groups that represented the poor generally wanted extension of benefits to individuals. Targeting in general, whether to individuals or regions, presented one of the most vexing problems. Groups such as the Northeast-Midwest Congressional Coalition expressed concern that programs concentrate sufficient resources in those regions to address their economic decline. On the other hand, many felt that broader coverage would be more appropriate and more politically palatable. Naturally, organizations like the Southern Growth Policy Board and the Southeast Industrial Development Council had their own perspectives on how eligibility criteria should be drawn. A case can be and was made that failure to assist today's growing regions in their development might well lead to their becoming tomorrow's declining regions. Furthermore, cities like Houston could point to the need for federal development aid to distressed "pockets of poverty" within otherwise economically healthy communities.

The state-role issue was hardly resolved either. After all, even with direct federal aid to cities, states could play a part in project packaging, approval, screening, and monitoring. Small cities and their national organization fought for substantial set-asides either to be funneled through states or to be doled out directly from Washington. They were not anxious to compete with big-city governments for funds. Larger cities pleaded their case on the basis of larger-scale problems and objected to any state involvement in "their" programs. Organized labor wanted programs that would create jobs at union wages for union members, while others wanted to emphasize jobs for the hard-core unemployed.

The basic arguments always came down to the same issue: who gets what share of the pie? The eligibility criteria used, the administering agency selected, the role of state governments, the presence or absence of set-asides for special purposes all help determine the answer to that question. The administration was trying to implement a comprehensive national urban policy. To do so, it would need support that cut across regional, political, income, and sectoral lines. To move any of the legislation through Congress, the package would have to contain something for everyone. In a way it did: a national bank that would favor large, capital-intensive companies investing in distressed areas; fiscal aid to cities having trouble paying their bills; a public-works program and employment-tax credits to create jobs for various sectors of the work force; investment-tax credits that would promote investment in new facilities and/or rehabilitation of older ones; state incentives that would reward states, but only those which "helped cities"; neighborhood programs to support voluntary associations in their self-help efforts; increases in social services for the poor and the aged; increased money for the Comprehensive Employment Training Act (CETA) public-jobs program to generate more private-sector involvement; increases in environmental, transportation, and crime-prevention programs; and expansion of existing programs at EDA and HUD.

How much of this ambitious set of programs made it through Congress? Unfortunately for the urban policy, the answer was: precious little. For one thing, Congress had its *own* ideas about urban policy. Not everyone on Capitol Hill was thrilled about having such a policy (some speculated that the very idea of an urban policy helped kill some of the legislation). As soon as the bills arrived at the House and Senate, they were assigned to committees for consideration. Then the committees planned long and exhaustive hearings, setting their staffs to work on the various components of the policy. Although it is true that more early staff to staff work between the White House and congressional committees might have expedited things, it is unlikely that many in Congress would have foregone careful examination of the president's proposals or their own. The ultimate irony is that the only set of proposals partially accepted were the tax credits. Unfortunately, taken out of context, they boiled down to just another case of tax-code tinkering. Let us look briefly at the fate of the urban-policy programs.

The National Development Bank. This legislation was split between two committees and three subcommittees in the House and between two committees in the Senate. It had to compete with at least two bank proposals already pending before Congress and with similar financing programs already in place at HUD and the Economic Development Administration. The triagency administration of the bank was unpopular, its limitation to fixed-asset financing was questioned, and its potential for helping smaller firms was doubted. The legislation was never reported out of committee in either house.

Fiscal Assistance. The administration was replacing one fiscal-assistance program with another, and many were not sure why. The new program was supposed to be more targeted—but figures varied over this, and potential recipients fought over eligibility. Congress had trouble deciding whether it wanted the old program (antirecessionary fiscal assistance), the new program (supplementary fiscal assistance), or no program at all. The bill was split between two committees in the Senate, which ultimately wound up with a compromise bill. The legislation failed by one vote to get out of subcommittee in the House. No program ever became law.

Labor-Intensive Public Works. Congress had previously enacted two rounds of capital-intensive local public works (construction oriented) for a total of roughly $6 billion. The House seemed intent of having a third round of local public works; the Senate was dead set against such a measure. Although the Senate was sympathetic to the labor-intensive program (maintenance and rehabilitation oriented) of the administration, it was not enthusiastic, and ultimately public works lost out to Senator Muskie's budget slashes. Both houses seemed willing to pass some kind of public-works bill, but no compromise was ever worked out. No one ever decided whether public works should be considered as an infrastructure program, a countercyclical program, or a jobs program.

Tax Incentives. Somewhat watered-down employment-tax credit and investment-tax credit modifications did pass both houses and were signed into law.

State Incentives. Unclear on exactly what the bill meant and undecided over how it dealt with states, Congress referred the bill to several committees in each house. No final legislation was passed.

Neighborhood Economic Development Initiatives. Some minor components managed to pass, but were never funded at significant levels. The programs have since been killed.

The verdict was a sorry one. Most of the legislation (including some not cited here) died and was formally buried by the next Congress. Numerous factors were responsible, including: conflicts between the administration and Congress; squabbling within the administration and Congress; interminable delays caused by formal procedures; delays and constant modifications owing to the intervention of hundreds of public- and private-interest groups; severe disagreements over how to target assistance; a continuing uncertainty over appropriate roles of national and state governments within the federal system; and personal reasons such as inept handling, poor planning, unwillingness to compromise conflicting political philosophies, individual disagreements, and communications failures. The sad bottom line is the same: the Carter urban policy was derailed somewhere in the fragmented American political system.

It would be capricious to place all the blame on either the pluralistic system or the groups that have access to it. Nevertheless, a partial list of groups that expressed formal or informal concerns at some state of the process (administrative and/or legislative) follows. The reader is invited to draw his own inferences. The groups include: U.S. Conference of Mayors (larger cities); National League of Cities (large, medium, and smaller cities); the National Association of Towns and Townships (very small communities); National Association of Counties; National Association of Regional Councils (councils of government and metropolitan-planning agencies); National Council for Urban Economic Development (urban-economic-development officials); Municipal Finance Officers Association; National Association of Housing and Redevelopment Officials (urban-housing and community-development officials); National Governors Association; National Conference of State Legislatures; Council of State Planning Agencies; Council of State Community Affairs Agencies; National Association of Development Organizations (EDA-funded development districts); National Conference of Black Mayors; International City Managers Association; National Association of Manufacturers; National Alliance of Businessmen; U.S. Chamber of Commerce; American Bankers Association; AFL-CIO; American Federation of State, County, and Municipal Employees; American Industrial Development Council (individuals involved in development); Committee for Economic Development (private corporations); and a host of others representing small businesses, attorneys, venture-capital companies, labor groups, accounting firms, land developers, shopping-center developers, real-estate firms, homebuilders, and thrift institutions. Not all these groups are lobbyists in the purest sense. Nevertheless, they all had some degree of input to administrative and congressional deliberations on urban policy; each had its own perspective.

The legitimate exercise of interest-group political influence certainly helped play havoc with the national urban policy. The many potential winners and losers pressured the administration, lobbied Congress, and courted the press in order to protect their piece of the pie. Washington staffs from association headquarters as well as public and private individuals from all over the country wanted constant input to the urban policy as it developed. The various national organizations that represent cities and towns, counties, states, districts, and regions worked hard to mold the eligibility criteria for the various programs. Some argued for narrow targeting that would apply maximum funding to the most severely distressed areas, suggesting that as little as one-third of the country qualified for aid. Others, pointing to the existence of need throughout the country, fought for broad eligibility, in some cases proposing that up to 85 percent of the country be eligible. To most congressmen and senators, the best eligibility test was whether their districts or states would receive funding. In briefing after briefing conducted by the White House for the interest groups, anxious lobbyists would gloss over the substance of the new proposals, focusing instead on the computer printouts of eligible areas.

Big business and small business and their various allies locked horns. Supporters of the view that small businesses hold the key to economic growth fought for federal programs that would be restricted to smaller firms. Larger, capital-intensive companies supported fixed-asset capital assistance, while others sought employment subsidies and working capital loans. Big labor fought hard for massive public-works spending for capital construction projects that would boost the construction industry, while minority-oriented groups favored more labor-intensive projects involving maintenance and rehabilitation that would guarantee jobs for the unemployed semiskilled workers.

Various federal-government interests locked horns to protect their political fiefdoms. Within the administration, the continuing battle between the Department of Commerce and HUD constantly delayed decisions and occasionally undermined initiatives on Capitol Hill. Veteran committee chairmen in the House and Senate insisted on sharing jurisdiction over bills sent originally to other committees so as to protect their political turf. And at times, it was evident that the White House, the agencies, the Office of Management and Budget, the House, and the Senate all had their own versions of the same program.

The real problem appears to have been that national urban policy was too broad an effort, encompassing too many winners and losers. But then, how could we hope to achieve a true national urban policy (or a regional policy of any kind) without choosing lots of winners and losers? It's funny, but we never did find out whether urban economic development was for old cities or new cities; whether it was for distressed cities only or also for "pockets of poverty" within healthy cities; whether it was for the snow belt or the sun belt; or for decline or growth—or for all of the above. We never did find out whether urban-business assistance should be provided primarily by an urban agency like HUD or a business-oriented agency like Commerce, or whether urban-economic-development legislation belonged in public works and economic-development committees or banking and urban affairs committees—or both. We never found out what a state incentive program might accomplish, nor whether it was meant to reward prourban states or convert antiurban states. Nor do we know to this day how the job-creation programs supported by many in 1977 and 1978 became the inflationary programs widely denounced in 1979 and 1980.

We cannot say with certainty why these things happened, but speculation is possible: the political climate changed. We can blame economic imperatives for the shift in federal emphasis away from distressed-area development and toward economic growth and federal budget control over the last four years. But the question concerning state incentives is symbolic of one of the deep problems inherent in this attempt at national policymaking. No one ever decided what the appropriate role for states in this urban policy should be, and this dilemma, which reflects a crisis in federalism, needs to be addressed.

Our unique federal system poses unusual political problems. Contrary to the general scheme of the Constitution, which described a partnership of national and state governments, the last twenty years have largely been a story of growing federal-local partnership. The states, for a variety of reasons, have sometimes become onlookers in this relationship. Some in the Carter White House favored restoration of the states as full partners, proposing that flexible block grants be given to the states for the purpose of local economic development. This may or may not have represented too abrupt a shift in the intergovernmental relationships, but the issues will not go away.

For one thing, states are politically necessary to the adoption and implementation of national regional or industrial policies. Local governments exist by virtue of state authority and their ability to tax and spend, incorporate or expand, borrow and lend, and even to zone, emanate from state constitutions and legislation. No national policy to promote revitalization of distressed communities can ignore such imperatives. Furthermore, states are increasingly aware of, receptive to, and helpful with, local development efforts. States provide planning and technical assistance, direct funding, federal program packaging, and general development aid to local governments in many areas. This emerging voluntary state role should be encouraged and nurtured by any federal program —and states need to be effectively involved in regional policy formulation. Otherwise, the federal initiatives will tend to be interpreted and even ignored in fifty different ways.

State involvement in national industrial policy is even more vital. The public-sector organizations most closely involved in working with industry are the state development agencies. Traditionally, the states have been very active in the areas of economic and industrial development, providing direct incentives, technical assistance, and other services geared toward stimulating economic growth. State development agencies (generally commerce departments) have worked in the areas of trade development, investment attraction, manpower training, financing assistance, tax incentives, and industrial-site preparation, developing in the process a unique insight into the problems and opportunities confronting private industry.

Most state agencies have already begun thinking in terms that go beyond individual firms and specific projects. Many states have formal or informal industrial and/or growth policies that target their development efforts. In addition, states have increasingly articulated their policy concerns through national organizations and are defying many predictions by sharing business-development information. The federal government needs to capitalize on this expertise in the formulation of national industrial policy and will need to coordinate with state programs in order to implement national industrial policy, that is, tailor the national policy to correct and/or reinforce a wide variety of state and local problems and initiatives.

We cannot recreate a working federal system with promises of federal incentives for unspecified actions. States need somehow to be full partners in the development of national regional and industrial policy and must play a meaningful role for success to be possible. Of course, it is difficult to say how, or whether, this can be accomplished. But the national government will need to find a way to make the federal system work for, rather than against, national-policy initiatives.

Conclusion

Some of the problems that confronted the urban policy could be avoided the next time. Perhaps some key players could have been more competent, or some discipline could have been imposed by the Democrats to avoid the jurisdictional fights among committees. But it is unlikely that the country will suddenly become so single-minded about either regional or industrial policy that an administration won't waffle or a Congress unify. Nor will Congress ever be likely to quickly accede to controversial requests from the president. The stakes involved in setting national goals for industrial, regional, or other policies are incredibly high. It is hard to imagine the government smoothly adopting any consensus position. After all, when picking winners and losers on a national scale, we can hardly expect those with something to gain or lose to sit idly by. This political roadblock to national-policy formation is exacerbated by the special conflicts inherent in pursuing industrial and regional policies simultaneously. However, it is worth noting that the early initiatives of 1981 in both the regional and industrial policy areas involve tax concessions.

On the other hand, there is something to think about. If a set of programs could be assembled that substantially served both efficiency and equity criteria and promoted fulfillment of both our industrial and regional-policy aspirations—we might "be in business," so to speak. The strategy of promoting economic development in distressed areas may not satisfy either set of goals completely, but it has promise. Although economic-development programs may not be able to totally rebuild sagging urban economies, they can slow the decline and help cities form new economic foundations. Encouragement of business in depressed regions may not always be the most efficient choice, but there may be some growth industries that can prosper in these areas, and better utilization of resources, especially labor, in these regions might mean a boost in productivity. If the economic development of distressed areas can be promoted with an eye toward equity and efficiency, the political system might prove more cooperative. But this does not suggest that the passage of uniform national policies will be possible—only that programs that are sensitive to the variation in regional problems and prospects may have a chance.

The suggestion here is that we not get so caught up in the design of broad national policies that we stop creating and implementing innovative single programs. The American political system has and will stubbornly resist the imposition of national regional or industrial policies. The people responsible for picking winners and losers will have a tough time making and effecting these decisions. The issue in terms of making regional and industrial policy is that winners selected under one will often be losers in the other. This further complicates an already difficult political situation. We spent much of the last twenty years in the unsuccessful quest for a regional policy—the next twenty may be spent in a similar quest for national industrial policy. Proponents of regional equity may be better off, if that is the case. Our challenge ahead may be to cope with the unique limitations of our political system, so that we can deal with problems of regional equity and economic efficiency in a practical manner.

We do not know who to blame (nor will anyone volunteer) for the failure to implement the Carter national urban policy. The administration blamed Congress for being divided and stubborn, and the interest groups for jumping ship. Congress blamed the administration for being slow, confused, and uncompromising, the House and Senate largely blamed each other, and everyone blamed the press for promoting rising expectations. Some in Washington blamed the states for demanding too great a role, and states blamed Washington for giving them too small a role. The cities blamed them all—and basically had to accept just another in a long series of bitter disappointments. Perhaps, just perhaps, if we had dealt with some individual urban-economic-development programs and not a national urban policy, more would have been accomplished.

Notes

1. Gail Garfield Schwartz and Pat Choate, *Revitalizing the U.S. Economy: A Brief for National Sectoral Policies* (Washington, D.C.: The Academy for Contemporary Problems, 1980), p. 1.

2. "Executive Summary of the Atlantic Conference on Balanced Regional Growth" (Racine, Wisconsin, January 4–6, 1978), prepared by the National Rural Center and the National Council for Urban Economic Development, p. 4.

    3. Schwartz and Choate, *Revitalizing the U.S. Economy,* p. 18.

    4. Alexander Hamilton, James Madison, and John Jay, *The Federalist Papers,* introduction by Clinton Rossiter (New York: The New American Library, 1961), Federalist Paper no. 10, pp. 77–78.

    5. David Truman, *The Governmental Process* (New York: Alfred A. Knopf, 1975).

    6. Theodore Lowi, *The End of Liberalism* (New York: Norton, 1951).

    7. Text of Jimmy Carter's Energy Address (Crisis of Confidence), Washington Post, July 16, 1979, section A, p. 14.

    8. Jimmy Carter, *New Partnership to Conserve America's Communities* (Washington, D.C.: The White House, March 17, 1978), preface.

    9. "Community Conservation Guidelines" (Washington, D.C.: The White House, November 26, 1979), p. 1.

    10. Miles Friedman, ed., *The NASDA Letter,* August 8, 1980, pp. 2–6. Also Schwartz and Choate, *Revitalizing the U.S. Economy,* p. 1.

    11. "Revitalizing the U.S. Economy," *Business Week,* June 30, 1980, p. 56.

    12. Gail Garfield Schwartz and Pat Choate, *Being Number One: Rebuilding the U.S. Economy* (Lexington, Mass.: Lexington Books, D.C. Heath and Company, 1980).

    13. Miles Friedman, ed., *The NASDA Letter,* October 1, 1980, p. 1.

    14. "Staff Summary of the Proceedings of the White House Conference on Balanced National Growth and Economic Development," January 29–February 2, 1978 (Washington, D.C.: The White House Conference Staff, April 10, 1978), Appendix A, p. 1.

    15. Jimmy Carter, *New Partnership.*

3 Congruencies and Conflicts in Regional and Industrial Policies

Harvey A. Garn and
Larry C. Ledebur

Current economic difficulties have evoked an array of proposals for national industrial policies that in many cases emulate those of other advanced industrialized nations. The most common taxonomy of proposed policies is: (1) industry-neutral policies not specific to any given industries or set of firms, taking the form of accelerated depreciation, increased investment-tax credits, and reduced corporate-profit taxes; (2) infrastructure development in areas such as transportation, energy, and public facilities; (3) assistance to growing high-technology, innovative industries (winner or sunrise industries); (4) assistance to troubled, contracting industries (loser or sunset industries).

The idea of national policies does not work naturally in the United States. Historically, national policy for most purposes has been to rely on the local genius for adaptation to different and changing circumstances on the often useful theory that those most directly affected by local circumstances will be best able to make the most efficient adaptations. Thus, as a nation, we have a great deal of difficulty in dealing with the idea of a national responsibility and policy for particular purposes, for example, Chrysler Corporation, New York City, and economically distressed cities, industries, or regions. It is not the case that the nation, acting through its representatives and executive officials, has not aided particular interests or groups. It is, however, the case, that this has seldom been done because it was national policy to do so.

Nevertheless, circumstances change. In recent years, there have been increasing attempts to develop national policies. Thus, we now have what is called a national urban policy, a national rural policy, and a national energy policy. In this context, various strands of public policy and practices are increasingly being aggregated into regional policy and there are insistent pressures to develop an industrial policy. Moreover, similar pressures exist to ensure that such emerging national policies are consistent with each other or, at least, not overtly or inadvertently contradictory.

The primary considerations motivating the recent interest in industrial policy spring primarily from three interrelated concerns about national economic efficiency. The first is that the future rate of growth in the gross national product (GNP) is likely to be low because of input-cost increases and slow rates of growth in demand for output. The second is that the rate of productivity improvement has slowed because of lags in innovation (development and adoption)

47

and because of a shift in industry mix toward services where there is less scope
for productivity gains than in manufacturing. These two concerns have significant
implications for international trade—imports become more attractive and exports more difficult to sell. A third general concern that underlies calls for industrial policy is the possibility that individual industries or major corporations within an industry (such as steel and automobile) may be unable to adjust effectively
to changing constraints and patterns of demand. Interdpeendence among industries through their linkages with suppliers and other industries make it likely that
such an outcome would cause ripple effects, threatening jobs and income opportunities in substantial numbers of other sectors and places throughout the economy.

Regional policies have tended to derive from a somewhat different set of
concerns. The major impetus for regional policy has been to respond to distributional issues in lagging regions. The criteria that have been taken to indicate a need for regional concern have been low income, high unemployment,
and high levels of out-migration of the potential labor force. Designing programs
to ameliorate the problems of lagging regions has always led to tension between
those who had either equity or efficiency concerns as of primary importance.
Some who support regional policies seem to feel that regional balance requires
regional policies, and that there may be efficient activities that have been overlooked, ignored, or precluded by the operation of the private market. Others
argue that the justification for regional policies must be on equity grounds only
because an emphasis on lagging regions would probably result in some overall
efficiency losses.

In recent years, there has been an increasing use of an adjustment rationale
for regional policies—assistance to those regions experiencing employment
losses because of international trade impacts, defense-installation closures, firm
relocation, and urban areas rapidly losing employment and population. This
rationale has two sides—that policy toward places experiencing adjustment
problems should be, on the one hand, temporary and ameliorative to permit
more orderly adjustments, or, on the other, devoted to efforts to find alternative, self-sustaining long-term economic activities. The former view tends to
predominate.

Considerations behind industrial policy rarely reflect the primary aims of
regional policy, except in the case of adjustment assistance and possibly economic efficiency (table 3-1). Conversely, considerations behind regional policy
rarely reflect the primary aims of industrial policy, except in the case of adjustment assistance. Two key questions emerge: (1) Would it be desirable to have
regional policy coordinated with industrial policy so that each reflects the primary aims of the other and works in concert to promote national and regional
efficiency? (2) Does pursuit of either kind of policy imply significant trade-offs
relative to the aims of the other, or can these policies be complementary?

Although the means to achieve a better reflection of the primary aims of
regional policy in industrial policy (and vice versa) are somewhat unclear,

Table 3-1
Aims for Industry and Regional Policies

Industrial Policy Aims	Regional Policy Aims
National economic efficiency	Regional economic efficiency
Gross-national-product growth	Not major aim
Export expansion	Not major aim
Import substitution	Not major aim
Adjustment assistance	Adjustment assistance
Not major aim	Spatial development (lagging regions)
Not major aim	Equity

there do seem to be potential trade-offs between the two. Recommendations for support of low-productivity industries do not mesh well with the primary aims of industrial policy—national efficiency, export expansion, import substitution, and GNP growth—even when justified by regional concentration of troubled industries. Similarly, recommendations for support of high-productivity activities (often very capital intensive, with limited employment opportunities concentrated in high-paying jobs) do not always support regional-policy objectives of employment growth, particularly among the low-skilled or long-term unemployed. These potential trade-off issues are explored in this chapter.

Whether industrial or regional policy is considered, key issues involve what industries should receive support, what kinds of firms should be supported within industries, and whether support should be devoted primarily to creating new activities and jobs or preventing the loss of activities and jobs already existent. In this chapter, potentially significant trade-offs will be illustrated in terms of alternative outcome streams in various industries, different-sized firms within industry, and efforts to increase new starts, expand existing firms, or reduce closures.

Outcome Streams in Different Industries

The possibility of significant trade-offs that may have major consequences for industrial or regional policy exists in the manufacturing industries. If manufacturing industries are cross-classified by value added per production worker (an indicator of concern in industrial policy) and employment growth (an indicator of concern in regional policy), five industries show relatively good performance on both indicators in the 1970s: printing and publishing, chemicals, petroleum refining, nonelectrical machinery, and instruments.[1] Five industries commend themselves on neither of these criteria: textiles, apparel, leather, primary metals, and miscellaneous industries. Of the other two-digit industries, lumber and wood, furniture and fixtures, rubber and plastics, stone, clay, and glass, and fabricated metals do considerably better on employment criteria than on productivity criteria. The reverse is true of the rest.[2]

These overall comparisons illustrate a general point—Support for particular industries will frequently be more suitable in achieving the primary aims of either industrial or regional policy, but not necessarily both simultaneously. For example, suppose that it was decided to support those industries which had the highest productivity as indicated by value added per employee in 1972. The five industries that rank highest on this criterion are: petroleum refining, tobacco products, chemicals, instruments, and transportation equipment. In terms of 1972 ratios of employment, wages, and value added to capital stock, this choice would produce, on average, 20 jobs, $200,000 in wages, and $580,000 in value added per $1,000 of capital stock. Suppose that the choice were to support the five industries that rank highest on employment growth rate. These are instruments, lumber and wood, rubber and plastics, fabricated metals, and petroleum refining. This choice would produce, on average, 40 jobs, $329,500 in wages, and $735,900 in value added per $1 million of capital stock (table 3-2). A comparison of these figures clearly shows the association of productivity with capital intensity and employment growth with lower capital requirements. It also shows the generally higher wages ($10,000 compared to about $8,250) in the high value-added industries.

Table 3-2
Expected Consequences of Picking Winners by Various Choice Rules

Industry Choice Rule (Top 5)	Outcomes per $1 million Capital Stock				
	1 Jobs	2 Average Wages	3 Value Added	4 Value Added per New Job	5 Employees Lost through Closure
1. Highest value added per employee	20	$10,000	$580,000	$29,000	3.5
2. Highest employment growth rate	40	8,250	735,900	18,397	7.0
3. Most labor intensive[a]	83	6,290	1,002,000	12,072	21.4
4. Highest average wages per employee[b]	21	5,300	527,300	25,110	3.5
5. Least loss owing to closure[c]	16	5,380	480,000	30,000	2.6

Note: The data from which this table is calculated are shown in appendix 3B.

[a]Industries are furniture and fixtures, apparel, leather products, miscellaneous, and textiles.

[b]Industries are petroleum refining, transportation equipment, primary metals, chemicals, and nonelectrical machinery.

[c]Industries are petroleum refining, tobacco products, transportation equipment, primary metal and chemicals.

It is of interest in terms of both industrial and regional policy to assess the likely permanence of jobs created. Do the industry choices suggested on productivity grounds differ from those suggested on employment grounds in terms of employment loss owing to the closure of firms? Using 1969–1975 industry-closure rates from the Dun and Bradstreet Market Indicators file provides an estimate of these potential losses. On average, the choice of the second set of industries (those with high current employment gain, labor-intensive practices, and relatively lower wages) would result in about two times as many jobs lost through closure per $1 million in capital stock (7 compared to 3.5).

The starkest contrast shown in table 3–2 is between a choice rule that maximizes the probability that jobs which are created will be permanent (least loss through closures) and that which provides the most current employment per dollar investment in capital stock (most labor intensive). The labor-intensive industries, on average, add more than five times as many jobs per dollar invested in capital as those in which the jobs are more likely to be permanent. At the same time, they are likely to lose almost ten times as many jobs owing to the closure of firms.

These examples illustrate in a fairly dramatic way the importance of deciding what the primary aims of an industrial or regional policy are going to be. Large increments of capital per employee will probably be required to ensure that support is given to industries that are the most productive, pay relatively high wages, and produce the highest probability of permanence. The short-run amelioration of employment problems in particular regions (or nationally) through the support of labor-intensive activities may require less capital—but at the cost of productivity, the income associated with employment, and a higher probability of job losses from firm closures.

These conclusions are generally endorsed by policymakers at all levels of government. However, these observations are based on the most aggregate level of analysis. The case against coordination of industrial and regional policies may not be supported so strongly by a spatially and sectorally disaggregate analysis.

Regional Variations in Industry Performance

Regional differentials in industry performance suggest the need for industry-specific national policies to be sensitive to regional variations. As is well known, the distribution of industry is not uniform across regions, nor does a given industry perform identically in different regions.[3]

Borts and Stein, examining manufacturing in four time periods between 1919 and 1957, concluded:

Interstate differences in growth rates of manufacturing production worker employment do not arise because states have different compositions of industries. These differences arise because, in the industries they contain, states grow at rates different from the national average in those same industries. . . . Maturity and decline have not resulted from a state's concentration in declining industries.[4]

This observation was confirmed by Perloff and others for the period 1939–1954.[5] The industry structure of the older industrialized regions (New England, Middle Atlantic, Great Lakes) in 1939 favored above-average employment growth between 1938 and 1954. Actual employment expansion, however, fell below the national average, indicating the importance of regional variations in the performance of individual industries.

More recently, Schiller and McCarthy examined the regional performance of eighty-six three-digit manufacturing industries and used measures of employment output, earnings, and productivity change. This study concludes that the concept of sectoral growth is central to economic-development strategies.

> Aggregate economic growth incorporates widely varying rates of industry growth as well as diverse patterns of within-industry regional growth. As a consequence, aggregate statistics are not very reliable indices of the experiences of any particular industry or region. To understand the process of economic growth, one must focus on specific sectors of the economy as defined in both industry and spatial terms.

> In view of this heterogeneity, the task of formulating national or state development policies is more complicated. The complications emerge from two directions. First, there is the spatial diversity of industry experience. As we have observed, an industry exhibiting rapid national growth may not be growing rapidly in all regions. Hence, picking a "winner" on the basis of aggregate statistics and promoting its further development may not achieve specific regional objectives.

> An analogous problem occurs in industries with average or below average national growth. Such industries tend to be passed over in development strategies, due to their relatively laggard performance. Yet laggard performance recorded in national statistics may disguise important subnational dynamics. In particular, an industry may be growing very rapidly in some regions while declining in others. In such situations, sectoral growth perspectives may reveal increasing productivity that can propel a local or regional economy.[6]

The extent of differentials in manufacturing productivity among regions has been recently documented by the American Productivity Center.[7] When differences in industry mix were controlled, significant productivity variations among regions were found. Manufacturing productivity according to these measurements is greatest in the West, followed by the North Central and Northeast regions, respectively. The South, with the lowest productivity, is the only region below the national average. Moomaw (1980) argues that manufacturing activity in the South is increasing because the region's relatively low wages more than offset its productivity disadvantage.

Regional averages tend to mask significant intraregional differences in productivity. When census divisions are compared, the Pacific and the Middle Atlantic manufacturing belt have the highest value added per worker. The three southern divisions and the mountain west have the poorest productivity performance. State productivity levels range from 73.7 percent of the national average in Delaware to 133.9 percent in Arizona. All divisions, with the exception of the Pacific, contain states with below-average productivity levels. The South Atlantic and East South Central are the only divisions with no states exceeding the national productivity level.[8]

Additional evidence on the variability of industry performance among regions is obtained through the examination of spatial patterns of firm starts and closures. The regional distribution of manufacturing establishments in 1969 and their changes between 1969 and 1975 are shown in table 3-3. Despite considerable regional variation in the number of manufacturing establishments in 1969, the regions all gained a roughly equal percentage of the new starts between 1969 and 1975. However, they had unequal shares of closures. This led to net increases in manufacturing firms in the South and West and reductions in the Northeast and North Central regions.

The degree to which individual industries contributed to total closures and starts varied considerably across regions. Appendix 3C shows industry closure and start rates by region relative to U.S. rates for the industry. The four regions each had a distinctive overall pattern of closures and starts relative to the U.S. rates as depicted in figure 3-1, with the Northeast doing least well and the West doing best on both counts. In most manufacturing industries, the northeast region had higher closure rates than the United States as a whole (twelve out of twenty), and had no industries with higher start rates than the United States. That pattern was nearly reversed in the western region where closure

Table 3-3
Regional Distribution of Manufacturing Establishments and Components of Change, 1969 and 1975
(*percents*)

Region	Distribution 1969	Closures 1969–1975	Starts 1969–1975	Stationary Firms 1969–1975	Distribution 1975
Northeast	31.6	32.8	24.1	30.7	29.1
North Central	28.1	27.2	24.6	28.6	27.4
South	23.6	24.7	26.5	23.2	24.1
West	16.7	15.3	24.8	17.5	19.5
United States	100.0	100.0	100.0	100.0	100.1

Source: Dun and Bradstreet data.

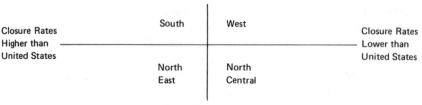

Figure 3-1. Patterns of Closures and Starts

rates exceeded those for the United States in only two industries of the twenty (rubber and plastics and electrical machinery) and start rates were higher in all industries.

The West had seven industries out of twenty that exceeded U.S. start rates by more than 50 percent. Start rates in the South also tended to be above those for the United States, although they were not as high as in the West. The South lagged behind the United States in new starts only in food, tobacco, and lumber and wood products, but had higher closure rates than the United States in fourteen of the twenty industries. The North Central region exceeded U.S. start rates only in tobacco products and textiles, but had lower closure rates than the United States in fourteen of the twenty industries.

Comparative start and closure rates tell part of the story of regional variation in industry performance. Information on the significance of closures and starts of industries for the regional economy and for the nation can be obtained by reviewing the distributions of closures and starts across industries for each region and within industries across regions.

Appendix 3D shows that five of the twenty industries account for more than 50 percent of the closures and starts of firms in each region. There are two industries that are represented among these five industries in all regions, namely, printing and publishing, and nonelectrical machinery. Fabricated metals are among the five industries with the most closures and starts in all regions, except for the group with the most closures in the West. Food products account for a substantial percentage of the closures (but not starts) in all regions except the Northeast.

The regional impact of the effects of organizing support for different industry groups (for example, those with high value added or with high employment growth) can be illustrated through examination of the percentage of closures and starts within regions among the four industry groups discussed in the first section (table 3-4).

Table 3–4
U.S. Closures and Starts by Industry Group within Regions
(*percents*)

Industry Group	Northeast		North Central		South		West	
	Closures	*Starts*	*Closures*	*Starts*	*Closures*	*Starts*	*Closures*	*Starts*
High value added, high employment growth	29.1	35.6	37.4	42.5	29.7	35.6	33.2	35.2
High value added, low employment growth	16.5	13.8	21.7	15.1	22.3	14.8	22.4	17.5
Low value added, high employment growth	20.3	21.9	28.3	29.6	31.8	31.1	29.4	29.6
Low value added, low employment growth	34.0	28.9	12.6	12.8	16.3	18.5	14.7	17.7
Total	99.9	100.2	100.0	100.0	100.1	100.0	99.7	100.0

Source: Dunn and Bradstreet data.

A programmatic approach directed toward preventing closures in existing firms would be likely to help the Northeast more if it were directed at the low value-added/low employment-growth industries (which had 34 percent of the closures in the region); at the high value-added/high employment-growth industries in the North Central and western regions; and the low value-added/high employment-growth industries in the South. Conversely, a policy designed to increase starts in the group of industries adding fewest new firms in each region would be focused on the high value-added/low employment-growth group in all regions but the North Central, where the low value-added/low employment-growth group had the fewest starts. The highest percentage of starts in all regions was in the high value-added/high employment-growth group, which would be suggested by these data as the group of industries to support if national growth is the objective. Thus, although these figures are only illustrative, they do show that specific regional concerns would probably not be best met with a uniform national industrial policy. It is likely that a policy directed primarily at improvements in either national productivity or employment enhancement would have to focus on different industries in each region—and, perhaps, in each local economy in each region.

A similar conclusion can be derived from an examination of the distribution of total U.S. closures and starts by region and industry, as shown in appendix 3E. An industry policy that has as its objective the reduction of closures in those industry groups where closures make the most difference nationally, would focus on low value-added/low employment-growth industries in the Northeast, high value-added/high employment-growth industries in the North Central region, the same industry group in the West, and low value-added/high employment-growth industries in the South, in that order (table 3-5). Generally speaking, pursuit of a national objective of reducing closures would tend to be applied differentially across regions. The same could be said of a national policy to encourage new starts, where they are currently the lowest. This policy applied nationally would suggest a focus on low value-added/low employment-growth industries in the North Central region, and high value-added/low employment-growth industries in the Northeast, West, and South, in that order.

The two illustrations just presented show that a policy designed to affect the most serious regional problems will have to be sensitive to the relative importance of different groups in each region and that a policy to improve the performance of industry nationally will have to be sensitive to the contributions to industry problems made by different regions.

The evidence of this section argues strongly that national industrial policy, to be effective, must be sensitive to regional variations in industry performance. In turn, policies addressing the problems of regions must be sensitive to the relative importance of different industries and industry groups in each region. Recognition of the spatial variability of industry performance causes the design of national industrial policy and, to a lesser extent, regional policy, to become significantly more complex.

Table 3-5
U.S. Closures and Starts by Region and Industry Group
(percents)

Industry Groups	Northeast		North Central		South		West		United States	
	Closures	*Starts*	*Closures*	*Starts*	*Closures*	*Starts*	*Closures*	*Starts*	*Closures*	*Starts*
High value added, high employment growth	9.5	8.6	10.2	10.5	7.3	9.4	5.1	8.7	32.1	37.2
High value added, low employment growth	5.4	3.3	5.9	3.7	5.5	3.9	3.4	4.3	20.2	15.2
Low value added, high employment growth	6.7	5.3	7.7	7.3	7.9	8.2	4.5	7.3	26.8	28.1
Low value added, low employment growth	11.2	6.7	3.4	3.1	4.0	4.9	2.2	4.4	20.8	19.1

Source: Dunn and Bradstreet data.

Small-Business Enterprise in Regional and Industry Policies

We have suggested that at an aggregate level the objectives of regional policy and industrial sectoral policy may not be congruent and have attempted to demonstrate the possible significant trade-offs that may arise in the pursuit of the objectives of these two national policies. In addition, we have discussed the need to develop regional policies that are sensitive to the variations in the sectoral composition of regions and industrial policies that are sensitive to the regional variations in the performance of industries and firms. Even this, however, understates the complexity of attempting to integrate diverse national-policy objectives.

Clearly, the complexity of this endeavor is compounded as the number of policies considered is increased (for example, adding the objectives of urban, rural, energy, and other policies). Recently, interest has been expressed in targeting at least some of the assistance in national programs to smaller firms. It is not inconceivable that this concern would arise also in the consideration and design of a national industrial policy. It is useful to consider, therefore, whether targeting industry policies to small firms provides a potentially useful focus.

In the context of examining national policies for regions and industries, small-business enterprises are important. The rationales for targeting assistance to small firms are related to the objectives of both regional and industrial policy. The small-business emphasis appears to derive from two primary rationales:

1. It is asserted that small-business enterprises are the primary generators of employment opportunities in the U.S. economy. This is based on the recent estimate that "on average about 60 percent of all jobs in the United States are generated by firms with twenty or fewer employees and about 50 percent of all jobs are created by independent small entrepreneurs."[9]

2. It is argued that small firms are responsible for a disproportionate share of new industrial technology, accounting for more than one-half of all inventions and innovations.[10]

The job-generation rationale implies that a regional policy oriented to the assistance of the private sector should focus on smaller firms. The implication of the second rationale is that an industrial policy with the objective of encouraging innovation and enhancing productivity should perhaps also be oriented to smaller firms. This suggests that the small-business sector may serve as a point of congruence between the two sets of national policies. This would be the case if smaller firms generating high rates of employment growth were characterized also by high productivity and/or high rates of increase in productivity.

This proposition was tested. Small firms (1 to 99 employees) in two-digit manufacturing industries were ranked on the basis of economic performance on four criteria—employment generation,[11] wage level in 1972, value added per employee in 1972, and change in value added per employee between 1967 and 1972. Employment generation and wage levels are used as measures of regional-development outcomes, and value added and change in value added, our measures of productivity, represent industrial-policy outcomes.

Small firms were ranked on the basis of performance on these four criteria across industries (that is, relative to similar-sized firms in other manufacturing industries) and also on the basis of their performance compared to size categories of larger firms.[12] The first ranking across industries is used to identify industries in which small firms perform best, and the second to determine if this scale of operation is optimal within the industry.

The five industries in which small firms performed best relative to small firms in other industries on each of the four criteria are presented in table 3–6. The most propitious outcome would be the identification of a common set of industries in which smaller firms contributed to the objective of both regional development and national industrial policy.

Tables 3–6 and 3–7 indicate that in all probability, targeting to small firms will not serve to minimize the trade-offs between the objectives of the two national policies. Only three of the twenty two-digit manufacturing industries meet at least one of the performance criteria in each set of policy objectives.

Petroleum stands out with high performance on all four criteria. The chemicals industry, with the expected relationship between high productivity and wages, exhibits high performance on both value-added criteria, but not on the employment measure. The remaining industry identified in the matrix—stone, clay, and glass—ranks high in employment and value added, represents the optimal employment size in the industry, and performs well on the wage measure and the change-in-value-added criterion (table 3–6) relative to firms of corresponding size in other industries.

There are further limitations to the feasibility of targeting to the small-business sector in the effort to achieve correspondence between the objectives of regional development policy and national industrial policy; limitations that raise questions about the desirability of targeting to small firms to achieve either set of objectives. In table 3–8, small firms are ranked on the basis of their performance relative to other firms of greater size in their own industry. Five performance criteria are used—value added per employee, change in value added per employee, new capital investment per employee, wage level, and change in wages per employee between 1967 and 1972.

In general, small-sized firms perform poorly relative to large-scale enterprise. For example, in the petroleum, chemical, and stone, clay, and glass industries, small firms tend to perform poorly when compared to larger firms in their industries, indicating that significant trade-offs may exist between potential employment and productivity gains in these industries. Alternatively, if industries are selected in which small firms are the optimal size class in their industry, for example, textiles, these perform poorly compared to small firms in other industries.

Table 3–6
Manufacturing Industries in Regional and Industry Policy

Regional Development Policy

Employment Criterion[b]

Rank[a]	Industry	Employment in Industry[c]	Wage[d]	Value Added[e]	ΔValue Added[f]
1	Stone, clay and glass	1	6	4	8
2	Apparel	3	20	20	19
3	Leather	4	18	19	15
4	Petroleum	1	1	1	3
5	Furniture	1	15	18	13

Wages Criterion

Rank[b]	Industry	Employment in Industry[c]	Employment in Size Class[b]	Value Added[e]	ΔValue Added[f]
1	Petroleum	1	4	1	3
2	Nonelectrical machinery	1	9	6	16
3	Chemicals	2	20	2	4
4	Fabricated metals	4	8	8	12
5	Instruments	2	11	7	9

Industrial Policy

Value-Added Criterion

Rank[a]	Industry	Employment in Industry[c]	Employment in Size Class[a]	Wages[d]	ΔValue Added[f]
1	Petroleum	1	4	1	3
2	Chemicals	2[a]	20	3	4
3	Food	4	17	12	2
4	Stone, clay, and class	1	1	6	8
5	Primary metals	4	18	8	18

Change in Value-Added Criterion

Rank[a]	Industry	Employment in Industry[c]	Employment in Size Class[a]	Wage[d]	Value Added[e]
1	Lumber and wood	2	13	16	15
2	Food	4	17	12	3
3	Petroleum	2[a]	4	1	1
4	Chemicals	2	20	3	2
5	Paper	2	16	9	9

Source: Data from 1972 *Census of Manufacturers*, Bureau of the Census, U.S. Department of Commerce.

[a] Rank ordering of the five industries in which small firms (1–99 employees) exhibited the highest performance compared with similar-sized firms in other industries. Industries compared are two-digit manufacturing.

[b] The employment criterion is jobs per thousand dollars of new investment in 1972. The rationale for this approach is as follows: Data on job generation by firm size between two periods at the two-digit level are unavailable because of the difficulty in identifying firms that change size categories within the time span. It would be preferable to use the criterion of jobs per unit of capital assets rather than new investment. Data on assets by firm size by industry are unavailable. New investment is used as a proxy for total assets. The rank-order correlation between total assets in 1972 and new investment in 1972 for two-digit manufacturing industries was 0.89. This ratio of employment per unit of new investment has validity only for obtaining rank orderings of industries.

[c] Rank of small firms (1–99 employees) in five firm-size categories within a particular industry.

[d] Average wage level of production workers in 1972.

[e] Value added per employee in 1972.

[f] Change in value added per employee in 1972.

Table 3-7
Regional and Industrial Policy Industry Matrix

Industrial Policy	Regional Development Policy		
	Employment and Wages	Employment	Wages
Value Added and Δ Value Added	Petroleum		Chemicals
Value Added		Stone, Clay, and Glass	Chemicals
Δ Value Added			Chemicals

Thus, it appears that although small firms may generate higher employment outcomes, there are significant productivity and wage trade-offs with this scale of operation. The existence of these trade-offs suggests that small firms may not be an exclusive focus for either regional or national industrial policy, much less a means of resolving the trade-offs between the objectives of the two policies.

Conclusions

In our enthusiasm to establish national policies to ameliorate particular problems, we often overlook the impacts of measures implementing one policy on the potential to realize the goals and objectives of other policies. It is important to recognize that the primary objectives of regional policy and national industrial policy are quite different. The impetus to develop an industrial policy derives from concern about economic efficiency, the rate of growth in output of the national economy, lagging productivity, and the international competitiveness of U.S. exports. The interest in aggregating strands of public policy and practice into a regional policy grows out of concern for disparities in regional levels of economic development and the attendant set of efficiency and equity issues.

In this chapter, we have focused on two principal questions: (1) Does the pursuit of either a national industrial policy or a regional policy imply significant trade-offs relative to the aim of the other?, and (2) Would it be desirable to have regional policy coordinated with industrial policy so that each reflects the primary aim of the other?

To address the first question of trade-offs, we examined the national performance of manufacutring industries, the performance of small firms in manufacturing, and start and closure of manufacturing firms nationally and by region. Although the examples used were only illustrative, the data support three conclusions.

1. Support of particular industries will contribute to the achievement of the objectives of either industrial policy or regional policy, but seldom will

Table 3-8
Ranking on Criteria Variables for Small Firms (1-99 Employees)

SIC[a]	Industry	Rank in Industry[b]						Rank in Size Class[c]					
		(1) Value Added per Employee 1972 ($1,000)	(2) Wages per Employee 1972 ($)	(3) New Capital Expenditures per Employee 1972 ($1,000)	(4) Δ in Value Added per Employee 1967-1972 (%)	(5) Change in Wages per Employee 1967-1972 (%)	(6) Average Rank for All Criteria in the Industry	(7) Value Added per Employee	(8) Wages per Employee 1972 ($)	(9) New Capital Expenditures per Employee 1972 ($1,000)	(10) Δ in Value Added per Employee 1967-1972 (%)	(11) Change in Wages	(12) Average Rank for All Criteria in the Industry
All Industries		5	5	5	4	5	4.8						
20	Food	5	5	2	2	3	3.4	3	12	7	2	4	5.6
21	Tobacco	5	4	5	4	4	4.4	17	19	16	20	16	17.6
22	Textiles	1	2	2	2	5	2.4	16	17	8	7	9	11.4
23	Apparel	2	2	3	5	5	3.4	20	20	20	19	20	19.8
24	Lumber and wood	5	5	4[d]	5	4[d]	4.4	15	16	9	1	1	8.4
25	Furniture	4[d]	3[d]	4	2[d]	5	3.4	18	15	17	13	15	15.6
26	Paper	5	5		1		4.0	9	9	6	5	6	7.0
27	Printing and publishing	5	5	4	4	5	4.6	10	7	12	10	11	10.0
28	Chemicals	4[d]	4[d]	4[d]	3[d]	4[d]	3.8	2	3	2	4	5	3.2
29	Petroleum	5	5	5		5	4.2	1	1	1	3	3	1.8
30	Rubber and plastics	5	5	1	5	5	4.2	11	13	4	11	14	10.6
31	Leather	4	3	2	5	4	3.6	19	18	19	15	13	16.8
32	Stone, clay, and glass	5	5		4	3	4.0	4	6	5	8	2	5.0
33	Primary metals	4	5	3	5	4	4.0	5	8	3	18	17	10.2
34	Fabricated metals	5	5	1	3	5	3.8	8	4	11	12	12	4.4
35	Nonelectrical machinery	5	5	3	5	5	4.6	6	2	13	16	18	11.0
36	Electrical machinery	5	4	2	5	5	4.2	12	11	14	14	10	12.2
37	Transportation	5	5	2	5	5	4.4	13	10	10	17	19	13.8
38	Instruments	5	5	4[d]	3[d]	2[d]	3.8	7	5	15	9	7	8.6
39	Miscellaneous	4[d]	2[d]	4[d]	3[d]	2[d]	3.0	14	14	18	6	8	12.0
	Average rank for all industries	4.4	4.2	3.1	3.6	4.2							

Source: Data from 1972 Census of Manufacturers, Bureau of the Census, U.S. Department of Commerce.

[a]SIC lists the Standard Industrial Classification codes for each of these industries as defined by the U.S. government.

[b]Rank of small firms' performance relative to four other size classes of firms: (1) 100-249, (2) 250-499, (3) 500-999, and (4) ≥ 1,000 employees within the industry. Worst-off equals 5, best-off equals 1.

[c]Rank of industry performance relative to small firms' performance in the other industry breaks. Worst-off equals 20, best-off equals 1.

[d]Data not available for one of the size-classes because of disclosure requirements; therefore, ranks range from 1-4 with worst-off equal to 4.

contribute to the achievement of both sets of objectives simultaneously. Among industries there appear to be sharp trade-offs between those which have a high potential for generating employment and those which have high productivity, pay relatively high wages, and offer the highest probability of permanence of employment. This trade-off dilemma is exacerbated by the differential capital costs of achieving these outcomes.

2. Despite the recent interest in the employment generation of small firms and the thesis that this sector accounts for a high proportion of new invention and innovation, targeting regional and industrial policies to smaller-business enterprises does not appear to provide a means of avoiding the trade-off dilemma inherent in the different objectives of these two policies. Although small firms may generate higher employment outcomes, there are significant productivity and wage trade-offs with this scale of operation. The existence of these trade-offs suggests that small firms are probably not an effective focus for either regional or industrial policy, much less a means of resolving the trade-offs between the objectives of the two policies.

3. Regional and industrial policies with the objectives of either industry retention or stimulating new firm starts also will confront serious trade-offs. A uniform national industrial policy is unlikely to respond effectively to regional concerns. An effective national industrial policy, to achieve its own objectives, will need to focus on different industries in different regions. In turn, a policy designed to affect the most serious regional problems will have to be sensitive to the relative importance of different industry groups in each region.

On the basis of these findings, each of which indicates the existence of sharp trade-offs between the objectives of national industrial policy and regional policy, we conclude that coordination between the two policies is not only desirable, but also essential to the realization of the objectives of either. Our analysis leads to the following propositions.

1. Aggregate national statistics on industry performance are unreliable indicators of regional performance of industries. The range of variability in industry performance argues that national industrial policies must be region specific. The need to be sensitive to regional industry differentials significantly increases the complexity of designing and administering national industrial policy.

2. Primary emphasis on the objectives of one of these policies will result in serious trade-offs with the objectives of the other.

3. Uniform national industrial policies will not be effective in achieving their objectives. To be effective, these policies will need to emphasize different industries in different regions. Uniform or region-specific national industrial policies will have differential impacts among regions and it is unlikely that these outcomes will be consonant with regional-development objectives.

4. Regional policies uniform for all regions will not be effective in achieving their objectives. Policies designed primarily to achieve regional-development objectives also will emphasize different industries among regions.

Thus, we argue that enthusiasm for either a national industrial policy or a regional development model must be tempered by consideration of objectives of the other. The two sets of objectives cannot be met simultaneously at the national level. Ultimately, the opportunity cost of pursuing one set of national objectives will be the sacrifice of the potential of achieving the other. It is improbable that ways will be found at the national level to avoid paying these costs. Realization of the existence of this harsh reality leads inevitably to the conclusion that national policy must find ways of establishing priorities among competing policy objectives.

Notes

1. This initial discussion draws on work by Deborah L. Buckrop, "Classification of Two-Digit Manufacturing Industries on the Basis of Performance Characteristics" (Urban Institute Working Paper, February 1979). Appendix 3A is a table reproduced from this paper, showing the cross-classification and ranks of other indicators of interest.

2. The other two-digit industries under consideration are food products, tobacco products, paper products, electrical machinery, and transportation equipment.

3. This literature is reviewed by the Advisory Commission on Intergovernmental Relations in *Regional Growth: Historic Perspective* (Washington, D.C., June 1980), chapter 3.

4. George H. Borts and Jerome L. Stein, *Economic Growth in a Free Market* (New York: Columbia University Press, 1964), p. 46.

5. Harvey S. Perloff et al., *Regions, Resources and Economic Growth* (Lincoln, Neb.: University of Nebraska Press, 1960).

6. Bradley R. Schiller and Amy A. McCarthy, *Subnational Variations in Industrial Growth,* study prepared for the Economic Development Administration, U.S. Department of Commerce, September 1980.

7. *Productivity Perspectives* (Houston, Texas: American Productivity Center, 1980). The productivity-index measure used is the ratio of value added in manufacturing in the region to the comparable national average.

8. Larry C. Ledebur and Ronald L. Moomaw, *Productivity in the Nation's Cities and Regions* (The Urban Institute, 1981).

9. David Birch, "The Job Generation Process" (Cambridge, Mass.: MIT Program on Neighborhood and Regional Change, 1979), report submitted to the Economic Development Administration, U.S. Department of Commerce. The findings of this research are provocative, raising a variety of questions and issues that require further research. Some of these are addressed in Harvey Garn and Larry Ledebur, "The Role of Small Business Enterprise in Economic Development" (The Urban Institute, Washington, D.C., 1980).

10. Although this assertion is frequently made, in our judgment it is inadequately documented and should serve only as a working hypothesis. The sources for these views are three studies, each with differing methodologies, definitions, and findings: Gellman Research Associates, Inc., *Indicators of International Trends in Technological Innovation* (Jenkintown, Pa. 1976), report prepared for the National Science Foundation, Washington, D.C.; *Technological Innovation: Its Environment and Management,* report of the Panel on Invention and Innovation to the Secretary of Commerce (U.S. Government Printing Office, January 1967); John O. Flander and Richard S. Morse, "The Role of New Technical Enterprises in the U.S. Economy" (Cambridge, Mass.: MIT Development Foundation, 1975). The literature on firm size and innovation is reviewed by Deborah Buckrop in "Innovation in the Private Sector: A Review of Firm Size Effects" (Urban Institute Working Paper, 1981).

11. The employment criterion used was employment per unit of new investment. See footnote b, table 3-6.

12. Size categories examined included (a) 1-99, (b) 100-499, (c) 500-999, (d) 1000+ employees.

Appendix 3A: Classification Results for Manufacturing Industries, from Production-Worker Data

Employment Growth 1969–1976	SIC[b]	Industry	Value Added per Production Worker, 1972 High[a]					
			Absolute Change Value Added	Average Wage	Value Added/ Wages	Nonproduction Worker/ Production Worker	Change Production Index	Durable or Nondurable
High	27	Printing and publishing	7	7	6	1	16	Nondurable
	28	Chemicals	5	4	1	2	2	Nondurable
	29	Petroleum refining	18	1	3	7	7	Nondurable
	35	Nonelectircal machinery	2	5	8	5	5	Durable
	38	Instruments	10	10	4	3	3	Durable
		Average rank	8.4	5.4	4.4	3.6	6.6	
Low	20	Food products	4	13	5	4	11	Nondurable
	21	Tobacco products	17	14	2	16	12	Nondurable
	26	Paper products	15	6	13	12	14	Nondurable
	36	Electrical machinery	6	11	7	6	8	Durable
	37	Transportation	1	2	12	8	18	Durable
		Average rank	8.6	9.2	7.8	9.2	12.6	

| | | Value Added per Production Worker, 1972 | | | | | |
| | | | | | Low | | |
SIC[b]	Industry	Absolute Change Value Added	Average Wage	Value Added/ Wages	Nonpro- duction Worker/ Produc- tion Worker	Change Production Index	Durable or Non- durable
24	Lumber and wood	8	15	15	17	15	Durable
25	Furniture and fixtures	16	16	16	15	6	Durable
30	Rubber and plastics	9	12	9	11	1	Non- durable
32	Stone, clay, and glass	11	9	11	13	9	Durable
34	Fabricated metals	3	8	14	9	17	Durable
Average rank		9.4	12.0	13.0	13.0	9.6	
22	Textiles	13	18	19	19	10	Non- durable
23	Apparel	14	20	17	18	13	Non- durable
31	Leather	19	19	20	20	20	Non- durable
33	Primary metals	12	3	18	14	19	Durable
39	Miscellaneous	c	17	10	10	4	Durable
Average rank		14.5	15.4	16.8	16.2	13.2	

Source: Deborah L. Buckrop, "Classification of Two-Digit Manufacturing Industries on the Basis of Performance Characteristics," The Urban Institute, February 1979.

[a]Ranks range from 1, the most favorable performance on an indicator, to 20, the least favorable performance. Ranks 1 to 10 are said to be high, and ranks 11 to 20 are in the low range.

[b]SIC represents the Standard Industrial Classification Code for each industry as defined by the U.S. government.

[c]Rank not possible because change in value added was not calculated for SIC 39 owing to inadequate data for 1967.

Appendix 3B: Ratios for Manufacturing Industries and Relative Ranks

		1		2		3	
SIC	Industry	Employees per $1,000,000 Capital Stock, 1972	Rank	Value Added per $1,000,000 Capital Stock, 1972 (in thousands of dollars)	Rank	Value Added per Employee (in thousands of dollars)	Rank
20	Food	35	12–13	794.5	10	22.7	6
21	Tobacco	11	19	440.0	19	40.0	2
22	Textiles	62	5	762.6	11	12.3	18
23	Apparel	93	2	920.7	7	9.9	20
24	Lumber and wood	38	11	566.2	16	14.9	16
25	Furniture	104	1	1372.8	1	13.2	17
26	Paper	34	14	700.4	13	20.6	7
27	Printing	54	6	1031.4	3	19.1	11
28	Chemicals	19	18	735.3	12	38.7	3
29	Petroleum	5	20	207.0	20	41.4	1
30	Rubber	51	8	963.9	5	18.9	12
31	Leather	86	3	920.2	8	10.7	19
32	Stone, clay, glass	42	10	848.4	9	20.2	10
33	Primary metals	25	16	507.5	18	20.3	9
34	Fabricated metals	52	7	936.0	6	18.0	14
35	Nonelectrical machinery	33	15	676.5	14	20.5	8
36	Electrical machinery	35	12–13	644.0	15	18.4	13
37	Transportation	22	17	510.4	17	23.2	5
38	Instruments	43	9	1006.2	4	23.4	4
39	Miscellaneous	68	4	1033.6	2	15.2	15

Average wages per $1,000,000 Capital Stock, 1972 (in thousands of dollars)	Rank	Wages per Employee (dollars)	Rank	Employees lost through Closures per $1,000,000 Capital Stock (1969–1975)	Rank	Percentage Employees lost through Closure (1969–1975)	Rank
288.2	14	8,233	13	8.4	12	24.1	17
83.3	19	7,573	14	2.0	2	18.6	8
393.8	9	6,352	18	13.3	16	21.5	14
490.2	4	5,271	20	24.3	18	26.1	19
274.2	15	7,215	15	7.6	11	20.0	11–12
721.6	1	6,938	17	25.9	19	24.9	18
321.6	12	9,460	6	5.7	6	16.9	3
502.1	2	9,310	8	12.7	15	23.6	15–16
198.3	18	10,437	4	3.9	5	20.3	13
58.7	20	11,738	1	0.9	1	17.8	7
426.5	7	8,362	12	8.8	13	17.3	4
499.9	3	5,813	19	27.3	20	31.8	20
373.8	10	8,901	11	7.4	9	17.6	6
266.2	16	10,646	3	3.2	4	12.8	1
481.3	6	9,255	9	10.2	14	19.7	10
334.4	11	10,135	5	6.2	7	18.9	9
320.0	13	9,143	10	7.0	8	20.0	11–12
254.4	17	11,565	2	3.1	3	14.1	2
406.7	8	9,458	7	7.5	10	17.5	5
485.2	5	7,136	16	16.0	17	23.6	15–16

Source: *1972 Census of Manufacturers,* Bureau of the Census, U.S. Department of Commerce.

Note: Ranking is from 1–20 where 1 equals best-off condition and 20 equals worst-off.

Appendix 3C: Regional Closures and Starts in Firms Indexed by U.S. Totals (Rates)

SIC	Industry	Northeast		North Central		South		West	
		Closures	Starts	Closures	Starts	Closures	Starts	Closures	Starts
	All Industries	1.04	0.76	0.97	0.87	1.05	1.13	0.92	1.49
20	Food	1.02	0.89	1.02	0.89	1.06	0.94	0.83	1.50
21	Tobacco	1.23	0.87	0.91	1.93	0.86	0.85	0.96	2.37
22	Textiles	1.12	0.78	0.91	1.12	0.88	1.07	0.79	2.56
23	Apparel	1.09	0.75	0.94	0.88	0.86	1.30	0.84	1.93
24	Lumber and wood	0.99	0.83	1.03	0.95	1.08	0.95	0.88	1.23
25	Furniture	0.99	0.67	0.94	0.84	1.09	1.10	0.85	1.57
26	Paper	1.12	0.87	0.99	0.95	0.93	1.15	0.85	1.33
27	Printing and publishing	1.02	0.80	1.00	0.85	1.04	1.19	0.92	1.39
28	Chemicals	1.04	0.84	0.98	0.89	1.01	1.09	0.92	1.40
29	Petroleum	0.95	0.78	0.97	0.97	1.13	1.24	0.85	1.03
30	Rubber and plastics	1.01	0.72	0.85	0.87	1.00	1.25	1.02	1.33
31	Leather	1.11	0.60	1.00	0.90	0.86	1.48	0.85	2.79
32	Stone, clay, and glass	0.95	0.79	0.97	0.81	1.08	1.04	0.91	1.45
33	Primary metals	1.08	0.84	0.98	0.86	1.01	1.40	0.91	1.37
34	Fabricated metals	1.00	0.71	0.97	0.88	1.11	1.33	0.92	1.48
35	Nonelectrical machinery	0.99	0.75	0.93	0.80	1.11	1.26	0.98	1.37
36	Electrical machinery	1.03	0.76	0.97	0.78	1.01	1.25	1.01	1.46
37	Transportation	0.88	0.67	0.94	0.80	1.16	1.11	0.94	1.41
38	Instruments	1.03	0.77	0.97	0.80	1.03	1.19	0.99	1.57
39	Miscellaneous	0.98	0.68	1.02	0.96	1.08	1.24	0.94	1.61

Source: *1972 Census of Manufacturers*, Bureau of the Census, U.S. Department of Commerce.

Appendix 3D: Percent Distributions of Closures and Starts in Firms across Industries for Census Regions

SIC	Industry	Northeast		North Central		South		West	
		Closures	Starts	Closures	Starts	Closures	Starts	Closures	Starts
20	Food	6.6	3.5	11.1	4.8	12.5	4.6	8.7	4.4
21	Tobacco	0.1	0.0	0.0	0.0	0.1	0.1	0.0	0.0
22	Textiles	5.0	4.0	0.6	0.7	3.8	3.6	0.7	1.3
23	Apparel	16.7	12.6	3.3	2.7	5.8	6.5	5.2	5.8
24	Lumber and wood	3.4	4.6	5.0	5.9	10.5	10.0	9.8	9.9
25	Furniture	3.9	3.1	3.7	2.9	5.5	4.5	4.5	4.5
26	Paper	2.3	1.7	1.7	1.3	1.3	1.1	1.0	0.7
27	Printing and publishing	10.9	16.2	12.2	16.2	11.3	16.7	10.9	14.1
28	Chemicals	5.0	3.5	5.5	3.4	5.6	3.5	4.7	2.8
29	Petroleum	0.5	0.3	0.7	0.4	1.0	0.6	0.6	0.3
30	Rubber and plastics	2.5	3.5	3.1	4.8	1.8	2.9	2.9	3.3
31	Leather	2.7	1.4	0.8	0.6	0.8	0.9	0.8	1.0
32	Stone, clay, and glass	3.0	3.0	5.9	5.1	6.9	5.3	4.5	3.8
33	Primary metals	2.1	1.8	2.8	2.0	1.4	1.4	1.8	1.3
34	Fabricated metals	7.5	7.7	10.6	10.9	7.1	8.4	7.7	8.1
35	Nonelectrical machinery	10.1	12.1	17.1	20.0	10.3	12.6	14.4	14.5
36	Electrical machinery	5.9	6.9	4.6	5.2	3.4	4.6	7.2	7.4
37	Transportation	1.6	1.7	4.3	3.8	5.0	4.4	5.5	5.0
38	Instruments	2.6	3.5	1.9	2.5	1.5	2.2	2.6	3.5
39	Miscellaneous	7.5	9.1	5.1	6.8	4.5	6.1	6.2	8.3

Source: *1972 Census of Manufacturers*, Bureau of the Census, U.S. Department of Commerce.

**Appendix 3E:
Regional Closures and
Starts in Firms as a
Percent of U.S. Closures
and Starts in Firms**

SIC	Industry	Northeast		North Central		South		West	
		Closures	Starts	Closures	Starts	Closures	Starts	Closures	Starts
	All Industries	32.8	24.1	27.2	24.6	24.7	26.5	15.3	24.8
20	Food	22.5	19.5	31.5	27.2	32.0	28.2	13.9	25.1
21	Tobacco	44.7	31.6	7.4	15.8	44.7	44.7	3.2	7.9
22	Textiles	57.7	40.2	5.5	6.8	32.8	39.9	4.0	13.1
23	Apparel	63.7	44.2	10.5	9.8	16.5	25.0	9.3	21.1
24	Lumber and wood	17.2	14.4	20.5	18.8	39.4	34.7	22.9	32.1
25	Furniture	29.3	19.8	23.2	18.9	31.4	31.9	16.0	29.5
26	Paper	44.1	34.1	27.1	27.3	19.3	23.8	9.4	14.9
27	Printing and publishing	31.5	24.6	29.3	25.2	24.4	28.0	14.7	22.2
28	Chemicals	31.5	25.2	28.4	25.3	26.3	28.3	13.8	21.2
29	Petroleum	22.4	18.4	27.1	24.5	36.2	39.9	14.3	17.2
30	Rubber and plastics	32.6	23.2	32.8	32.8	17.3	21.5	17.3	22.5
31	Leather	63.2	34.3	14.7	15.0	14.0	24.2	8.1	26.5
32	Stone, clay, and glass	20.0	16.5	32.2	29.0	33.9	32.5	13.9	22.0
33	Primary metals	33.5	26.2	36.7	30.7	16.8	23.3	13.0	19.7
34	Fabricated metals	29.8	21.1	34.8	30.5	21.2	25.5	14.2	22.9
35	Nonelectrical machinery	26.1	19.7	36.6	33.3	19.9	22.7	17.3	24.3
36	Electrical machinery	37.7	27.8	24.5	21.1	16.6	20.4	21.3	30.7
37	Transportation	14.3	10.8	31.2	25.0	32.4	31.1	22.1	33.0
38	Instruments	39.1	29.0	24.6	20.8	17.6	20.3	18.8	29.8
39	Miscellaneous	41.9	29.0	23.5	22.3	18.7	21.4	15.9	27.4

Source: *1972 Census of Manufacturers*, Bureau of the Census, U.S. Department of Commerce.

The Regional–Development Implications of Industrial Policy

Paul S. Lande

The use of employment statistics as an indicator of the performance of state and regional economies is widespread among policymakers at all levels of government. The behavior of state and regional employment provides as indication of the long-term growth as well as the short-term cyclical variability of regional economies. Recent controversies regarding the relative performance of regional economies in the United States have, in large measure, concerned themselves with the behavior of regional employment. For example, rates of growth in employment lower than the national average have been used as a sign of ill-health of the Northeast regional economy; or variability of regional employment greater than the national average is taken to be an indication that a state or region is subject to cyclical sensitivity greater than the national economy. Such comparisons have also provided the basis for regional development and stabilization policies.

Regional economic development and stabilization policies are frequently tied to attempts to accelerate the industrial development of regional economies as well as to seek government aid and assistance. Frequently, such assistance is received from federal sources. It is a commonplace belief among state government officials that more is better. Therefore, regional-industrial-development programs are frequently indiscriminate with respect to the kind of industrial/commercial development that takes place. A full understanding of the behavior of regional economies leads one to the observation that the relative stability of any given region will be determined by the industrial structure extant in the region. Thus, any region may achieve greater or lesser stability than the national economy, depending on the industrial structure of that region. In addition, the rate of growth of the regional economy is not independent of the industrial structure of the region. Thus, an informed debate over the relative merits of a national industry policy and regional development and stabilization policies requires a full understanding of the relationship of the industrial structure to growth and stability of regional economies as well as of the national economy. For example, in the current debate over the relative performance of the Northeast vis à vis the South, it is unclear whether the Northeast has been suffering from a long-term secular decline or is subject to greater cyclical fluctuations than the South, or both.[1] Distinguishing between the two in terms of industrial structure is a prerequisite to deriving appropriate long-term versus short-term development and stabilization policies.

Regional Portfolio Analysis

One can view the resources of a region, both human and physical, as an endowment to be allocated among alternative uses to meet specified objectives. Regional objectives may include increasing the rate of growth of income or employment, achieving a more uniform distribution of income, and increasing the stability of the regional economy, among others. It is in this sense that the resources of a region can be usefully viewed as a portfolio in which employment in the various sectors of the economy is analogous to investment in an array of securities. Thus, the behavior of the regional portfolio indicates the performance of the regional economy with respect to a specified objective function. The regional portfolio can be evaluated with respect to the return on the allocation of regional resources (the growth of total employment), and with respect to the stability of the regional economy.

The portfolio-analytic approach provides a framework for identifying the determinants of regional economic activity at a highly disaggregated level of analysis. The adoption of disaggregated approaches has been shown to be very useful in the study of regional economies. Perhaps the most outstanding example of such an approach is input-output analysis. In analysis of regional impact multipliers, identification of industrial complexes, and for other purposes, input-output analysis has proved to be an invaluable tool. The development of a portfolio-analytic approach to the study of the problem of regional economic instability will make possible an equally disaggregated interindustry framework.

Once the analytical framework is established and the empirical relationships estimated, it will be possible to determine the effect alternative, industrial-development strategies have on regional growth and stability. This is accomplished by estimating the portfolio variance, an index of economic instability for alternate regional industrial structures. In what follows, an analytical model will be developed that expresses the idea of an employment-portfolio variance and an optimal-portfolio variance. The optimal portfolio minimizes the instability of employment. An employment-growth constraint can be introduced so that the trade-off (should one exist) between growth and stability can be explicitly considered. The optimal solution will be expressed in terms of the proportion of employment in the various sectors. This portfolio variance can be calculated for each region, thereby showing that interindustry relationship as well as industrial structure vary from region to region.

Related Research

The study of the determinants of the stability of regional economies dates from the work of Simpson,[2] Vining,[3] and Neff and Weifenbach.[4] These studies represent the first attempts to identify the causes and consequences of regional economic instability and regional cyclical behavior. All these works attempted to examine the relationship between regional industrial structure and the sensitivity of regional economies to fluctuations in the national economy. These studies did not produce conclusive results, owing to the highly aggregated nature of the data analyzed and lack of clarity in the underlying models. The result, by the end of the 1950s, was that the basic premise on which the studies rested had yet to be conclusively tested.

This situation was partially alleviated in 1960, when George Borts published an important study of the cyclical behavior of state economies.[5] In this study, Borts developed an index of cyclical severity that was based on an analysis of the amplitude and length of the cycle of manufacturing employment for each of thirty-three states for the period 1914–1953. The index of cyclical severity allowed Borts to rank states according to their cyclical behavior. Borts attempted to isolate sensitivity by introducing a hypothetical cyclical index for each state. By assuming that the cyclical behavior of a particular industry in any given state was the same as the behavior of that industry in the national economy, he was able to develop a hypothetical cyclical-behavior index. This was done by weighting the cyclical behavior of each national industry (two-digit manufacturing) by the relative importance of the industry in each state. A comparison of the hypothetical index with the actual index allowed Borts to analyze the relationship between cyclical behavior and industrial structure, employment growth, and cyclical amplitude (that is, the severity of the state cycle). Borts reached the following conclusion: "Thus, we can assert quite confidently that industry mix plays an important role in explaining the positive relation between growth and actual amplitude."[6] However, Borts also found exceptions.

The Borts study is instructive for several reasons. The research was the most comprehensive analysis of the cyclical behavior of state employment up to that time. The development of an index of cyclical severity was an important step forward as was the introduction of a method for determining the role of industrial structure in the cyclical behavior of a state economy. In addition, the conclusion regarding the relationship of employment growth to cyclical severity is quite important to regional development policy. If such is the case, it would appear that policymakers face a trade-off bewteen the two. Further investigation of this possibility is essential to the development of regional economic policy.

Notwithstanding the important contributions of his 1960 study, Borts's research is subject to several significant shortcomings. Chief among these is the way in which Borts introduces the effect industrial structure may have on regional cyclical behavior. Using the behavior of national industries to introduce industrial structure as an explanatory factor in the cyclical behavior of state economies, he ignores the effect of local interindustry relationships which may produce state behavior that is not typical of the behavior of the industry at the national level. The Borts approach implies that the relationships of industries to one another do not vary significantly from state to state. Furthermore, the Borts study does not provide a highly disaggregated analysis of the state employment data. This is particularly important to a complete examination of the apparent trade-off between growth and stability.

More recently, disaggregated approaches to the study of regional economic instability have appeared. Most important among these is the 1975 study by Michael Conroy.[7] In this study, Conroy develops a measure of economic instability for 52 Standard Metropolitan Statistical Areas (SMSAs) based on employment data for 118 industries. First, an index of the instability of total employment is developed for each SMSA. This is simply the variance of total SMSA monthly employment for the period January 1958 to December 1967, adjusted for a time trend. This allows Conroy to rank each SMSA according to the variability of total employment in a manner quite similar to the way in which Borts ranked the cyclical sensitivity of state economies. Following this, Conroy estimates a portfolio variance for each SMSA. This is based on a 118×118 variance-covariance matrix of national employment. The portfolio variance is defined by Conroy as:

$$\sigma_p^2 = \sum_{j=1}^{118} \sum_{i=1}^{118} x_i^k \, x_j^k \, \sigma_{ij}$$

where x_i^k and x_j^k represent the weight of the ith and jth industries in SMSA k. σ_{ij} is the covariance of adjusted employment for the pair of industries i and j. In $i = j$, σ_{ij} equals the variance of industry employment. Thus, the portfolio variance is equal to the weighted sum of a variance-covariance matrix. This provides an index of metropolitan instability derived from disaggregated employment data. Conroy's approach is a direct application of the method developed by Markowitz to analyze financial portfolios.[8] Conroy went on to analyze the effect of diversification on the instability of regional economies.[9] However, the Conroy study is subject to several criticisms. First, he uses a national variance-covariance matrix and local weights to derive the portfolio variance. This is very similar to the approach developed by Borts and subsumes the interregional variation in interindustry relationships.[10] This is a particularly damaging shortcoming given the otherwise highly disaggregated nature of his study. Also, Conroy does not consider the possible trade-off between growth and stability.

This brief overview of research related to the empirical study of regional economic stability has shown that several important contributions have been made. However, policy-oriented research into the questions of regional employment growth and instability has yet to be undertaken. This includes study of the stability of regional economies which allows for interregional variation in industrial structure and a detailed examination of the possible trade-off between growth and stability. The development of regional economic policies requires that a highly disaggregated approach to these questions be developed. This will make it possible to distinguish between long-term secular growth trends and cyclical instability at a level of aggregation that identifies the role of regional interindustry relationships.

Regional Employment Portfolio Analysis

As noted earlier, the important contributions to the analysis of the stability of regional economies have been concerned primarily with regional business cycles. These studies have not considered in a satisfactory way the role of regional industrial structure in respect to the instability of the regional economy. The development of an empirical technique whereby the industrial structure determines the measure of regional instability allows one to solve for the effect of changes in industrial structure. Thus, it is possible to derive the consequences development policies have not only for development, but also for the stability of the regional economy. Moreover, by determining a measure of instability for each region, one can avoid the problem of assuming that interindustry relationships do not vary from region to region.

The Regional Employment Instability Index

The portfolio variance has been developed as an index of the instability of the return on a financial portfolio. The greater the portfolio variance, the greater the instability in the return on that portfolio. For example, the portfolio variance has come into use as a measure of the risk associated with a given distribution of securities.[11] The results of these analyses imply that industrial diversification will reduce the instability associated with a given industrial structure only if the variations in employment in the respective industries are not correlated with one another. Thus, in a world where employment in various sectors is correlated to some extent, simple diversification cannot a priori be expected to reduce instability.

It follows, therefore, that it is necessary to investigate the extent to which employment in the sectors of the economy varies together. In addition, a measure of the magnitude of the covariability is desirable. The portfolio variance (the regional employment-instability index) is defined on the covariances of employment in the individual sectors. The variance-covariance matrix used in this analysis is derived from a time series of regional industry employment data.

Following Markowitz, the covariance of employment in a pair of industries i and j over the interval of months M is given by

$$\sigma_{ij} = \frac{\sum_{m=1}^{M} (x_{im} - \bar{x}_i)(x_{jm} - \bar{x}_j)}{M - 1} \tag{4.1}$$

and the portfolio variance is given by

$$\sigma_p^2 = \sum_j w_j^2 \sigma_j^2 + \sum_{i \neq j} \sum_{i \neq j} w_i w_j \sigma_{ij} \tag{4.2}$$

where w_j = a weight equal to the proportion of total employment in industry j; and, σ_j^2 = the variance of employment in industry j.[12]

The regional employment-instability index for any given region is the weighted sum of the variances and covariances of employment in the various sectors under consideration. It can be seen that this measure is sensitive not only to the degree to which employment in the various sectors will vary together, but also to the degree of variability in employment of the individual sectors. The regional employment-instability index is the degree of employment instability in the regional economy and identifies the stabilizing industries within the region.

It follows from this definition of instability that there is an important distinction between a stable sector and a stabilizing sector. A stable sector is one that has a relatively small variance in employment. A stabilizing sector is one that reduces the instability of total regional employment. Proponents of diversification encourage the entry of industries that are relatively stable. Such a stabilization strategy may have the opposite effect if the new (or expanding) sector has a positive (and relatively high) covariance with the other sectors. That is, the derivation of stabilizing sectors depends not only on the variability of the individual sector, but also on whether that variability (however large or small) is positively (or negatively) related to the other sectors in the regional economy.

It should be pointed out that the regional employment-instability index will be biased if employment has been growing over the interval of time under investigation. From equation 4.1, one notes that the covariance (as well as the variance) of employment is calculated in terms of mean deviations. With the growth of employment as well as fluctuations in employment over time, the variance of employment will be affected by the rate of employment growth. In figure 4–1 $\bar{E}_i^r$ represents the trend of total employment over time in sector i, and $\bar{E}_i^r$ represents the mean employment for the time series. Sector j (E_j^r) has shown no growth trend; however, the variance of employment E_i^r will tend to be high

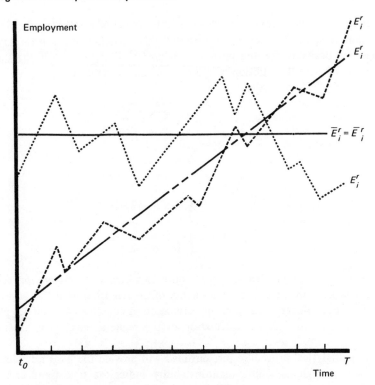

Figure 4-1. An Example of Employment Growth Trends

relative to the variance calculated for E_j^r (which has the same mean employment for the time period), even though the fluctuations in E_j^r may have been greater than E_i^r.

Since we are interested in the instability in employment resulting from fluctuations such as those exhibited by E_i^r, a time-trend equation should be estimated (E_i^r in figure 4-1), and the deviations in employment about the estimated time trend (that is, the residuals) should be used to compute the variances and covariances of employment. Further, a variable can be added to the regression equation which will capture the seasonal variation in employment. Thus, a comparison of the estimate of regional employment-instability index that is based on the equation including the seasonal variation variable, with that which does not include this variable, will make possible the identification of those regions and industries which are particularly subject to seasonal fluctuations. Equation 4.3 is one possible time-trend-estimating equation:

$$E_{im}^r = a + b_1 m + b_2 m^2 + \epsilon_{im}$$ (4.3)

where m represents a month-sequence variable. The choice of the trend-estimating equation is somewhat arbitrary; however, this particular relation displays the properties desirable for the purposes at hand.[13] Equation 4.4 is the same as equation 4.3 with the addition of a deseasonalizing variable S,

$$E_{im}^r = a + b_1 m + b_2 m^2 + \sum_{k=3}^{14} b_{ik} S_{m\mu K i} + \epsilon_{im} \qquad (4.4)$$

where

$$S_{m\mu K i} = \begin{cases} 1 \text{ if } K - 2 = \mu \\ \\ 0 \text{ if } K - 2 \neq \mu \end{cases}$$

where $\mu = 1, \ldots, 11$, denoting the month to which each observation belongs. The constant term captures the seasonality of the twelfth month.[14]

The residuals resulting from the estimation of equations 4.3 and 4.4 provide the data to be used in the calculation of the regional employment-instability index.

The analytical procedure just outlined will provide the basis for calculating two sets of regional employment-instability indices: a time trend and a seasonally-adjusted time trend. The magnitude of the regional employment-instability index will not be independent of the number of workers in each region. For interregional comparisons to be made, one must normalize each index. This can be done by expressing the index in terms of mean total employment for the period under investigation. This is given by:

$$\bar{\sigma}_p^2 = \frac{\sigma_p{}^2}{\bar{E}^r}$$

where $\bar{E}^r$ is mean total employment for a particular region r.

The Instability-Growth Frontier

Computation of the regional employment-instability index makes possible an analysis of the effect of changes in the industrial structure on the instability of the regional economy. Such effects can be derived by changing the weights of particular sectors (see equation 4.2). Using this technique, one can determine, for example, the consequences for total regional employment growth of such a change in industrial structure.

From equation 4.5, one observes that the rate of growth of employment in region r is the weighted average of the actual employment growth in the various sectors.

$$G^r = \sum_{i=1}^{I} W_i g_i \qquad (4.5)$$

where g_i = the growth rate of sector i, $i = 1, \ldots, I$.

Therefore, given the vector g_i for the region, a change in the elements of the vector W_i will produce a new value for G^r. This assumes that the values of g_i are representative of long-run growth trends for individual industries. This procedure can be formalized by considering the equation for the regional employment-instability index (equation 4.2) to be an objective function to be minimized.

$$\text{Minimize } \Phi^2 = \sum_{j} W_j^2 \sigma_j^2 + \sum_{i \neq j} \sum_{i \neq j} W_i W_j \sigma_{ij}$$

$$\text{subject to } \sum_{i} W_i = 1$$

$$W_i >/ 0$$

$$\sum_{i} W_i g_i = G$$

The minimization of the nonlinear objective function Φ^2 will provide the optimal set of weights for the region under consideration. The constraints of this objective function insure that the optimal solution will be within meaningful bounds. The first constraint requires that the vector of weight sum to one, thereby preventing a solution that uses more or less than 100 percent of regional employment. A number less than one could be used in this constraint to impose an unemployment rate on the regional economy. The second constraint insures that none of the weights is less than zero. The third constrains makes possible the imposition of a growth constraint on the region. The lower bound of total employment growth G can be varied so as to make possible the estimation of the relationship between growth and stability. One possible relationship is given in figure 4-2.

In figure 4-2, the existing regional employment instability and growth rate are given by point A. FF is the instability growth frontier. In this example, it is possible for the industrial structure to be altered so as to increase the rate of growth, reduce instability, or show some combination of the two.

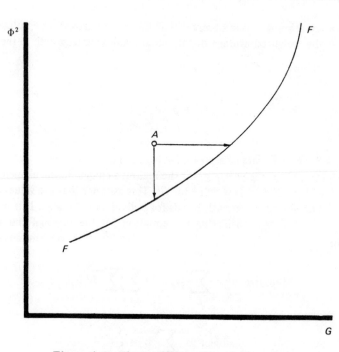

Figure 4–2. The Instability-Growth Frontier

Implications and Conclusions

The analytical framework just described provides a way in which the employment growth and instability implications of changes in industrial structure can be assessed. This framework is not limited only to the analysis of employment. For example, the growth and stability of income or tax revenue could also be analyzed with the same approach. In addition, the analysis does not have to be limited to the derivation of the implications of regional development policies. In particular, the consequences of national policies for regional growth and instability can be derived.

National industry policies designed to stimulate certain sectors of the economy will not be uniform in the regional consequences. Because of the lack of uniformity in the distribution of various industries across the country, there will be differential regional impacts resulting from industry policies. Given the current discussion of industry policy or revitalization, it is unclear whether, on balance, there will be positive or negative regional consequences.

As shown in this analysis, changes in industrial structure have implications for both the growth and stability of regional economies. It therefore follows that national industry policies should be rationalized not only in terms of macroeconomic consequences but also in terms of regional economic consequences.

Notes

1. A review of disagreements over the causes of interregional differences in growth and stability can be found in Robert W. Rafuse, "The New Regional Debate: A National Overview" (Washington, D.C.: National Governors Conference, April, 1977).

2. Paul R. Simpson, *Regional Aspects of Business Cycles and Special Studies of the Pacific Northwest* (Eugene: University of Oregon, 1953).

3. Rutledge Vining, "The Region as a Concept in Business Cycle Analysis," *Econometrica* 14 (July 1946): 201–218, and "The Region as an Economic Entity and Certain Variations to be Observed in the Study of Systems of Regions," *Papers and Proceedings of the American Economic Association* 39 (May 1949): 89–104.

4. Neff and Weifenbach, *Business Cycles in Selected Industrial Areas* (Berkeley: University of California Press, 1949).

5. George H. Borts, "Regional Cycles of Manufacturing Employment in the U.S., 1914–1953," National Bureau of Economic Research, Occasional Paper Number 73, 1960.

6. Ibid., p. 185.

7. Michael E. Conroy, "The Concept and Measurement of Regional Industrial Diversification," *Southern Economic Journal* (January 1975): 492–505.

8. Harry M. Markowitz, *Portfolio Selection, Efficient Diversification of Investments* (Chicago: Cowles Foundation for Economic Research, 1959).

9. A variant of the Conroy approach was used by Barth, Kraft, and Wiest, "A Portfolio Theoretic Approach to Industrial Diversification and Regional Employment," *Journal of Regional Science* 15 (April 1975): 9–15.

10. See Paul S. Lande, "Regional Growth in the United States: A Reexamination of the Neoclassical Model," *Journal of Regional Science* 17 (April 1977), for an analysis of regional differences in industrial structure.

11. Markowitz, *Portfolio,* and William Sharpe, *Portfolio Theory and Capital Markets* (New York: McGraw-Hill, 1970).

12. 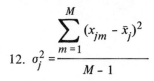 $$\sigma_j^2 = \frac{\sum_{m=1}^{M}(x_{jm} - \bar{x}_j)^2}{M-1}$$

13. Pindyck and Rubinfeld, *Econometric Models and Economic Forecasts* (New York: McGraw-Hill, 1976); Michael Lovell, "Seasonal Adjustment of Economic Time Series and Multiple Regression Analysis," *Journal of the American Statistical Association* 58 (December 1963): 993–1010; M.L. Lovell, "Least Squares Seasonally Adjusted Unemployment Data," *Brookings Papers on Economic Activity* 1 (1976).

14. Ibid.

Industrial Policy and Regional Development in Less-Developed Countries

Harry W. Richardson

The aim of this chapter is to provide a counterpoint to the rest of the book since it is obvious that industrial and regional policies in the developing world are very different from those in the United States. However, it is important to stress at the outset that intercountry differences within the developing world are very striking. After all, the potential sample size could be as many as 126 countries of extreme diversity, ranging from Saudi Arabia to Senegal, Cuba to Chad, or Bangladesh to Brazil. Economic, social, and political conditions vary so widely within less-developed countries (LDCs) that almost any kind of generalization is bound to have several exceptions. Yet in order to cover such a broad set of issues in a brief chapter, the writer must generalize, since the alternative of focusing on the unique and the particular is even less appealing. The generalizations of this chapter refer to a large subset of developing countries; namely, mixed economies that are faced with capital constraints. Hence, neither the centrally planned economies (such as China and Cuba) nor the capital-rich oil exporters (such as Saudi Arabia and Kuwait) are explicitly considered. The illustrative detail is somewhat unsystematic, being largely drawn from countries where the writer has had field experience.

Differences between Developing and Developed Countries

Whereas it would take up far too much space to discuss all the differences between developing and developed countries (DCs), and how they affect industrial policy and regional development, the data of tables 5-1, 5-2, and 5-3 may be used to highlight a few of the more salient distinctions among countries.[1] Table 5-1 presents data on six important variables: population, labor force, urbanization, education, investment, and energy. Although population growth rates declined universally (with the notable exception of the oil-exporting countries) in the 1970s, the rates are much higher in the developing countries than in the DCs in general or the United States in particular. Although these differentials are not carried over into differentials of similar magnitude in labor-force growth (largely because of the rapid rise in female labor participation in the DCs), the future is expected to be different in this respect from the past. The continued high population growth rates in developing countries suggest that the problems

Table 5-1
Economic Indicators

Type of Country	Population Growth Rate (Percent)		Labor Force Growth Rate (Percent)			Urbanization				Education — Percent of Age-Group Enrolled				Investment				Energy			
						Percent of Population Urban		Percent of Urban Population in Largest City		Secondary		Higher		Percent GDI/GDP		GDI Growth Rate (Percent)		Consumption per Capita (kilogram Coal Equivalent)		Energy Imports as Percent of Merchandise Exports	
	1960–1970	1970–1978	1960–1970	1970–1980	1980–2000	1960	1980	1960	1980	1960	1977	1960	1976	1960	1978	1960–1970	1970–1978	1960	1978	1960	1977
Low-income	2.5	2.2	1.7	1.9	2.2	17	21	14	16	14	24	2	4	14	21	4.6	3.6	98	161	9	16
Middle-income	2.5	2.4	2.0	2.4	2.5	37	51	29	30	17	40	4	11	21	25	7.6	7.2	395	903	11	20
Industrialized	1.0	0.7	1.2	1.1	0.6	67	77	19	18	68	87	17	36	21	22	5.6	1.5	4,462	7,060	11	23
Capital surplus oil exporters	2.9	3.2	2.6	2.8	2.9	35	58	28	36	12	45	1	6		31			404	1,620		
Centrally planned economies	1.7	1.4	1.4	1.7	1.2	29	36	9	7	45	72	11	20					1,347	2,117		
United States	1.3	0.8	1.7	1.5	0.9	67	73	13	13	86	93	32	56	18	19	4.8	1.6	8,172	11,347	8	37

Source: World Bank, *World Development Report, 1980* (New York: Oxford University Press, 1980). Reprinted with permission.

Note: These are weighted averages, with the exception of Gross Domestic Investment growth rates (median). GDI = Gross Domestic Investment; GDP = Gross Domestic Product.

of population distribution, and hence of spatial policy, are more important in LDCs than in the rest of the world. The anticipated higher rates of labor-force growth in LDCs imply serious problems of labor absorption so that the type of development strategy adopted could well be crucial. More specifically, LDCs will have to search for more labor-intensive patterns of development if additions to the labor force are to be absorbed.

The urbanization data point to significant differences in the level of urbanization and in the degree of primacy (as measured by the urban population share living in the primate city) within the developing-country categories as well as between the developing and the developed countries. The middle-income countries, on the other hand, have little more than one-fifth of their populations, urban areas and have high but stable levels of primacy. The low-income countries, on the other hand, have little more than one-fifth of their populations, on on average, living in urban areas. Low urbanization levels in general imply that spatial policies are of high priority because policymakers have the opportunity to influence the pattern of urbanization, given the incontestable assumption that urbanization will increase in low-urbanization countries. As will be argued, industrial policy may have a marked, often unintended, impact on the pattern of urbanization.

The education data reveal, not surprisingly, wide differentials in both secondary- and higher-education enrollments among country groups. The contrast between the low-income countries at one end of the spectrum and the United States at the other is particularly striking. If a skilled labor force and highly educated managerial and administrative cadre are key preconditions for industrial development, the limited educated talent in LDCs, especially the lower-income countries, means that sustained industrialization has to be confined to a small number of locations. Since the scarce talent is not evenly distributed over space, but is heavily concentrated in the primate city, that city has yet another competitive advantage over alternative industrial sites.

With respect to investment, the developing countries are not seriously disadvantaged. As table 5–1 shows, the ratio of investment to the gross domestic product (GDP) and the rate of growth in investment are higher in the middle-income countries than in the industrialized countries and are not significantly lower in the low-income countries. Moreover, in the developing countries the rate of growth of investment declined only modestly in the 1970s rather than cataclysmically as in the DCs. Although the base is much smaller, the higher LDC investment rates offer some prospects for a more dispersed pattern of investment. Certainly, industrial decentralization could not take place in a stagnant atmosphere for investment.

Energy costs and supplies have been a major constraint on industrial growth in both the developed and developing countries in the last decade or so. Although per-capita energy consumption is much lower in the LDCs, it has been increasing at a rapid rate. Moreover, the balance-of-payments impact, at least in the middle-income countries, is as severe as in the industrialized countries. Where the developing countries have indigenous energy resources, whether underground or offshore, their exploitation is likely to stimulate complementary industries in the periphery. In all other cases, constraints may tend to perpetuate the concentration of industrial development in the core region and the primate city.

Table 5-2 sheds some light on the role of industry in developing countries compared with industrialized countries. Manufacturing is already as important in the middle-income countries as in the DCs (when measured by output) and is growing much faster. In the low-income countries, on the other hand, the manufacturing sector is much smaller and less dynamic. However, even in the middle-income countries the labor-force share in industry is much smaller than in the DCs, an indication of the capital-intensive character of industry in the LDCs despite their more lavish reserves of surplus labor and scarcity of capital. This paradox is explained by the rigidities of technology transfer that have resulted in the developing economies adopting newer capital-intensive technologies that are not responsive to differences in local-factor endowments and prices. With the exception of resource-based activities, these industries are located mainly in or near the primate city in LDCs.[2] In the DCs, on the other hand, the manufacturing sector is much more dispersed and their primate cities specialize heavily in finance, commerce, and high-order services. Manufacturing activities in a DC primate city, however, tend to be dominated by small-scale "external economy" industries bound to the metropolitan core by the agglomeration economies offered there.

Table 5-2
Importance of Industry
(*percents*)

Type of Country	Manufacturing's Share in GNP		Growth Rate in Manufacturing Output		Labor-Force Share in Industry	
	1960	1978	1960–1970	1970–1978	1960	1978
Low-income	11	13	6.6	4.2	9	11
Middle-income	22	25	7.6	6.8	17	23
Industrialized	30	27	6.2	3.3	38	39
Capital-surplus oil exporters		8		16.1	20	29
Centrally planned economies					20	31
United States	29	24	5.3	2.9	36	33

Source: World Bank, *World Development Report 1980* (New York: Oxford University Press, 1980). Reprinted with permission.

Note: These are weighted averages, with the exception of growth rates in manufacturing (median). GNP = Gross National Product.

Since there are strong linkages between foreign-trade patterns and policies and the geographical distribution of economic activity, the dependence of a country on international trade can influence both its industrial and regional development. Table 5-3 shows that the middle-income countries are more dependent on exports than the industrialized countries and far more export-dependent than the United States (although the latter's export per GDP share has risen sharply since 1960). Nevertheless, most LDC exports still consist of food and raw materials. Manufactured products account for less than one-fifth of exports in the low-income countries and for less than two-fifths in the middle-income countries (despite a two-and-a-half-fold increase in this share since 1960), compared with a three-quarters share in the industrialized countries. On the other hand, manufactured products account for the majority of imports in LDCs despite many years of import-substitution strategies. The distribution of markets for manufactured exports is not dissimilar among the three main country groups except for a tendency for industrialized countries to sell more to other industrialized countries and for the developing countries to trade more among themselves. Nevertheless, the industrialized countries remain the dominant markets for manufactured exports.[3] Because both exports and imports are more important to the developing economies than to the United States, tariff and other trade policies in LDCs have a much greater potential impact on economic activities and their location.

The scope for industrial decentralization is much greater in DCs because they typically have well-endowed infrastructure and trained human resources in almost all regions. In LDCs, on the other hand, these resources are heavily concentrated in the primate city and the core region.[4] The interregional problem is one of dispersion out of a strongly polarized region into the rest of the country. In DCs, however, there are at least three types of region: stagnant, mature industrial regions (the early starters of industrialization); rapidly growing regions, usually with strong industrial and service bases (the late starters); and rural and sparsely populated peripheries that have always had a negligible industrial base. The first and third of these types are problem regions, but they require very different strategies; clearly, the difficulties of the first type are more created than solved by industrial dispersion. In the LDCs, the scale of the dispersion problem dictates than an effective dispersion strategy requires locational selectivity since it is impossible to develop all regions outside the core region at the same time. This need for selectivity reflects the scarcity of resources and the fact that the generation of agglomeration economies is a precondition for sound industrial development. Of course, one solution to the problem is to focus on intraregional industrial decentralization within the core region. This is much easier to achieve but it does little to promote interregional policy goals. On the contrary, it would tend to reinforce spatial polarization to and the dominance of the core region.

Table 5-3
Parameters of International Trade, 1960-1978
(percents)

Type of Country	Exports Share in Gross Domestic Product		Growth in Exports		Manufacturing Share in Exports		Manufacturing Share in Imports		Destination of Manufactured Exports, 1977			
	1960	*1978*	*1960–1970*	*1970–1978*	*1960*	*1977*	*1960*	*1977*	*Industrialized*	*Developing*	*Oil Exporters*	*Centrally Planned Economies*
Low-income	10	12	5.0	–0.8	17	19	55	56	51	27	10	12
Middle-income	15	21	5.5	5.2	14	37	62	63	58	30	6	6
Industrialized	12	18	8.7	5.7	66	76	43	55	65	25	6	4
Capital Surplus oil exporters		48	9.5	–1.2	1	1	84	84	31	24	42	3
Centrally planned economies						60			14	18	4	64
United States	5	8	6.0	6.5	63	70	44	52	58	33	8	1

Source: World Bank, *World Development Report 1980* (New York: Oxford University Press, 1980). Reprinted with permission.
Note: These are weighted averages, with the exception of growth rates in exports (median).

Industrial Policy in Developing Countries

In general terms, industrial policy in developing countries has been dominated by a few key principles. One of these is the entrenched belief that it is necessary for any industrializing economy to promote a set of basic industries, such as steel, chemicals, and cement. These industries are often fostered in inhospitable environments where the natural resources are absent and there are no compensating locational advantages. Frequently, the projects are financed by foreign governments and companies interested in selling turnkey operations or in building their own plants behind tariff walls. This emphasis has had several adverse consequences. The neglect of the principles of comparative advantage has resulted in the misallocation of scarce investment resources. The undue attention to large-scale industry often requires inappropriate support of public investments in heavy industrial infrastructure (often in industrial estates), which is unsuited to the country's relative factor endowment, and offers very limited employment potential. Even where some choice of technology is feasible, LDCs have often imported the latest, most advanced technology with little attempt to adapt the technology to available local resources or to local relative factor prices. The emphasis on basic industries combined with a heavy and increasing reliance on energy imports have resulted in a profligate use of scarce energy resources in many developing countries.[5] Where economic growth rates have been reduced by the size of the energy-import bill, there is much to be said in favor of promoting a less energy-intensive pattern of industrialization.

Although there has been a shift in some countries toward export-promotion strategies, the prevailing emphasis has been on import-substitution strategies. These strategies have reinforced spatial polarization toward the primate city and the core region by pulling manufacturing firms to the largest market to gain maximum access to government. More generally, they have favored manufacturing and discriminated against agriculture. For example, in Brazil "regional disparities in the impact of protection are the result of differences in the structure of the regional economies. Protection tended most consistently to drive down the output of agriculture and non-tradeables and to stimulate the output of manufacturing industry. Since the latter generated a much smaller proportion of income in the North-East than the Center-South, even if the relative output changes in each sector had been the same in both regions, income would have risen more (or fallen less) in the latter."[6] These strategies have also resulted in most of the benefits of protection and subsidies being reaped by the primate cities. For instance, in Nigeria the Lagos region receives about 90 percent of the indirect subsidies associated with national trade policies.[7] In the Philippines, Manila and the rest of the metropolitan region (southern Tagalog) receive almost four-fifths of the export industry incentives, called the "seventh export priorities."

The preoccupation with industrial development in general, with the pursuit of industrialization as an instrument of modernization, has left LDC policy-makers—at least those connected with ministries of industry—with little concern for where industries are located. This lack of concern is apparent even though interregional economic and welfare differentials are very wide in many countries. As a result, policies designed to influence the location of industry have been pursued with little drive and enthusiasm. Other consequences follow. For instance, there has not been much regard for the environmental consequences of industrial development. Starting from scratch with the experience of the industrialized countries before them, developing countries could avoid many of the grossest pollution impacts of industrialization at minimum cost, some of them by appropriate siting of industries, others by choice of technology. But the national environmental boards have little power or prestige in developing countries. Hence, LDCs are repeating the environmental mistakes of the industrialized countries. Similarly, very few developing countries have attempted to use foreign industrial investment as an instrument of regional development. There have been only limited efforts to persuade multinational corporations to set up plants (except in resource-based industries) at decentralized locations on the grounds that such efforts would scare the corporations away to other countries that would not attempt to interfere with their free choice of location.

The emphasis in LDC industrial policy on heavily protected, capital-intensive basic industries implies a relative neglect of investment opportunities in industries more in tune with the principles of comparative advantage. These industries include agro-based industries, some natural-resource industries and their forward-linkage activities, and small-scale industry. Although developing countries have given much higher priority to rural development in recent years, reinforced by a rural bias in international-agency and bilateral-lending programs, they have rarely followed up many of the more obvious opportunities in agro-based industries. There has been some attention to rural industrialization, but the contents of such a program have remained ill-defined. In any event, rural industrialization often implies part-time off-farm employment in craft industries rather than agro-processing industries, which may be quite large in scale and are usually located in towns in rural regions, not in the open countryside. Agro-processing industries are very important to peripheral regions because they offer more prospects of stimulating backward and forward linkages in a city's rural hinterland than the capital-intensive manufacturing activities fostered by traditional growth-center strategies.[8] However, they often require careful nurturing since they are frequently plagued with problems of reliable raw-material supply and of seasonal-labor absenteeism.

Natural-resource industries have been exploited in developing countries since the last century, usually by foreign enterprises supported by colonialist governments. Yet in many LDCs, their full potential has not been realized because of continued reliance on exporting the resources in a relatively raw state.

For example, in southern Thailand most of the rubber and tin are exported as raw materials even though local industrial growth could be stimulated by the development of processing industries to generate local value added.

Small-scale industries (SSIs) are critical to the industrialization process in most developing countries,[9] especially in the secondary cities where they are often the only component in the local industrial base. LDC policymakers are beginning to realize their potential, and many ministries of industry have developed technical assistance and financial-aid programs to promote SSIs. But these programs are usually handicapped by insufficient financial and human resources, burdened by administrative processing delays, and are not decentralized enough. The key problem of credit and capital for expansion might be dealt with more efficiently via the involvement of commercial banks, but such banks are reluctant to initiate SSI programs because of high administrative costs, pressures to offer below-market interest rates, and the difficulty of obtaining acceptable collateral.[10] Also, small firms frequently have problems developing new markets, especially in cases where the best opportunities are found in export markets.

Diagnosis of the Problem

The goals of industrial policy as formulated in most developing countries are in conflict with the goals of regional policy. Industrial policy aims for rapid industrialization and the development of basic industries behind high tariff walls. Regional policy aims at narrowing interregional income and welfare differentials, and this requires the dispersion of industry into many regions. But industrial policy fosters the spatial concentration of economic activity to exploit the primate-city market, to maximize agglomeration economies, and to reduce production costs. Of course, there are many sound economic reasons for industries to cluster in or near the primate city even in the absence of reinforcing industrial policies. These include: the pull of the national market, since income densities are high only in the primate city and the surrounding core region; the agglomeration economies of the primate city, such as the presence of ancillary industries, finance and banking services, and access to skilled managerial and labor pools; proximity to government (in most countries[11]) for negotiating benefits and privileges; the locational preferences of the business class and their families, related to the consumption externalities of the primate city, such as cultural and leisure amenities, schools, and medical services; the lack of information about, or interest in, investment opportunities in other parts of the country; and the critical importance of communications, either face-to-face or, failing that, an efficient telecommunications system.

The spatial implications of the concentration of industry in the primate city are of several kinds. Since the jobs associated with industrial growth attract migrants, the industrial concentration reinforces primacy.[12] Many of the developing countries, but few of the DCs, have primate-city size distributions.[13] There is widespread dissatisfaction with primate-city patterns in LDCs, although there is no evidence that increasing primacy is associated with economic inefficiency. On the contrary, it has been shown that increasing primacy is statistically associated with faster gross national product (GNP) growth,[14] and there is virtually zero correlation between the primacy indices and the index of regional inequality.[15]

On the other hand, there is little doubt that the clustering of modern economic activity in the primate city's metropolitan region tends to create a core-periphery pattern of development in which many regions of a country are left outside the mainstream of the economy.[16] This results in a kind of spatial dualism, where the core region's economy is dominated by a modern, technologically advanced industrial sector and a sophisticated financial and banking sector that are more in touch with the world metropolitan centers than with other areas in their own country, while the perhiphery's economic structure is based largely on traditional agriculture and an urban informal sector in both small-scale industries and services. This dualism is a persistent obstacle in the way of achieving national spatial integration.

Third, industrial concentration in the primate city and the core region contributes heavily to interregional differentials in levels of living. Interregional per-capita differentials are much wider in developing countries than in industrialized countries. This statement is true, despite the zero correlation between primacy and regional income inequality noted earlier. Possible reconciliations of this contradiction are that the correlation analysis included DCs and, probably more important, that the spatial concentration of industry has more of an impact on interarea-income differentials than on population-growth differentials. In any event, the coefficient of variation of regional per-capita incomes averaged only 0.19 in 11 developed countries but averaged 0.52 in 15 developing countries.[17] The main thrust behind industrial decentralization strategies is to narrow interregional income differentials in LDCs. The vigor with which these strategies are pursued as opposed to the alternative policy of rapid industrialization for its own sake depends on how policymakers trade off interregional equity against national economic efficiency.[18]

Conditions for Industrial Decentralization

The clear inference from this diagnosis is the need for industrial decentralization as a means of implementing the goals of regional policy; namely, a reduction in interregional economic and social disparities. However, for the efficiency-equity trade-off dilemma to be minimized, decentralization would have to be promoted in a way that was reasonably consistent with the goals of industrial policy; namely, rapid industrialization and economic efficiency. It may be possible to reconcile these apparently contradictory policies, if not perfectly, at least more successfully than in the past. The rationale for this belief is that, as suggested earlier, industrial policies in LDCs have often been in conflict with resource-allocation efficiency and that viable investment opportunities in the periphery have been overlooked.

This reconciliation has to be achieved by the search for a cost-effective and successful policy to influence the location of industry. However, devising location policies requires an understanding of the preconditions necessary for industrial decentralization to occur. A preliminary point is that industrial decentralization in a developing country is likely to take a form that is different from that in DCs. In the latter, location policies typically concentrate on persuading industrial plants to relocate physically out of the prosperous into the stagnant or underdeveloped regions. In developing countries, this hardly ever happens.[19] Industrial decentralization in LDCs is instead a relative growth phenomenon. It may involve several elements: the development of agro-processing and other resource-based industries (such as mining or lumber) in peripherally-located resource regions; the growth of small-scale industries by the expansion of existing firms and by new entrants that account for a substantial proportion of industrial growth in secondary cities; the diversion of *new* establishments in export-oriented or import-dependent manufactures from their obvious first-choice location in the primate-city port to ports in other cities, often requiring investment in new-port construction; and the opening up of branch plants in regional cities to exploit local demand by corporations with their headquarters in the primate city or abroad. Thus, industrial decentralization really means an acceleration of industrial growth in the periphery. This means that industrial location policies in developing countries should be much broader in scope than those tried in the industrialized countries which have more emphasis on industrial promotion than on industrial relocation.

Given this situation, there are several lines of approach available to LDC policymakers to facilitate the process of industrial decentralization. One that has been tried often but has recently been discredited is the growth-center strategy. This aims to reconcile both regional-policy objectives and the traditional goals of industrial policy by promoting large- and medium-scale industrial development in a spatially concentrated form at a limited number of key locations. This approach has at least two sound merits: that industrial decentralization has to be spatially selective because the volume of interregionally mobile industry is small and because locations differ in their potential for industrial growth; and the related point that agglomeration economies are important in generating regional development with the implication that regional economic development will be more vigorous with a spatially concentrated pattern than with a geographically uniform one. However, the key argument in selling this strategy as the main plank of a regional development policy was the idea that polarized development at the growth center would at some stage, presumably relatively early in the process, result in diffusion of the benefits of economic expansion into the surrounding region (or hinterland). In most cases, this diffusion has not taken place, possibly because policymakers were overoptimistic about its time frame, but certainly because the industries promoted had few linkages with the hinterland. They tended to be high-technology, capital-intensive enterprises with much closer linkages with the primate-city economy or abroad than with their host regions.[20] Their failure to generate enough jobs meant that the lack of pole-hinterland industrial linkages was not offset by the diffusion of income effects.[21]

Even the rejection of a comprehensive growth-center strategy does not imply that all its components should be avoided. For example, the principle of extreme locational selectivity remains very important. The biggest risk of industrial decentralization policies is to dilute their impact by attempting to promote too many industrial sites at the same time. There is a strong temptation to follow this course because it appeases local political interests. But the short-run political benefits are offset by economic costs and, in the longer run, by the disillusion of the local communities where industrial development fails to take off. The emphasis on industrial infrastructure in growth-center strategies is also of more general value, since the presence of industrial infrastructure in an economically underdeveloped area is a necessary if not sufficient condition for industrial development. However, social infrastructure (schools, health facilities, public services, hotels, cultural amenities, and so on) may also be important, especially as a magnet for professionals and managers; and social overhead capital has received little attention in growth-center strategies. The critical policy questions involve how much reliance should be placed on infrastructure strategies, both in total and in terms of their composition compared with other policy approaches, and the degree of complementarity between infrastructure and other instruments of decentralization.

Among these other instruments, location subsidies and incentives are the most widely used and the most important. The main objective of these incentives is to reduce, if not eliminate, the differentials in the rate of return between peripheral locations and the primate city. Their economic justification is to compensate for the unpaid-for external economies enjoyed by firms in the primate city and to encourage a threshold of industrial development sufficient to generate agglomeration economies in the periphery. The success of a locational incentive scheme depends on the scale and form of the incentives, the efficiency with which it is administered, and the economic conditions of the country.

Other requirements for industrial decentralization are easily comprehensible. First, in view of the scarcity of information about investment opportunities on the periphery, any measures to increase the spread of information are likely to be helpful. Second, changes in the direction of national trade policies may be an important prerequisite. In particular, a shift in emphasis from import-substitution policies to export promotion will normally tend to reduce the attraction of the primate city's national market and increase that of export industries in the periphery (for example, agro-based and natural-resource industries). Third, the implementation of a *domestic* import-substitution policy may be instrumental in promoting industrial decentralization. As population and incomes expand locally, the opportunities for producing domestic import substitutes catering to regional markets increase. These substitutes, initially relatively simple products, such as domestic implements and agricultural tools, replace goods previously imported from the core region. Finally, improvements in interregional transportation and communications networks may be a critical precondition of industrial decentralization. Deficiencies in the trunk-road network and the intercity telephones systems are the most important bottlenecks. However, the absence of farm-to-market roads within regions may make it difficult to develop a sustained agro-based industrialization.

Infrastructure and Industrial Estates

It was suggested earlier that industrial infrastructure is a necessary but insufficient condition for regional development and industrial decentralization. Many developing countries have relied too much on infrastructure, neglecting the contributions of locational incentives and favorable implicit spatial policies. Yet this reliance has been ad hoc in character, stressing the build-up of infrastructure at a number of industrial sites (that is, an industrial-estates policy) rather than a major redistribution of public infrastructure investment out of the primate city and the core region into the periphery. Not only have the primate cities received the lion's share of public infrastructure, but more recently the new priority given to rural development has resulted in the peripheral urban regions receiving an even smaller proportion of the total. Redressing this imbalance is an important priority if industrial decentralization is to occur, because the secondary cities are the most likely centers for industrial development, and the lack of a sound infrastructural base is a major bottleneck to industrial growth.

Developing countries in general have been more concerned with the provision of industrial infrastructure than with social infrastructure, presumably in the belief that modernization and industrialization are higher-order goals than direct measures to improve individual welfare. This priority persists despite recent shifts, in part symbolic, in favor of poverty alleviation and the provision of basic human needs as important goals in development plans. A recurrent component of industrial infrastructure investment is the attempt to maximize scale economies in the supply of basic industrial services through the promotion of industrial estates. The interest in this policy instrument is based on the hypothesis that the presence of industrial infrastructure is the key locational attractor for new industry. Although industrial infrastructure is important and indeed imperative in newly opened-up industrial areas, there is a danger in assuming that this is all that is required in an industrial-location policy. The prospects of success are greater if industrial estates are treated as complements to other locational instruments, such as fiscal incentives and human-resource investments. Moreover, even if the importance of industrial infrastructure is accepted, it does not follow that the most efficient form of provision is a government-sponsored industrial estate.

It is difficult to evaluate the performance of industrial estates as location instruments. They have been promoted in so many countries in very different circumstances and in a variety of institutional forms. Even within the same country, the success rate varies widely from one estate (and one region) to another. In Peru, for example, the estate of Arequipa has been very successful, whereas those at Trujillo and Tacna have hitherto been total failures. A major difficulty is that when a country begins to implement an industrial-estates policy, it almost invariably starts with one or two estates near the primate city. These are often very successful, since firms in such estates benefit from many of the agglomeration economies of the core region. But such estates are clearly anti-industrial-decentralization instruments since they make interregional industrial dispersion less, rather than more, likely. For instance, in South Korea, widely regarded as one of the success stories in industrial-estates promotion, many industrial estates were established under the Local Industrial Development Law of 1969. Industries moving to the estates received substantial exemptions from income and corporate taxes. By 1973, industrial estates in Seoul provided 36.3 percent of jobs created in industrial estates nationwide while the capital region provided 63.9 percent. Subsequently, however, as the program expanded, the dominance of the capital region was reduced; by 1978, Seoul's share in jobs had dropped to 19.9 percent and that of the capital region to 44 percent.[22] Of course, industrial estates may be developed for urban land-use problems rather than for interregional policy purposes, and in such cases a primate-city location is appropriate since the problems associated with disorganized land uses tend to be more serious in large cities. In most large LDC cities, a high proportion of industrial establishments are sited outside industrially zoned areas; in Seoul, for instance, this proportion is as high as 70 percent of industrial establishments.

Industrial estates have been less successful than they might have been because policymakers have neglected some important considerations. Too often an industrial-estates strategy has been treated as a supply-led policy where it was anticipated that a supply of industrial infrastructure would in itself attract industries. But the other ingredients for industrial decentralization were frequently absent. On the other hand, if an effective demand for industrial sites already exists in an area, industrial estates may be very efficient—offering economies of scale in infrastructure provision and serving as focal points for industrial expansion. Another problem is that policymakers often mount too large an industrial-estates program with the simultaneous development of many estates. As a result, the learning experiences possible from a sequential program are lost. Also, the proliferation of estates dilutes their impact and multiplies the chances of failure. This proliferation usually reflects local political pressures and the weakness of governments that buckle under this pressure regardless of the economic merits of potential locations for industrial estates. Obviously, if the estates fail to attract industry, this approach is very wasteful of scarce capital resources.

Furthermore, government-promoted industrial estates are often badly located within a region. There is a temptation to build them on very cheap land far away from the natural expansion area for industry. The infrastructure and services offered are often too expensive and of too high a quality for local industries. As a result, many firms prefer to locate on sites off the estates, even if it means providing their own infrastructure. A similar problem is the tendency to build estates for large-scale industry, even though most of the scope of industrial growth in secondary cities lies with small-scale enterprises. The neglect of small firms in industrial-estates policies is inappropriate, since the cost savings from agglomeration for such firms may be substantial. Of course, the engineering aspect of industrial estates for small firms may be very simple, even if crude. All that may be required is the construction of clusters of worksheds to enable small artisans to benefit from power economies, interfirm linkages, and other economies of agglomeration. Finally, the preoccupation with an industrial-estates policy may result in a neglect of social infrastructure and its locational pull on industry, by making a peripheral region's environment attractive to managers and technicians.[23] Industrial and social infrastructure investments are complementary as locational attractors, but unfortunately they are competitive in their claims on scarce public capital resources.

The Multinational Corporations

Multinational corporations play a very important role in the industrial structures of many countries, both developed and developing. However, some developing countries, or at least their intellectuals, are paranoic about the influence of the multinationals. This paranoia has undermined the potential contribution of foreign investment to industrial decentralization. If foreign investment is additive rather than substitutive for domestic investment, it can help overcome the capital constraint that inhibits the dispersion of industrial investment out of the core region. However, the standard argument in terms of location is that multinational plants cluster in the primate city and the core region because there they can retain a degree of indirect political control, they can benefit from the area's social amenities, and because the area is highly profitable (owing to agglomeration economies) and the access to markets. Further, if governments attempt to influence their location decisions, the multinationals will run away to more hospitable environments in other countries. This widespread belief has undoubtedly discouraged LDC policymakers from attempting to implement strong locational measures that might affect the multinationals.

Although this argument may be valid in special cases, it has several weaknesses if applied generally. First, many multinationals operate in natural-resource and other primary-product industries. These are, of course, materials-oriented industries that are much more likely to be located in the periphery than in the core region. Second, even within the manufacturing sector, it is not clear that the multinationals are less willing than the wholly domestic firm to move out of the primate city and core region. This may reflect their greater ability to evaluate the impact of subsidies and incentives on interregional rates of return, though admittedly in most LDCs the incentives are not large enough to make a significant difference. Perhaps more important, those deciding on the location of multinationals are unlikely to have to move themselves from the primate city to the periphery (they may, in fact, live abroad), whereas the local entrepreneur would have to move. Locational preferences in favor of the primate city are much stronger in developing than in developed countries. Finally, the power of the multinationals to relocate out of a country if they are unhappy about the direction of the government's location policies is much exaggerated. Relocation costs are very high. Moreover, many multinationals have a plant in a particular country to supply the home market behind high tariff walls rather than to export. In such a case, the threat to move out is empty.

Location of Industry Policies

In almost all developing countries, an agency exists to promote industrial development and to administer industrial incentives where offered. This agency is usually responsible for location of industry policy, or at least for administering it. The agency may be called the Ministry of Industry, the Board of Investment (as in Thailand and the Philippines, for example), or some other name.

Despite the wide variety of locational-incentive schemes in LDCs, few of them have worked. Part of the failure rests with the Board of Investment (or its analogous agency). Generally, the Board of Investment is a promotional agency for industry in general, expressing its goals in terms of national industrial investment and manufacturing jobs created. It operates in the belief that interfering with the free locational choice of companies would conflict with the dominant goal of promoting as much industry as possible. Consequently, it fails to push location policies very hard. In many cases, the locational incentives in operation are so complex and many-sided that industrialists are unable to calculate the benefits they might receive. Moreover, since incentives are usually discretionary rather than automatic, the Board of Investment retains a great degree of power. Bureaucratic delays often inhibit firms from submitting applications. Large firms frequently receive preference in incentives offered nationwide, and this discriminates against the peripheral regions, where small and medium firms are dominant. Even the locational incentives for underdeveloped areas are often subject to a high minimum-threshold size as an eligibility criterion. The Board of Investment often imposes restrictions on the types of industry that may receive aid and on the eligible areas; the scope of these restrictions may change frequently and hence be a source of confusion to potential applicants.

The actions of the Board of Investment are further restricted by the level of industrial-location incentives. They are often too low, given the high risks and uncertainties associated with untested peripheral locations. They tend to be quite varied in type, including not only the standard tax holidays and investment allowances but also such benefits as import-duty relief and interest-rate subsidies. Nevertheless, their net effect typically is to increase the rate of return in the periphery by only 1 or 2 percent, insufficient to cover the risk premium—not to mention the interregional differential in the real rate of return. Also, some of the incentives are inappropriate. For example, import-duty rebates have distorting effects on the efficiency of resource allocation and are of no advantage to many firms (such as agro-based industries) that do have a comparative advantage by being in the periphery, but do not import much machinery or other inputs. Interest-rate subsidies are less valuable than easy access to credit, especially for small firms. Rebates on profit taxes are of little value, since few new firms in the periphery earn profits in the first years of operation. Similarly, incentives that help with the initial start-up costs are probably more useful than operating subsidies, though if the latter are offered they should be semipermanent in the sense of being in existence for at least a predetermined, minimum time period. The most serious source of inefficiencies in resource allocation is the capital-intensive bias of most locational incentives in developing countries. If there is any choice in technology, this encourages the use of the generally scarce factor (capital) and discourages the use of the relatively abundant factor (labor). An efficient incentive scheme would eliminate this bias. The major explanation of the low level of incentives is the severely constrained budgets of LDC governments. An effective scheme would need to address this problem.[24]

Despite their weaknesses in practice, fiscal incentives remain preferable to direct locational controls and licensing schemes for several reasons. They leave entrepreneurs with a free choice in location, but merely attempt to influence this choice by changing the structure of relative prices among regions. Provided that the incentives are automatic rather than discretionary (a proviso rarely observed), the location decision-making process can be accelerated without valuable managerial (and government administration) time and efforts being wasted. Whereas incentives reduce production costs in the periphery (however modestly), thereby increasing the prospects for profit at new locations, direct controls do not have this advantage. On the contrary, since the costs of direct controls are hidden their efficiency penalty cannot be estimated. Also, the administrative costs of an incentives system are lower than that of a licensing or direct-controls system. The one major disadvantage of an incentives system, its budgetary cost, can be obviated if a self-financing scheme is adopted. Unless this is adopted, another possible question mark about locational subsidies may arise in developing countries that have a very active and interventionist public sector. In such cases, it does not follow as a matter of course that a locational investment subsidy will both stimulate national investment as a whole and increase economic growth, because the opportunity cost of the locational subsidy is the return on direct public investment—which may be high.[25]

Although there are common themes that recur in LDC industrial-location policies, there are many differences in style and emphasis among countries. This important point may be illustrated with a few examples drawn from different continents. In Kenya the only major locational subsidy is a 20-percent investment credit, introduced in 1975, available everywhere in the country except Nairobi and Mombasa. Since the credit is distributed in the form of a profit-tax remission, it does not provide an *initial* locational incentive and hence has not been very effective except in urban areas close to Nairobi. In Thailand, since 1973 the Board of Investment has operated an industrial-incentives scheme, based on three types of investment-promotion zones (general, agro-processing, and export-oriented zones) and offering a wide variety of incentives, such as import-duty reductions, sales- and profit-tax relief, deductions from taxable income for utility and infrastructure costs, and additional export incentives. But aid is discretionary, and both the level of assistance and the number of eligible industries may vary. A high minimum-size criterion and the emphasis on profit rebates are of little help to the small, new upcountry firms. Bangkok firms are eligible for aid if they are export-oriented as are agro-processing firms in the core region. Not surprisingly, between 1960 and 1978, 78 percent of applications for incentives were from firms in the greater Bangkok area. In late 1978, the number of general investment-promotion zones was reduced from ten to four in recognition of the fact that the locational-incentives program was diluted by too many designated industrial-development areas. As yet, the concentration of assistance has not had a discernible impact.

Mexico has operated industrial-location policies for many years, but their direction and content have changed several times. In the 1960s, the main emphasis was given to industrial estates (fourteen were established between 1960 and 1969) and to the National Frontier Program initiated in 1961 to develop the frontier zones to serve the United States market. Location policies in the 1970s continued to stress industrial estates and fiscal incentives, and a broader industrial-development program to promote assembly industries (maquila) was established. The most recent development is the Program of Incentives for the Territorial Decentralization of Industrial Activity of 1978–1979, a component of the National Plan for Industrial Development. This program set up a hierarchy of preferential zones and offered firms tax credits to locate in these zones.

It is too early to evaluate this program. However, Mexico has a substantial industrial base that is distributed spatially in a pattern far different from that intended by location of industry policies. The concentration of industries in or near the largest cities is the result of spontaneous forces and agglomeration economies. The combined effects of market forces and implicit spatial policies reinforcing polarization outweigh the impact of location of industry policies, a phenomenon common to many developing countries.

In Brazil, a well-known regional industrial-development program called the 34/18 scheme was implemented in the northeast by SUDENE, the regional-development agency for that region. Its basic feature was investment subsidies, but it was supplemented by a large-scale infrastructure program and by federal tax transfers. It has been very successful in the narrow sense of fostering rapid industrial growth in the northeast, but more than one-half of the jobs created were in the three state capitals of Salvador, Recife, and Fortaleza.[26] However, because the program encouraged highly capital-intensive industries, the spatially polarized pattern of industrial development was accompanied by extreme economic polarization, with a deterioration in the economic situation of the working classes even in the major industrial cities.[27]

The final two examples illustrate dimensions of a location of industry policy different from the traditional reliance on fiscal incentives. They refer to the less common approach of direct controls. In India, the central government has introduced a ban on new industries in large cities (defined as those with a population greater than one million). The problem associated with this blanket restriction could arise only in a large country with several large cities. The Indian metropolises are very heterogeneous in terms of their economic vitality. Thus, in a strong metropolitan economy such as Bombay the ban may be appropriate, but in Calcutta with its rapidly declining industrial base the ban rules out any prospects, admittedly dim, for industrial recovery. Of course, in a heavily primate-city system with a single dominant city, a ban on industrial development would not have this kind of differential impact. However, its superiority over a taxation approach is highly dubious. The latter is more efficient, offers firms a degree of choice, and generates revenue to finance regional development.

In the Philippines, the direct controls on industrial development apply not only in Manila but also within a 50-kilometer radius of the central core. However, since the prohibition applies only to nonexport industries, there are many exceptions that undermine the policy. Nevertheless, the effect of the 50-kilometer ban has been to produce artificial industrial zones just beyond the perimeter of the zone in cities such as Angeles City, Olongapo, San Fernando, and Pampanga in the north, and Calamba, San Pablo, Lucena, and Batangas in the south. Interestingly, the ban was introduced in 1975 not in the pursuit of interregional-development objectives but as a pollution-control strategy. Nevertheless, many of the newly promoted industries are light, footloose industries rather than heavy polluters. In any event, the spatial pattern of industrial development created by the 50-kilometer rule is not particularly efficient, though the impacted cities are close to major transportation arteries and have a reasonably good infrastructure endowment.

A Tax-Subsidy Locational Scheme

The examples just given suggest that location policies vary from one country to another. Economic, social, and cultural conditions differ so widely among developing countries that it is unlikely that any general location of industry policy would have universal validity. Nevertheless, it is believed that there is one approach that has a wide degree of applicability. The requirements of such an approach are a simple, automatic, and substantial location subsidy that does not severely strain government revenues. The subsidy should also promote the use of surplus labor rather than scarce capital. These requirements suggest a periphery-region subsidy financed out of a core-region tax, with the periphery subsidy favoring labor and the core-region tax discouraging investment in the primate city and its surroundings. If the tax revenues are equal to the subsidy payments, the scheme takes the form of transfer payments within the industrial sector rather than a net subsidy from the government. The industrial-promotion agencies' objection that the core-region tax would heavily penalize industrialization is not generally valid. The explanation is that in most developing countries, such a large proportion of industrial development is found in the primate city and its core region that a mild tax can generate enough revenue for a substantial subsidy to the limited amount of industry in peripheral regions. As such a scheme became successful in generating peripheral industrial growth, the revenue base would become relatively smaller and the peripheral industrial base much larger. This would require a reduction in the rate of the subsidy if the self-financing nature of the scheme were to be preserved. However, this might be inappropriate if the scheme were proving successful in promoting industrial growth in the periphery.

These generalizations may be illustrated by a hypothetical application of such a tax-subsidy scheme in a particular country, Kenya.[28] The example assumes three types of area: Nairobi and Mombasa, the areas where the tax applies (called the core); the central province (except for the town of Nyeri) as a neutral zone (neither tax nor subsidy) to avoid the boundary effect of the type observed with the 50-kilometer ban in the Philippines; and all other regions plus Nyeri as areas receiving the subsidy (called the periphery).

Consider what might happen if the 20-percent investment allowance were replaced by a labor subsidy in the periphery for the same budgetary cost. If it is assumed that the rate of growth of manufacturing employment in the periphery was twice the historical national rate (that is, 2×6.2 percent), the cost of the investment credit would finance a lump-sum wage subsidy of K£1,076 (a sum approximately double the manufacturing wage) to workers in new manufacturing plants and expansions, or an operating wage subsidy of K£133 per man per year to workers in all manufacturing plants (existing as well as new plants) in the periphery.

To introduce the effects of a development tax levied in Nairobi and Mombasa, assume that all incentives were financed by a tax on new manufacturing investment in this core region. The 20-percent investment allowance would require a 9-percent investment tax for the incentives to be self-financing. However, as argued earlier, an investment-tax/labor-subsidy scheme would be preferable. If the rate of growth in manufacturing employment was 1.5 times the historical national average (which would equal 9.3 percent), then a lump-sum subsidy of K£500 per man in new plants and expansions would require a 3-percent investment tax. Finally, a 3.2-percent investment tax would be needed to finance an operating wage subsidy of K£50 per man per year in all peripheral manufacturing plants. As pointed out earlier, to the extent that the scheme was successful in achieving industrial decentralization, and as the periphery share in national manufacturing increased, the tax base would shrink while the subsidy base expanded. Hence, to preserve the self-financing integrity of the scheme, the subsidy would have to be gradually reduced over time.

The surprising aspect of this example is that a substantial locational subsidy could be financed with such a mild disincentive in the core. This fact helps to counter the most serious objection to the scheme, its political feasibility. It is explained by two key factors. First, the high share of manufacturing investment in the core (greater than 70 percent) means that the subsidy base is small relative to the tax base. Second, the relatively high marginal capital/labor ratio keeps the relative cost of a labor subsidy low in terms of capital. Another virtue of the scheme is that factor-substitution possibilities in both the core and the periphery are in the right direction, that is, encouraging the use of labor relative to capital. Finally, the criticism that the core investment tax would have a deterrent effect on the rate of industrialization is not very strong. Any deterrence would be marginal because of the low rate of the investment tax and its zero net impact on the manufacturing sector (since all tax revenues are rebated in the form of locational inducements). Moreover, these features of the scheme are not peculiar to Kenya but are found in most developing countries, since the spacial concentration of the manufacturing sector in the core region and its capital-intensive character are endemic in the developing world.

Conclusions

The developing countries are industrializing in a spatially concentrated pattern, with most of the manufacturing industry located in the primate city and the core region. This reflects spontaneous market forces such as agglomeration economies that make locational concentration efficient and profitable. However, spatial polarization has been reinforced by industrial policies, such as import-substitution strategies, and by other implicit spatial policies that have strengthened the competitive advantages of the primate city. Except in the most advanced LDCs, such as South Korea and Brazil, there is little prospect that industrial decentralization will occur on any scale as a result of market forces, since the preconditions for "polarization reversal" appear only in the relatively late stages of economic development.[29]

Since LDC policymakers and society in general regard the continued polarization of population and economic activity toward the core region as socially undesirable and inimical to national unity, the task of industrial decentralization policy is to achieve a degree of industrial dispersion ahead of the reversal in market forces. It is believed that in many developing countries with a growing industrial base, strong regional policies can be at least moderately successful in the sense of bringing about a substantial degree of industrial decentralization with minimal losses in economic efficiency. Unfortunately, policies have rarely been strong or pursued with vigor. Industrial infrastructure has been built wastefully far ahead of demand in too many places and locational incentives have been complicated, discretionary, and weak.

This chapter argues that it is possible to develop industrial policies and regional-development policies that are compatible with each other. What is required is a shift of industrial policy to favor export promotion and industries in which developing countries have a comparative advantage. On the regional-policy front, infrastructure provision should be synchronized with simple, automatic, and substantial locational incentives. The only way that most developing countries could afford the latter is by adopting a self-financing scheme in which peripheral subsidies were paid for by a core-region development tax. Influencing relative prices and rates of return is preferable to direct locational controls which are clumsy and inefficient. The need for spatial selectivity can be met by concentrating industrial infrastructure provision at a few high-potential locations. Industrial locators would then be attracted to these places without any additional steering. A strategy of this kind may not avoid the efficiency-equity trade-off altogether, but it would keep the trade-off within reasonable bounds.

Finally, given that the focus of this book is on the U.S. experience, it may be worth speculating whether the experience of the developing countries has any relevance to industrial policy and regional development in the United States and, conversely, whether experience in the United States sheds any light on the problem in developing countries. In view of the earlier arguments on the importance of country-specific characteristics and on the major differences between the developed and the developing countries, such speculation is not likely to be very fruitful.

A parallel exists between the underdeveloped regions in LDCs where governments are attempting to decentralize industry, and certain areas in the United States. The U.S. regions include those which received attention at the Federal level in the 1960s, such as the Four Corners area near the Indian reservations of the Southwest, and smaller isolated pockets of underdevelopment found in almost every state. The experience of the developing countries suggests the importance of infrastructure and perhaps human-resource investments. But creating these preconditions in the less developed areas of the United States would be difficult and very risky. Much industrial infrastructure is provided in industrial parks by private developers who are likely to be even less enthusiastic about these areas than the industrialists themselves. Human-resource investments in a highly mobile society such as the United States lead to high out-migration rates, an efficient solution but not the intended outcome. Very few of these pockets have substantial locational advantages such as indigenous materials and easy access to markets. Moreover, in the United States there are so many alternative attractive locations that firms have a very wide choice among existing industrial centers with little incentive to seek out untested locations. In the developing countries, on the other hand, the simple choice is between a relatively underdeveloped peripheral location and the core region, with at least a possibility that emerging diseconomies in the primate city may induce industrial firms to consider the periphery.

If this diagnosis is correct, it would take sizable, perhaps massive, subsidies to attract firms to the low-potential, less developed areas of the United States. There is little prospect that such subsidies would be forthcoming. Interregional fiscal incentives have never been offered on a substantial scale by the federal government, even in the heyday of regional-development policy in the 1960s. The Economic Development Administration is a much weaker agency than it was at that time, and much of its limited assistance is now given to distressed central cities. State and local governments have been more active in offering locational subsidies. But lower-level governments are in competition with each other, and there is a strong tendency to match one's neighbors' locational incentive packages. Hence, within a broader region these incentives tend to cancel each other out, suggesting that subsidizing mobile industry may be a zero-sum game for the competing governments. The only beneficiaries are the industrial corporations that now are subsidized for developing at their first-choice locations. Locational-incentive schemes are more likely to work if implemented at the national level, thereby permitting spatial selectivity, but in the United States there are severe political, and even constitutional, obstacles to a federally-sponsored interregional locational-incentives policy. It is very doubtful that the least-favored areas can be developed industrially. In the LDCs the medium-term prospects are limited to a few major industrial decentralization centers, and a focus on low-potential areas would be doomed to failure. Perhaps the lesson for the United States is that even in a rich country a "worst first" strategy would be too costly and would never work. The process of interregional industrial dispersion is still taking place with beneficial effects in terms of income convergence. The problems of the populations living in the underdeveloped pockets can be more efficiently dealt with by a combination of migration subsidies and welfare assistance.

What can the developing countries learn from the United States? The inter-regional shifts in industrial location that have occurred in the United States, especially since the end of World War II, out of the industrial heartland into many areas (some of which had no history of extensive industrialization), offer some hope that the process of spatial polarization will be eventually reversed. However, the United States and developing countries have such vastly different income levels, economic structures, and transport and communication networks (among other things), that it is improbable that the conditions for polarization reversal can be created in most developing countries in the short or even medium run. If the key elements in the polarization-reversal process were better under-stood, it might be possible for LDC policymakers to stimulate some of the required preconditions by policy measures. Hence, study of the polarization-reversal process in developed countries in general and the United States in particular may offer clues to the key factors behind interregional industrial dispersion that could help LDC policymakers devise measures to accelerate the process.[30]

Although regional policies in the United States have been weak, there is strong evidence that implicit spatial policies have had major spatial impacts. For example, federal defense spending and contracting decisions have been very important in strengthening the industrial base of cities in the South and the West. Similarly, most federal economic policies have had a variety of conse-quences that have affected the economic performance, growth, and welfare of the country's major metropolitan areas, some favorably and others unfavor-ably.[31] If LDC policymakers fully understood the implications of what has happened in the United States, they would realize that the spatial impacts of nonspatial policies can easily overpower the effects of explicit regional-develop-ment policies. Since so many implicit spatial policies in developing countries reinforce polarization toward the primate city, LDC policymakers should be modest in their expectations of what can be attained with explicit regional-development policies. This could result in fewer and less-radical policy shifts in response to the "failures" of regional industrial policies that simply have had insufficient time to achieve results.

Recent locational shifts in the United States suggest the critical importance of amenities as a locational attractor.[32] Most developing countries have given priority to industrial infrastructure. Obviously, this is important, but perhaps the role of amenities and social infrastructure in attracting industry to decen-tralized locations has been underestimated. Given the extreme capital constraints that exist in most developing countries, perhaps the policy implication is that special attention should be given to those secondary cities which have either natural amenities (climate, tourist facilities, and so on) or a superior stock of social infrastructure.[33] This implies promoting the relatively well-favored areas rather than those with the worst economic and social conditions. Unfortunately, the dynamics of regional development offer no feasible or cost-effective alterna-tives for helping the most disadvantaged regions, except in the very long run.

Reconciling regional and industrial policies demands that priority be given to the high-potential regions and cities outside the core region.

Notes

1. The sizes of the groups are: 38 low-income countries, 52 middle-income countries, 18 industrialized countries, 5 capital-surplus oil exporters, and 12 centrally planned economies. Obviously, the groups are not comprehensive but merely include those countries for which the World Bank has substantial data sets. The low-income cut-off is a per-capita income level of less than $360 in 1978.

2. In Africa, for example, 12 out of 23 countries had more than 60 percent of manufacturing activity in their primate city (Mabogunje, 1973). In Asia, the story is similar. Manila accounts for 60 percent of investment in large-scale manufacturing in the Philippines. In Thailand, more than two-fifths of manufacturing output is produced in Bangkok with another two-fifths in the surrounding central (core) region. Kuala Lampur and the surrounding state of Selangor account for 36 percent of Malaysian GDP in manufacturing. Karachi produces 31 percent of manufacturing value-added in Pakistan. Lima accounts for more than 54 percent of Peru's manufacturing output. The capital region of South Korea absorbs 48 percent of manufacturing employment. Even in a large and relatively dispersed country such as India, Bombay, Madras, and Calcutta absorb 60 percent of manufacturing value-added. These examples could be multiplied several-fold.

3. The smaller country groups (the centrally planned economies and the oil exporters) have export-market distributions different from the three main groups, with a much stronger tendency to export to other countries within their group.

4. For example, Manila, Nairobi, and Bangkok each absorb about 60 percent of national infrastructure investment although their population shares are only 11 percent, 8 percent, and 10 percent, respectively.

5. In the industrialized countries, households are usually given priority in energy consumption. In the developing countries, it is more common for industrial consumers to receive priority. For example, controls on nonindustrial energy consumption in Thailand have included limitations on opening hours of places of entertainment and even on the use of television.

6. Reboucas, (1974), p. 6, quoted in Renaud (1979), pp. 121–122.

7. Bertrand et al. (1978).

8. Richardson (1978).

9. In Thailand, for instance, 95 percent of industrial establishments employ less than twenty workers (Saeng Sanguanruang et al., 1978).

10. See Farbman (1980) for a discussion of the state of the art on SSI promotion.

11. In a few developing countries (such as Brazil and Pakistan), the primate city and the seat of the national government are not the same, usually because of an earlier decision to relocate the national capital.

12. Primacy is the degree of dominance of the primate city over the rest of the national urban system.

13. A simple measure of primacy is the so-called four-city index (Davis, 1969), that is, the ratio of the population of the largest city to the combined populations of the next three largest cities. Another measure is the ratio of the population of the largest city over the total urban population of the country. If the latter index is used, only Ireland among the industrialized countries scores above 0.4, but 32 out of 90 low- and middle-income countries have scores above that level (World Bank, 1980, table 20).

14. Mera (1973).

15. UNFPA (1980), p. 237.

16. The core-periphery dichotomy is a direct consequence of the spatial polarization associated with primate-city economies. For a description of the core-periphery model, see Friedman (1966 and 1973).

17. Williamson (1965), p. 44, and Gilbert and Goodman (1976), p. 118.

18. There are a few exceptions where this trade-off can be avoided. These cases of efficiency-equity compatibility are discussed in Richardson (1979).

19. There are obvious reasons for this difference. For instance, a frequent reason for interregional relocation in industrialized countries is the lack of space for plant expansions on core-region sites; in developing countries, the shortage of space for expansion is a much rarer phenomenon.

20. A classical example of the growth-center industrial enclave is the Philippines Sinter Corporation plant near Cagayan de Oro, in Mindanao in the Philippines. Owned by the Japanese, it employs many Japanese workers, imports its raw materials from Australia and Vietnam (except for limestone which is brought from the island of Bohol), and exports its output directly to Japan.

21. These arguments do not imply that growth-center strategies should be written off completely. Boisier (1980) and Richardson (1978) suggest modifications that salvage the strategy.

22. Hwang (1979), p. 11.

23. In many developing countries, the secondary cities that have been most successful in strengthening their economic bases have a high-quality and relatively lavish stock of social infrastructure, sometimes associated with their dual functions as tourist resorts. Examples include Chiang Mai (Thailand), Baguio (the Philippines) and Cartagena (Colombia).

24. For a comprehensive evaluation of location policies in developing countries, though with different conclusions and emphasis from those implied in this chapter, see Townroe (1979).

25. Of course, in many situations, especially in the industrial sphere, private investment and public investment are highly complementary. A region's

industrial base will not be developed without supporting-public-infrastructure investment, whereas the social return on such investment depends on its stimulus to private-sector activity.

26. Similarly, in the Amazon region, two-thirds of the firms aided by SUDAM were located in two major cities, Belém and Manaus.

27. Gilbert and Goodman (1976), pp. 129–135.

28. The data for this hypothetical illustration mainly refer to the year 1975.

29. For a discussion of polarization reversal and its preconditions, see Richardson (1980).

30. This argument does not imply that the dispersion processes are exactly the same in the United States and in developing countries. A major factor in the United States is change in the locational preferences of households, a major element in what has been described as counterurbanization (Berry, 1978).

31. Glickman (1980), and Vaughan (1977).

32. Richardson (1974).

33. In tourist cities, rapid industrial growth may lead to conflict between industrial-promotion goals and environment goals. Although this conflict is troublesome, it may be handled by strong zoning and industrial-siting measures and by priority attention to environmental protection.

References

Berry, B.J.L. "The Counterurbanization Process: How General?" In *Human Settlement Systems: International Perspectives on Structure, Change and Public Policy* edited by N.M. Hansen, pp. 25–29. Cambridge, Mass.: Ballinger, 1978.

Bertrand, T. et al. *Industrial Policy in Nigeria.* Washington, D.C.: World Bank, 1978.

Boisier, S. "Growth Poles: Are They Dead?" Mimeographed. Santiago, Chile: Latinamerican Institute for Economic Planning, 1980.

Davis, K. *World Urbanization,* 1950–70. 2 vols. Berkeley: University of California Press, 1969.

Farbman, M. "Providing Assistance to Informal Sector Enterprises: The Neglected Side of Urban Development." Mimeographed. Honolulu, Hawaii: East-West Population Institute Workshop on Intermediate Cities in Asia, 1980.

Friedmann, J. *Regional Development Policy: A Case Study of Venezuela.* Cambridge, Mass.: MIT Press, 1966.

——. *Urbanization, Planning and National Development.* Beverly Hills: Sage Publications, 1973.

Gilbert, A.G., and Goodman, D.E. "Regional Income Disparities and Economic Development: A Critique." In *Development Planning and Spatial Structure* edited by A.G. Gilbert, pp. 113–141. New York: Wiley, 1976.

Glickman, N.J., *The Urban Impacts of Federal Policies*. Baltimore, Md.: Johns Hopkins Press, 1980.

Hwang, M.C. "A Search for a Development Strategy for the Capital Region of Korea." In *Metropolitan Planning: Issues and Policies*, edited by Y.H. Rho and M.C. Hwang, pp. 3–32. Seoul: Korea Research Institute for Human Settlements, 1979.

Mabogunje, A.L. "Manufacturing and the Geography of Development in Tropical Africa." *Economic Geography* 49(1973): 1–19.

Mera, K. "On the Urban Agglomeration and Economic Efficiency." *Economic Development and Cultural Change* 21(1973): 209–224.

Reboucas, O.E. "Interregional Effects of Economic Policies, Multi-Sector General Equilibrium Estimates for Brazil." Ph.D. dissertation, Harvard University, 1974.

Renaud, B. *National Urbanization Policies in Developing Countries*. Washington, D.C.: World Bank Staff WP 347, 1979.

Richardson, H.W. "Empirical Aspects of Regional Growth in the United States." *Annals of Regional Science* 8(1974): 8–23.

——. "Growth Centers, Rural Development and National Urban Policy: A Defense." *International Regional Science Review* 3(1978): 133–152.

——. "Aggregate Efficiency and Interregional Equity." In *Spatial Inequalities and Regional Development* edited by H. Folmer and J. Oosterhaven, pp. 161–183. Boston: Martinus Nijhoff, 1979.

——. "Polarization Reversal in Developing Countries." *Papers, Regional Science Association* 45(1980): 67–85.

Saeng Sanguanruang et al. *A Study of Small and Medium Industries in Thailand*. Bangkok: National Institute of Development Administration, 1978.

Townroe, P.M. *Employment Decentralization: Policy Instruments for Large Cities in LDCs*. Oxford: Pergamon Press, 1979.

United Nations Fund for Population Activities (UNFPA). Mimeographed. "Population and the Urban Future." Rome: UNFPA, 1980.

Vaughan, R.J. *The Urban Impacts of Federal Policies*. Santa Monica, Calif: Rand Corporation, 1977.

Williamson, J.G. "Regional Inequality and the Process of National Development: A Description of the Patterns." *Economic Development and Cultural Change* 13(1965): 3–43.

World Bank. *World Development Report, 1980*. Washington, D.C.: World Bank, 1980.

Regional Effects of an Energy Policy: The Case of Coal and Oil in the Western United States

Cynthia A. Kroll

Energy-development policy is an example of a sectoral policy that is shaped by economic forces and government programs at the national level and yet is critical in determining the economic and social development of some regions. Most energy resources have a locational aspect. Energy resources such as coal, petroleum, and hydroelectric power occur in a limited number of geographic areas. The initial resource-extraction activity and sometimes power production must take place at the location where the resource is found. Such resource-based economic activity has important implications for the surrounding regions, as it is integrally tied to the local economy.

Throughout the history of the industrial and postindustrial United States, the federal government has been closely involved in decisions about energy-resource development. Federal programs, actions, and regulations influence how much of a resource is developed, the price of the resource, who is involved in production, and where and how a resource is produced. Clearly, each of these factors may affect how a region grows and what happens to the people living in a region.

Coal development in the United States strikingly illustrates the range of regional consequences that may result from a pattern of energy-resource development determined at the national level. In early periods of coal development, federal policy toward transportation networks and the distribution of mineral ownership affected patterns of extraction. More recently, national policies have been instrumental in shifting coal-development activity toward the western United States.

The rapid increase in western coal development is largely a result of two areas of national policy—environmental regulation and energy independence. The enforcement of strict environmental standards related to the sulfur content of coal encouraged a shift from the extraction of high sulfur-content coal in eastern states (particularly Kentucky, West Virginia, and Illinois) to the less-efficient but low-sulfur western coal. The oil embargo of 1973 and the subsequent rapid rise in OPEC oil prices led to a national policy decision to shift from

This paper draws from research completed by Cynthia A. Kroll for her doctoral dissertation, "Local Distributional Effects of Energy Development—Coal Boom Towns in the Northern Great Plains," University of California at Berkeley, 1981.

121

oil to coal as a major energy base in the United States. This decision caused an increase in coal production throughout the nation, and placed particular focus on the vast coal resources of the west. Recent federal programs to spur on synthetic-fuels production have given further impetus to the growth of western coal-producing areas.

This chapter explores some of the consequences of a federal policy favoring the production of western coal in a substate regional area of Wyoming. The local distribution outcomes of economic development tied to energy resources are examined. The discussion touches only briefly on the question of how well specific geographic areas in the West cope with rapid growth, and explores in much more depth the question of what happens to different population groups in the course of this development. The chapter begins with a generic description of the local effects of energy development, followed by a brief theoretical description of the distribution issues raised in energy-resource-development regions and a proposed research approach for identifying differential effects experienced by each population group. A third element of the chapter is the application of the research approach to a case-study region in Wyoming. Finally, the implications of western energy development for public policy at the federal, state, and local levels are addressed.

Energy-Resource Development and the Local Economy

Several features characterize the mining industry's role with respect to the local economy. First, the industry is based on the extraction of nonrenewable natural resources. This implies that the industry has a limited life span at best, and a volatile and uncertain future at worst. Many towns in mining regions have an economic basis only as long as mining continues. Second, the industry uses large amounts of land. It often displaces other land-based activities, such as forestry, agriculture, and recreation, which could provide longer-term bases for local employment. Third, the location of the mining activity is limited by the location of the mineral. It may be impossible to relocate the industry in a less-disruptive setting. Fourth, at least some of the new jobs require skills different from those required by agriculture or recreation employment. Therefore, many of the new industrial jobs are taken by outsiders, rather than by the local wage earners. Fifth, the long-term demand for many minerals is uncertain. The level and duration of mining activity in a region are subject to changes in the national economy or international relations.

Coal-based energy-resource development typically occurs in regions where agriculture dominated the local economies in the past. In these regions, the majority of the population reside in rural areas and towns of fewer than 10,000 people. The new industry is large enough, in comparison with previous population levels and economic activity, to create major changes in the local economy and social structure.

The Development Sequence

Figure 6-1 illustrates the growth sequence in the early stages of energy-resource development. Mineral extraction and closely related industrial activities (construction, refining, power generation, transportation) create a relatively large demand for labor. These activities may directly employ between several hundred and several thousand salaried employees, often more than doubling the local labor force. Although some jobs are filled by local residents and commuters, the increasing labor demand spurs migration into the region. Job seekers, new employees, and their families settle in the small towns close to the growing industries. Growing incomes and a larger population increase the demand for housing and for both public and private goods and services. Growth in these sectors of the economy increases local construction activity and the demand for labor, reinforcing growth pressures on the local communities. Each stage of development produces changes that permanently affect the economies of local towns, counties, and the region as a whole. In the short term, the most visible effects on the growing community are the changes in the dominant economic base, the demographic composition of the population, and local markets for goods and services.

The local economic base. The economic base (or export base) of a region is the economic activity that depends on demand from outside the region. Mining and agriculture are both examples of economic bases. Regional theory often assumes that demographics, social characteristics, and service economies of local communities are dependent on, and therefore can be partly explained by, the existing economic base of the community. The history of mineral-development areas in the United States shows that mining activity can quickly dominate other basic activities in the local economy (where mining primarily occurs for export). For example, in Campbell County, Wyoming, one of the most rapidly growing energy-development areas in the West, the energy industry now exceeds economic activity in other export factors (such as agriculture) in terms of number of employees, total income, and assessed valuation (see table 6-1).

The change in the economic base has other effects on the local economy. The increasing demand for labor attracts new migrants into the community. Thus the changing economic base becomes a major force behind population growth. Population growth ensures the need for more services, more housing construction, and greater public expenditures.

Population growth. The number of people brought in by increases in minerals activity depends on several factors. First, the industry may absorb some of the local work force (people who do not need to move in order to work at the new mine or plant). The extent of local hiring depends on the number of workers needed, size and training of the labor pool before the new growth, wage levels in other sectors of the economy, and training required by the industry. For example, in North Dakota, more than half of the operating work force in the coal industry remain in the same county where they were previously employed.[1]

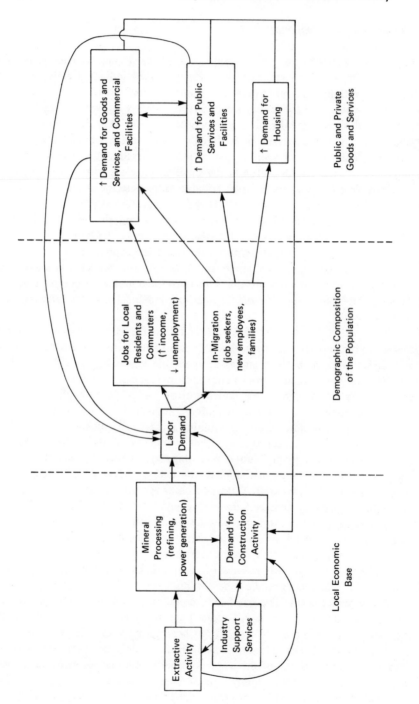

Figure 6–1. Employment and Population Growth Sequences in Energy-Development Regions

Table 6-1
Economic Trends in Campbell County, Wyoming, 1950-1975

	1950	1960	1970	1975
County employment[a]				
Total	1,919	2,370	5,060	6,740
In agriculture	912	890	780	790
In mining	57	180	1,020	1,400
County-assessed value[b]				
Total	$12,523,175	$22,640,899	$125,321,947	$322,349,355
Oil, gas, and coal	3%	NA	76%	85%
Local assessments	80%	NA	20%	10%
County personal income[c]				
Total	$ 6,849,000	$10,823,000	$ 47,000,000	$ 80,300,000
Agriculture	45%	50%	12%	1%
Mining	4%	5%	23%	32%

[a]U.S. Bureau of the Census, *Census of Population,* 1950; for 1960-1975, Gladstone Associates, *Analysis of Economic Base and Growth Potentials, 1976-1990, Gillette and Campbell County,* Washington, D.C., 1976.

[b]Annual Reports, Department of Revenue and Taxation, 1950, 1960, 1970, and 1975.

[c]Data in 1950 and 1960 columns are for 1949 and 1959, from R.E. Lund, *Personal Income in Wyoming Counties 1929-1959,* University of Wyoming, Laramie, 1963; source for 1970 and 1975 is *Wyoming Data Handbook 1977,* Wyoming Department of Administration and Fiscal Control, Cheyenne, 1977.

In contrast, the coal industry in Wyoming employs many more workers from outside locations. Second, some workers are single or come without their families. The proportion of these workers appears to be much greater among the construction work force than among miners or power-plant operators. Finally, the age of the workers and the size of their families are important, in terms of both the immediate induced growth and the long-term demographic patterns. Many of the workers in the coal industry are young with growing families. This increases school enrollment in the short term, and has longer-term effects on the demographic patterns of the region and the labor force in subsequent generations.[2]

Other private economic sectors. The growth of the basic industry induces growth in other segments of the economy. Activities that supply the basic industry may grow. For example, mining may be supported by construction contractors, heavy-equipment firms, and transportation services. In addition, industries using the products of mineral extraction, such as refineries or power plants, may locate near the source. These two areas of growth are often observed more clearly in a substate, statewide, or multistate region than in the immediate locality of the mining activity. For example, oil pumped in Campbell County,

Wyoming, is refined in Natrona County, and coal extracted in Campbell County is used to generate power at the Laramie River plant in Platte County, Wyoming, which provides power to several western states.

Population growth induces increased demands in other areas of the economy. A boom in the housing industry follows a boom in population. This is likely to lead to an additional growth in local construction employment, but other support services for housing construction (for example, materials, design) often come from beyond the region. Retail establishments and service industries clearly increase, often well beyond the relative increase in the population, in response to new demands and economies of scale.

The total employment "multiplier" effects induced by a new basic industry are hotly debated.[3] In the case of mineral industries in rural areas and small agricultural towns, the induced activities appear to be relatively high compared with the initial size of the towns involved. The overall level and variety of services increase for all residents, filling in some previously existing gaps. Services to transient populations (such as hotels and restaurants) increase substantially, although perhaps with some lag between the growth in demand and expanding supply. For example, in Campbell County during the 1960s and early 1970s, jobs in trade, services, local government, and secondary industry grew two-and-a-half times as quickly as jobs in the basic sectors.[4]

Public services. Several characteristics of the growing community encourage the public sector to increase more than proportionately to the population growth. The pregrowth town or county tends to have minimal needs for local government, and may get by with a single law-enforcement officer and with education, health-care, and fire-protection services shared among several geographic areas and jurisdictions. Publicly provided water- and sewage-treatment facilities may be nonexistent. Public roads have small levels of traffic and receive little maintenance. The entry of a large industry and new population group places tremendous demands on a weak local government structure.[5] In some cases, new servicing districts must be formed. A major increase in facilities is required. Public agencies become responsible for providing a number of services that previously were unnecessary or were obtained by private individuals (often at low or no cost). The number of local government jobs increases and the structure of local agencies often changes. Provision of new services leads to greater per-capita costs than previously existed.

Social effects. The amount of growth in the community changes the way people interact and the lifestyle options available in the community. Some effects that can be observed at the community level include the types of social and recreational activities in the area, the styles of social interaction (where people meet, types of interactions on the street), and the addition or removal of obstacles to daily life (for example, the simple increase in congestion seems to be a major irritant for many boom-town residents).

Long-Term Outcome

The longer-term consequences of the resource activity depend on the detailed characteristics of the local energy industry. Many regions may never experience a period of long-term, steady mining activity. Frequent fluctuations in the size of individual mines and in the level of output of energy-production facilities may prevent a region from ever balancing its service supply with the needs generated by local industries and residents.

   In contrast, if resource development continues at a steady level for two or more decades, the local inflationary-cycle and service lags will probably decrease. Other economic activities (such as agriculture) will adjust to the new level of competition by contracting, dissolving, or readjusting production technologies to employ higher-costing labor. However, this new state of equilibrium will leave the region in some jeopardy when the energy industry declines. At this point, even if the previous economic base has not dissolved, high levels of unemployment will likely occur when the newer group of "long-term" residents show reluctance to move. Only areas that have developed diversified economic bases may be able to limit the dependency on mining activities enough to avoid contracting when the local resources are exhausted or become noncompetitive.

The Boom-Town Effect

Many analyses of the local effects of energy-resource development focus primarily on problems related to rapid growth—the boom-town phenomenon.[6] In a boom-town situation, the development process just described is hindered by the rate at which new people move into a town or county. People move into the local area more quickly than producers in the region can respond with necessary goods and services—from housing space and classrooms to health care and automobile repair. Lags occur, especially during the first decade of growth. Private developers are reluctant to speculate during early periods of growth, when the future level of demand from the community is still uncertain. It may be difficult to obtain financing even after a new population has arrived, because the duration of mining activity is uncertain. Public government frequently finds that income from new growth (in the form of property taxes, sales taxes, and royalty payments) lags far behind the influx of new residents. Although anticipatory development could be financed by public debt, the preboom population is reluctant to take on this commitment until it is certain that growth will actually occur.[7]

   As long as many products are in short supply, the region will suffer from high rates of local inflation, poor access to goods and services, congestion, and a variety of social ills associated with rapid growth.

Local Distribution Effects

Most of the regional literature on energy-resource development focuses on the process just described, either through the detailed study of one or more energy-development experiences or through an in-depth analysis of one aspect of the boom-town process. With the exception of a few vivid and tragic accounts of some individual experiences in energy-resource towns,[8] most of these studies focus on the adjustment problem—how large the gap is between growth-induced demands and existing supplies, and what types of assistance will best enable the local economy to meet new demands. Where distribution questions arise, they tend to be applied to the public sector and they address the issue of who should pay for mitigation programs. Discussion centers on whether money for mitigating responses should come from the federal government, state government, local agencies, or the energy industry. The actual proposed mitigation programs focus on allowing local towns to accept growth induced by energy development in an efficient and timely manner.

This approach to the study of energy-resource towns uses geographic units as the basis of analysis. Yet underlying the place-specific effects are some important economic changes to and interactions among different population groups within the region. Over time, the set of population groups in an energy-development region shifts considerably. Policies that cope well on aggregate with changes occurring to a place may be ineffective in assisting the groups of people most adversely affected by energy-resource development. Boom-town research (and perhaps, the field of regional development more broadly) needs an added dimension whose focus is the incidence of changes to specific population groups within the regional and local economies.

The Distribution Questions

Theoretical literature and empirical research in urban and regional economics suggest several alternative patterns of distribution effects that may occur as a region develops. One possible pattern is the filtering of benefits from the basic economic sector to all other branches of (and groups within) the economy.[9] Other possible patterns emerge if certain groups have characteristics that exclude them from these benefits. Still different patterns may emerge if we reject the importance of the relationship of basic and nonbasic sectors of the economy and consider alternative sets of factors affecting distribution.

Pattern of filtered benefits. Local proponents of economic development frequently describe the distribution of benefits to local population groups as one of the primary goals of an industrial-location program. These supporters argue that economic growth filters gradually throughout the local economy, benefiting all sectors of the population. This occurs in several stages. The increased economic activity creates new jobs at higher wages. Some workers benefit directly through jobs in the industry. The rest of the population benefits indirectly—unemployment falls, competition for labor increases, wages rise in all sectors of the economy, higher incomes give a larger tax base, and public services improve for all. Implicit in this is the assumption that the increase in output is translated into a real wage increase (the nominal gain in wages is not counteracted by a proportional level of local price inflation).

Pattern of benefits gained by in-migrants. If labor from other regions of the nation is mobile, the adjustments in the local economy just described may not occur. In the extreme case, if all new labor demands are filled by in-migrants, there may be no benefits filtered to the local population. This distribution pattern could occur where the labor-force skills required by the incoming industry are quite different from the skills held by the local labor force. In this case, structural barriers to the filtering of benefits may appear. The original community labor force, because of lower skills and lower rates of productivity, cannot compete with the people who migrate into growing regions; these in-migrants tend to have higher skills and higher levels of education than the local population. Therefore, the higher-wage jobs in the new resource-based industry and other new jobs go to in-migrants. Wage levels in both the older basic industries and in much of the service sector remain the same. The growth process may result not only in a failure to filter down benefits, but also in an increase in the costs of living in the community. Wages offered to in-migrants may take account of higher costs, but incomes of nonmigrant segments of the population are effectively reduced. Expanding public services may more serve the needs of the newer population than the original population. These effects are similar to those observed from American and European economic development programs in chronically depressed areas and from some cases of suburban growth.[10]

Alternative patterns and modifying tendencies. A closer look at both local economic-development experience and development theories indicates that a number of other factors may interfere in the processes just described, modifying these patterns of distribution or producing alternative patterns. First, barriers may exist that keep certain old-timer population groups from participating in the filtering process. These groups may differ from other groups in the region because of age, skills, education, or work experience. For example, young workers may have more mobility than older workers. Also, workers in construction and service industries may obtain wage increases, whereas workers in agriculture may be unaffected because demand for their skills has not increased.

Second, some variations in distribution patterns may be explained by ownership of, access to, and use of physical and financial capital. For example, small-farm owners who try to maintain agricultural activity on their land may lose money whereas those who sell or lease land to the energy companies may make profits. Some retail businesses may expand, and others may fail because of rising costs of inputs and barriers to financing.

Third, geographic patterns within the region may affect characteristics of local population groups. Geographic variation may influence the distribution effects among groups within the region. For example, secondary employment growth may increase in the nearest metropolitan center, rather than in the local resource town.

Each pattern or variation may create a number of the short-term boom-town effects so frequently described. Yet the outcomes of a mitigation policy will vary considerably, depending on which pattern actually occurs. Clearly, in addressing policy considerations, we need to examine distribution patterns.

A Research Approach

To define the distribution outcomes of energy-resource development in the production region, we need to look beyond the community-level impacts of energy development, such as total population growth, employment growth, housing costs, and the fiscal balance for public government. The research must take a more disaggregated view of the region, and measure a different set of development outcomes. The measures should be tied as closely as possible to the population groups in the region, and should reflect the major economic factors that affect each group as the local economy changes.

For this research, a taxonomy of population groups present in western energy-production regions was developed. The population groups are classified largely by economic characteristics, including sector of employment, occupation, and source of income (wages, rents, or profits). Some further distinctions are made that consider a group's historical relationship with the community (long-term resident or recent in-migrant), and demographic and cultural characteristics. Table 6-2 outlines the major groups and their basic characteristics.

Because the research is concerned with a variety of effects to population groups, the analysis of distribution focuses on a range of factors that are indicative of a group's economic well-being. Changes in the short-term earning power of different groups are indicated by changes in wages, other forms of income, and prices. Effects on the long-term wealth of a group are related to changes in employment opportunities, the value of durable commodities, land, and human skills. The types of public services provided benefit different groups at different levels, and costs of these services accrue differentially.

In addition to having economic effects, changes in social structure may have major effects on the well-being of certain groups. The negative or positive values of specific life-style changes vary in part according to the characteristics of different population groups. Changes in social networks, visual amenities, traffic congestion, and crime levels are all examples of community characteristics that influence the quality of life and can be used as broad indicators of a group's welfare. At this initial stage of inquiry, the research focuses primarily on the

Table 6-2
Characteristics of Population Groups in Energy-Resource and Mining Communities

Boom-Town Group Long-Term Residents	Occupation	Income Level	Income Source	Types of Assets	Education and Training[a]	Age (Range or Approximate Median)	Family Structure	Length of Residence in Area[b]	
								Previous	Future
Farmers and ranchers	Owners, managers	Moderate (variable)	Profits, transfers	Land, farm, machinery	Low to medium	50	Male household heads, wives-homemakers, adult children	Long	Long
Agricultural workers: permanent residents	Unskilled labor; semi-skilled equipment operators	Low to moderate	Wages		Low to medium	35–40	Male household head, wives-homemakers, adult children	Long	Long
Agricultural workers: migrants	Unskilled labor	Low	Wages, transfers		Low (except for summer student labor)	18–60	Working adults, young children, (single students)	Temporary	Temporary
Downtown business local industries	Owners, managers	Moderate	Profits	Business site, inventory	Medium	50	Male household heads; wives-homemakers, adult children	Long	Long
Workers in local industry	Laborers, semiskilled	Low to moderate	Wages		Low to medium	18–60	Male household heads; wives-homemakers, adult children	Long	Long
Workers in trade and service	White-collar	Low to moderate	Wages		Medium	18–60	Male household head, working wife or older children	Long	Long

Table 6-2 Continued

Boom-Town Group Long-Term Residents	Occupation	Income Level	Income Source	Types of Assets	Education and Training[a]	Age (Range or Approximate Median)	Family Structure	Length of Residence in Area[b]	
								Previous	Future
Public employees	White-collar professional	Low to Moderate	Wages		Medium to high	35–50	Male household heads, wives may work, older children	Long	Long
Retired and fixed incomes		Low	Savings, transfers	Home	Low to medium	65+	Married couples or widowed, adult children	Long	Long
Native Americans	Broad range— few owners, managers	Low	Wages, rents, transfers	Tribal lands, resources	Broad range	18–60 (most under 35)		Long	Long
Construction workers: mobile	Skilled, blue-collar	Moderate to high	Wages		Medium	30+	Single males or family elsewhere	Short	Short
Construction workers: temporary "get rich quick"	Unskilled, labor	Moderate	Wages		Low	20–30	Single males or family elsewhere	Short	Short
Construction workers: permanent residents	Unskilled, semiskilled	Moderate	Wages		Medium	20–30	Male household head, young children, wives may work	Short	Medium to long
Miners and plant operators	Unskilled, semiskilled, and skilled labor	Moderate	Wages		Medium	20–30	Male household head, young children, wives may work	Short	Medium to long

Workers in education, public administration and health	Professional	Moderate to high	Wages		High	20–30	Single adults, young couples, working wives, some children	Short	Medium
Other incoming workers	Blue- and white-collar	Moderate	Wages		Medium	20–30	Same as above two categories	Short	Medium to long
Energy-facility owners and managers	Owners, managers	High	Profits, salaries	Mines, plants, equipment, minerals	Medium to high	20–40	Same as above for resident owners and managers	Short	Medium (tied to plant life)
New investors in trade and services	Owners, managers	Moderate to high	Profits	Business site, inventory	Medium to high	20–40	Same as above for resident owners and managers	Short	Medium
New investors in industry	Owners, managers	Moderate to high	Profits	Industry plant and equipment	Medium to high	20–40	Same as above for resident owners and managers	Short	Long

aApproximate levels of education and training: low—less than high-school graduation; medium—high-school graduate, some college or vocational training; high—college graduation, professional degrees.

bLength of residence: Previous—before present level of resource development was reached; Future—expected length of stay in community; short—about one year; medium—about five years; long—ten or more years; temporary—less than one year.

measurable economic indicators of change, with only brief mention of qualitative observations on life-style effects.

The case study presented here is based on this classification of population groups and focuses on some of the measures of economic change just mentioned. Some specific questions related to the distribution patterns outlined earlier are examined, including: (1) Who is employed in the growing sectors of the economy? (2) How is income spread throughout the region and among different population groups? (3) How are public services and costs distributed?

The analysis is based on a detailed accounting of trends and experiences observed in a five-county region. It draws on public records, published data, existing surveys, and field visits, and relies on qualitative impressions as well as quantitative measures. Case studies have both strengths and weaknesses compared with studies based only on sampling techniques. Case-study findings do not lend themselves to generalizations as do statistical analyses of a broad survey of experiences. Hypothesis tests based on case-study evidence are weakened by a narrow focus on a few communities. There is no way of showing whether a particular experience is representative of a normal or deviant case. In general, case-study findings do not allow us a strong degree of confidence in confirming hypotheses.

However, case-study findings allow us to make some determinations in areas that sampling techniques rarely touch. A case study may offer a broad understanding of the dynamics of a situation—how change occurs and how different mechanisms operate. In addition, a case analysis tends to be more sensitive to group characteristics. We can consider effects on groups even where large gaps exist in available data bases. Case-study findings frequently point to a wider scope of action than the narrower findings from statistical samples. Nonetheless, theoretical and policy conclusions drawn from a single case study must be followed by deeper investigations before they can be translated into action.

Boom and Bust in the Wyoming Powder River Basin

The Powder River Basin in northeastern Wyoming lies over rich deposits of energy minerals. Development of these minerals affects much of the northeastern and eastern parts of the state. The largest mineral deposits within the area lie in Campbell and Converse counties. These consist entirely of energy fuels, including oil, gas, low-sulfur bituminous coal, and uranium. Bordering counties are closely tied into this growing minerals economy, either through mineral resources or as service and refining areas for the regional energy-resource industry. Crook, Weston, and Niobrara counties have oil and gas deposits, Sheridan County provides housing and many services to surrounding mineral-resource counties, Natrona County was the center of earlier oil booms and continues to provide secondary services and refining capacity to the energy industry, and Platte County is the site of a 1,500-megawatt power plant, fueled entirely by Campbell County coal. The following analysis focuses on five of these counties—Campbell, Converse, Natrona, Platte, and Sheridan (see figure 6-2).

National Energy Policy and Wyoming's Energy Industry

As in other parts of the West, northeastern Wyoming has experienced brief periods of energy development in the past. Concern for energy independence during World War II led to the expansion of oil exploration and production in this part of the state during the 1940s. With the end of the war, much of this activity ceased, and by 1950, mineral extraction in northeastern Wyoming had declined to prewar levels. As a result, many of the local counties went through a boom and bust cycle that lasted less than a decade.

Energy activity remained low through the 1950s and into the 1960s. By the mid-1960s, energy companies were once again active in the region. Oil drilling began quickly, and the region became a major oil-producing area for the state. The coal industry built up more slowly in the region. Most of the exploration and leasing took place in the 1960s, but the first Electric Consumers Association has recently completed construction of a large plant near Wheatland in Platte County.[11]

Many groups in the region and the state have supported the export of local fuels for out-of-state processing. This policy reduces the immediate rapid-growth effects in local areas, but the reliance on outside demand also increases uncertainty about the region's economic future. Wyoming Powder River Basin coal is currently shipped to several other energy-rich regions in the United States—as far south as Texas and as far east as West Virginia. Changes in environmental standards or pollution-control technology could quickly change the demand for Wyoming's low-sulfur coal. Thus, although the potential growth of the coal industry in Wyoming is high, the future is uncertain. This uncertainty has made it particularly difficult for local agencies to plan for the future development of the region and has affected the rates, levels, and types of private investments that accompany and anticipate the energy-related growth.

The Region since 1960

Until 1960, most of the regional growth in northeastern Wyoming occurred around the city of Casper, in Natrona County. Between 1960 and 1977, the stagnant and declining population trends in the rest of these counties turned around, and the total population of the five-county area increased by more than 50 percent. At the center of growth, in Campbell County, population increased by more than 300 percent (table 6-3).

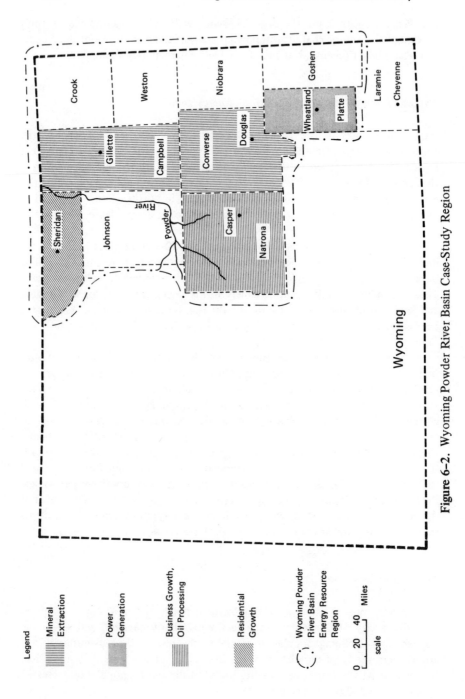

Figure 6-2. Wyoming Powder River Basin Case-Study Region

Table 6-3
Population Trends in the Powder River Basin, 1920-1977

County	1920	1960	1970	1977
Campbell	5,200	5,900	13,000	27,800
Converse	7,900	6,400	5,900	9,300
Natrona	14,600	49,600	51,300	64,400
Platte		7,200	6,500	8,500
Sheridan	18,200	19,000	17,900	21,400
Five-county total		88,100	94,600	132,400

Source: *Wyoming Data Handbook*, Department of Administration and Fiscal Control, Cheyenne, 1977.

This turnaround in the population trends of the rural and small towns coincides with new levels of mineral-resource extraction in the region. With this growth has come major changes in the local economy, particularly in the more rural counties. Growth has been accompanied by several changes observable throughout the region. Employment opportunities have increased, not only in mining and energy development but also in many other areas of employment. Unemployment is low—for most of the region the unemployment rate is lower than the state average and far lower than national trends. The range of wage levels represented by jobs has expanded, and there are many more high-paying jobs available in the region.

The private sector has expanded rapidly. This is particularly apparent in the service sector. Services catering to transient populations have mushroomed in the region. More options are available to the local populations, although in many cases the costs of products are very high. At the same time, many of the problematic effects of boom-town growth are apparent. The region has experienced high levels of inflation, and many goods and services, including housing, are in short supply.

Public agencies were quickly overwhelmed with demands. Police and fire services were understaffed. Crime levels increased dramatically, particularly in theft, vandalism, assault, and drunken driving. Although the crime level was no higher than in other urban areas of similar size and rates of growth, the change compared with previous experience was important for both the crime-prevention staff and the older residents.

Other agencies were inundated with demands for permits and licenses, planning assistance, land-use regulation, mental-health care, and other social services. The number of government employees grew much more rapidly here than in any other part of the state.[12]

The cost of expanding the public sector was offset in part by increasing revenue sources. The energy industry brought a tremendous rise in property values within the region. The imposition of local sales taxes enabled local governments to benefit from expanding retail trade as well. Grants and outside loans from state and federal agencies and private industry have also offered new revenue sources.

Major new public investments have offset some of the negative effects of rapid growth. Schools, after several years of being crowded, are now more than adequate in some parts of the region. Some new forms of medical care are available, and local cultural facilities have expanded. However, other problems still remain. Mental-health services are now provided, but cases of depression and child abuse remain at high levels. Law-enforcement services have expanded, but so has the crime rate. Over time, then, the region has provided some institutional means of addressing problems. The problems, however, are recurrent.

Population Groups in the Regions: Some New Mixes

As the economy of the region shifted in focus from an emphasis on agriculture to energy resources, new population groups became more important and the shares of different occupations held by long-term and new residents changed.[13] Over time, some of the groups normally dominated by newcomers came to include long-term residents as well. However, roles of in-migrants and long-term residents often differ within these groups.

Agriculture. As in the other energy-resource regions, agriculture was the dominant employer in the rural counties in the predevelopment period. The largest population group involved in agriculture in Wyoming consists of farm owners and operators, only 15 percent of whom are tenant farmers. Wage earners in agriculture form a relatively small population group, many of whose members are also involved in other part-time occupations throughout the year.

In the Powder River Basin, agricultural activity consists mainly of cattle grazing, sheep grazing, and dairy farming. This type of agricultural activity is extremely land intensive. The average farm size in Wyoming in 1969 was 4,034 acres, whereas the average farm size for the United States was 369 acres.[14] In each of the five counties making up the case-study region, agricultural land made up at least 85 percent of all land uses in the county. In Campbell County, agricultural land use was 97 percent of the total land area,[15] making farm owners and operators sensitive to any other land-involving activity such as mining.

Most of the farm operators in Wyoming tend to be substantially older than workers in other sectors of the economy. For example, in 1969, the average age of farm operators in Campbell County was 52.6 years, and more than one-fifth were 65 or older. Although few of these farmers hold or seek full-time work outside agriculture, almost half of the farm operators supplement their farm income by part-time work outside the farm.

Trade and services. Trade and services have grown substantially, most noticeably in Campbell, Converse, and Platte. Several different types of local businesses now exist in the region to meet the demands of a growing population. First, there are the original businesses established in the community before the expansion of the energy industry. In the Powder River Basin, these establishments varied by county and city size. Businesses in Campbell, Converse, and Platte counties and the small towns in Sheridan and Natrona were patronized almost entirely by county residents. These businesses appear to have been largely locally owned and owner-run, with few employees per establishment. In contrast, more businesses in the cities of Sheridan and Casper drew customers from outside the county. By serving a relatively large market area, the operation of these businesses in the preboom period made it easier to meet the demands of a rapidly growing community than was the experience of predominantly local services.

Second, there are local businesses, mainly located in Casper and Sheridan, that are branches of larger national or regional firms. Although some of these businesses may have been located in the region preceding the energy development, the business owners are often nonlocal, and the firm may draw operating personnel from a much broader region. For example, some "local" contractors are branch offices of firms in Denver, Minneapolis, or some more distant city.

Third, many new businesses take the form of franchises. These are businesses associated with national or regional chains but locally owned or managed. None of the available studies for this region has indicated how many of these businesses are owned by long-term residents. However, only a small proportion of such businesses in Gillette can reasonably be accounted for by the original ranching, trade, and service populations.

Wage earners in the trade and service sectors work mainly in new businesses. Although some of the businesses operated by long-term residents have kept on older employees, most of the new businesses have hired young workers, of high-school age or in their early twenties. This is among the most transient group of workers. The turnover is high, with many employees soon moving to higher-wage jobs or to school.

Government. New and old roles in local government differ substantially. In the small predevelopment communities, particularly in Campbell, Converse, and Platte counties, there were very few people employed by public agencies.[16] Of the public employees in these communities, most were employed by city and county agencies, school districts, and the United States Department of Agriculture, largely in jobs that did not require advanced academic degrees. Casper and Sheridan had many more state agencies and employees proportionate to population size than Gillette, Douglas, or Wheatland. City and county government employees in all these counties tended to be paid very low wages and they often held part-time positions.

With energy-related growth has come, slowly, a "professionalization" of city and county governments and a larger presence of state and federal agencies. The transformation of local government is clearest in counties that have both a heavy influx of energy workers and large increases in income from energy activities. In Campbell County, after almost ten years of continual rapid growth, the style of local government is almost entirely changed. Many of the new positions are at professional levels, and white-collar and laborer jobs have also increased. More state and federal agencies establish branches in the smaller towns, as demands for their services increase. Most of these positions are filled by newcomers to the region.

Retired workers. Retired workers are a distinct group in the population, consisting almost entirely of long-term residents. In the most rapidly growing parts of the region, the proportion of older residents has been decreasing steadily. By 1975, only 5 percent of the residents of Campbell County were sixty-five or older, whereas in Sheridan County 15 percent of the population was made up of residents in this age group.[17] Members of this group often have lower incomes than much of the rest of the population, need more centrally located housing, and also have special transportation, recreational, and medical needs.

The energy industry. The energy-resource-extraction industry in the Powder River Basin consists of oil drilling and strip-mining of coal and uranium. Although oil drilling has been a greater source of gross revenues to the region, coal and uranium production require a greater number of employees. The majority of mining employees in the region are engaged in strip-mining. Workers in these industries vary in skill level and income. Jobs begin at a "laborer" classification and reach the highest classification level for heavy-equipment operators on shovels, cranes, and draglines. Most of the mine workers in Wyoming tend to be newcomers, especially at higher skill levels.

Two types of energy-resource processing occur in this region—oil refining and electric-power generation from coal. Oil refining is probably the only energy activity in the region that employs primarily long-term residents, largely in the urban areas. For the last twenty-five years, the oil-refining industry has provided stable employment for its workers, but no growth in jobs. Labor agreements in the 1950s led companies to cease layoffs and deal with decreasing work force needs through natural attrition processes of retirement and resignations. Until the mid-1970s, this policy resulted in no new hires, although substantial hiring has occurred since then. Employees appear to find the stability of employment an important feature, and plants in Casper have very low turnover rates of wage employees.

Management-level employment is handled somewhat differently by most of the regional energy companies. Managers move from plant to plant throughout the country, staying in one site for no more than a few years. Although an entry-level manager might be recruited locally, he would not necessarily gain employment at the local plant. Thus, over the long term, hiring practices split energy-industry employees into two separate groups—long-term-resident wage earners and a continually changing crop of newcomers among salaried employees.

Most of the electric-generating facilities in the region are not yet or only recently in operation. Once in operation, these facilities will provide less than 5 percent of the five-county region's energy-industry work force. For example, total work force projected for the Wyodak mine and Black Hills Power and Light generating plant in 1980 was only 80 out of the projected 2,800 permanent employees of the energy industry in Campbell County. The other major power plant in the region, the Laramie River plant outside Wheatland, was projected to employ a long-term level of 200 people.

Construction. Construction generated by energy development has been a major new source of employment for the region and has attracted many newcomers. For the five-county region as a whole, the construction work force grew less rapidly during the first decade of this energy-industry boom than the state's construction work force. However, Campbell and Converse counties, with power plants under construction, showed much sharper rises in construction employment (see table 6-4).

Characteristics of construction workers vary among different locations and for different types of work. Several types of construction work have expanded recently in the study region, including construction related to mining operations (road work, storage facilities, office facilities, equipment), construction of power plants, and construction of residential units. Construction employment fluctuates for several reasons. Like mining and agriculture, construction is affected to some degree by seasonal variations. For example, the number of unemployed construction workers, statewide, in January 1977 was almost twenty times greater than the number unemployed in October 1977. In addition, construction employment varies with the stage of development of the facility. Of the

Table 6-4
Changes in Construction Employment, 1968-1975

	1968	1975	Percent Change 1968-1975
Campbell	294	1,031	251
Converse	165	286	73
Natrona	1,233	2,161	75
Platte	117	111	-5
Sheridan	609	700	15
Five-county region	2,418	4,289	77
State	6,403	14,569	128

Source: Data for 1968 and 1975 (actual numbers; not percentage change) from *Wyoming Data Handbook*, Department of Administration and Fiscal Control, Cheyenne, 1977.

construction projects occurring in the region, power-plant construction requires the greatest fluctuation in employment. Employment may vary from a few dozen people at the early and final stages of construction to a peak level of more than 2,000.

Highly skilled professions. The growing communities offer employment in a number of other professional, management, and white-collar positions. Opportunities in legal professions, finance and real estate, and medical professions expand. Many of the people holding these jobs are highly-paid recent graduates of training programs, and are recruited nationwide.

The Spread of Effects among People and Places

Campbell County and the surrounding region give the impression of being a place that is evolving from an agricultural rural setting to a more urban style of life. However, taking a more disaggregated view of those effects, we find that participation in many aspects of the growing economy varies considerably among the population groups described here.

Who Is Employed in the Growing Sectors of the Economy? Information on employment in the region was incomplete. However, there is clear evidence that some barriers exist for people wishing to move into new occupations. Patterns of employment in the region vary with the occupational sector and the location of new employment. Commuting is an important factor in the distribution of a few types of jobs in some counties. Other counties are so isolated that almost all jobs are held by people residing locally (whether they are long-term residents or in-migrants).

Distribution of jobs in construction and mining. Construction jobs were the least likely to be filled by long-term residents of the energy-development counties. This is a result both of the low availability of workers trained in construction among the predevelopment population and of the contracting and recruitment policies of the energy companies. Hiring practices for construction work varied from project to project. In cases where a sharp increase in the number of workers was required for a limited time period (as with peak periods of power-plant construction), companies tended to contract outside the region for workers. In addition, some of the large housing developments built by energy companies in Campbell County were designed and constructed by outside contractors. Workers brought in for these short-term jobs frequently were single or they came without their families, and they lived in motels or temporary facilities provided by the construction firm, thus spending a relatively large proportion of their income outside the county.

Monitoring reports by the Missouri Basin Power Project (MBPP) on the construction of the Laramie River plant give some insight into the locational patterns of the construction work force.[18] The MBPP began construction of the Laramie River station in 1977. Following the requirements established through the Industrial Siting Act permitting process, the company has monitored several aspects of community change and the construction work force on a monthly basis. Employment during construction of the plant rose from 164 in January 1977 to 2,117 in July 1978. The MBPP also recorded the residence patterns of its employees. The employees showed three patterns—daily commuters, who maintain a permanent residence from which they commute daily (they either had lived in Platte County before construction work began or have since established a permanent residence outside the county); weekly commuters, who maintain a permanent home elsewhere but also have a temporary residence in Platte County to which they commute weekly without their families; and temporary residents, who have moved into the county with their families since construction work began. During the first year, 1977, as employment rose to more than 900, the proportion of daily commuters remained fairly constant, close to 50 percent in 1978. As construction work approached its peak employment level, the proportion of weekly commuters increased sharply and the proportion of daily commuters dropped. Thus, it appears that as the prospects for long-term employment became weaker, the proportion of people choosing to establish only temporary residency in the community increased.

The residence patterns of daily commuters indicates the willingness of many construction workers to commute at great distances. Of the 554 daily commuters in July 1978, only one-fifth lived in Platte County. Almost four-fifths of these workers communted from 50 miles or more to work at the plant. With widespread competition for construction jobs, long-term residents in Platte County are less likely to gain jobs in this sector. The number of Platte County residents employed in construction varied between about 40 and 120 in the decade preceding MBPP employment.[19] Of the 2,000 MBPP workers in July 1978, 112 had permanent residences in the county before construction began. Although we do not have records of total construction employment among long-term residents in Platte County for that month, it seems likely from these figures that few of the new construction jobs were filled by local people transferring from other industries.

The experience of the Laramie River plant supports a couple of specific conclusions on the spread of employment benefits within the region. First, the temporary nature of many construction jobs implies that there are few potential opportunities for local people. Local workers already working in construction fields lack many of the skills needed for power-plant construction and they cannot obtain necessary training in a short period of time. Second, if large labor pools exist within a broad commuting distance of the construction site (up to 150 miles away), the filtering of jobs to local people will be further reduced.

In other parts of the region, the commuting effect is much less intense. Sheridan and Campbell counties are in a less populous section of the state than

Platte County. This means that there are fewer workers available for hiring and fewer choices of residential locations for new workers. For the Campbell County area, particularly in the early stages of growth, alternative residential choices were few. There are only 3 towns within 100 miles of Gillette that have populations of more than 1,000, and no towns within this distance with populations greater than 5,000. In contrast, there are several places of more than 20,000 people within this distance from Wheatland.

Although commuting effects are greatly restricted in Campbell County, there is no evidence that local hiring for power-plant construction jobs increases in its place. In general, Wyoming tends to have a relatively small proportion of local workers hired for power-plant construction. At the Wyodak plant, outside Gillette, only 3 percent of the 200 construction workers in 1975 were local residents.[20]

The mining industry shows different hiring and commuting patterns. Mining companies do much more of their hiring locally. For example, Carter Oil Company recruited about 60 percent of its current work force through its Gillette office. The rest were either transferred from other affiliates or recruited throughout the country. However, even local hiring does not necessarily bring long-term residents into the mining industry. As a Carter official pointed out, "though all our non-exempt employees are hired locally, they come to Gillette from all parts of the country in search of the employment opportunities available there."[21]

Although the area around Gillette is fairly isolated and attracts few commuters from other counties to jobs in mining, southern Campbell County and Converse County both have more commuters from outside the county. Commuting rates are particularly high for mines located within sixty miles of a larger city. Southern Campbell County, where much future mining is projected, currently draws one third of its mining work force from other counties. Many mining employees in Converse County reside in Casper or its suburbs and almost all the workers employed by the Decker mine in Montana reside in Sheridan, Wyoming. Although the commuting from Natrona County consists at least in part of long-term residents of that county for whom the energy growth offers new opportunities, most of the commuters from Sheridan County are new residents.[22]

In summary, a clear division emerges between the more diversified urban counties and the predominantly agricultural counties. The energy sector appears to offer much greater opportunities for workers from Natrona County, many of whom have held previous jobs in energy-extraction activities. The companies are clearly taking advantage of the more diversified skills available around the city of Casper. Where the mix of skills is much narrower, as in Sheridan and Campbell Counties, the companies are much more likely to hire nonlocal workers. In particular, the agricultural activities common in northeastern Wyoming appear to offer few skills transferable to mining and other energy-development activities.

Movement into jobs in other sectors of the economy. Observation of other sectors of the economy shows that the distribution of jobs, particularly in trade, services, and public government, varies considerably. The cities with larger pre-development populations seem to have maintained a much greater mixture of long-term residents and newcomers within many occupations. In the more rapidly changing cities that were once small towns, almost all the employees in new businesses appear to be newcomers. Although there is no evidence that these new patterns of employment have resulted in displacement of long-term workers from previously held positions, there is also little indication that new business growth in the resource-based counties has offered them wider opportunities.

A similar pattern is evident in public-sector jobs. There have been big changeovers in local government positions in Campbell and Converse counties. Virtually all the new professional jobs and many of the longer-term positions are now held by newcomers. This tendency seems much stronger in Campbell and Converse than in the other counties in the region. In Sheridan and Natrona counties, long-term residents still hold many of the city and county positions.

Movement out of traditional sectors. In most of the sectors just described, movement of workers out of traditional jobs into new occupations and job categories is slow, particularly in the fastest-growing counties. Older workers show the least mobility in terms of new employment opportunities. Opportunities for younger workers are somewhat greater, especially over longer periods of time. For example, some training is offered for mine technicians through local college curricula.

In contrast to energy-development activities at some other sites in the West, the energy industries in Wyoming offer little opportunity for local farmers and ranchers to supplement their income. The age of local farm operators makes it unlikely that many of them will choose to change careers for full-time employment opportunities in the energy industries. Although part-time employment is sometimes available in mining or construction, the seasonal variations in these two occupations correspond closely with seasonal variations in agriculture. The winter months, when farm workers and operators are most likely to be looking for supplemental employment, are the periods of highest unemployment in the mining industry. In contrast, mining activities expand at the same time that worker demands on the farm are at their highest.[23] Thus, the structures of the two industries create further barriers to the filtering of employment opportunities to the local work force.

The Spread of Income through the Region and among Different Population Groups. *Income levels.* The income structure has clearly changed in some of the energy-development counties. The resource-extraction counties, Campbell and Converse, show the greatest gains in income relative to other counties in the region and the state. In 1949, median family incomes in these two counties were about 80 percent of the median family incomes for the state as a whole. At least

since 1969, median family income in Converse has been roughly equal to the
state level, whereas median family income in Campbell has been 10 to 25 percent higher than the state level (see table 6-5).

The counties where resource extraction has only indirect effects (Natrona,
Platte, Sheridan) do not show the same degree of change. Median income in
Natrona County has remained somewhat higher than the state average during
the whole period. Median income in Platte County has remained about 20 percent lower than the state average during the entire period (1976 was the last
year for which this measure was available, thus the date precedes the major
construction boom). Sheridan County shows a relative decline in income over
the period. Sheridan had the second-highest median family income in the five-
county region in 1949 but now has the second lowest. Although income in
Sheridan has always been slightly lower than the state level, the gap has steadily
widened since energy development expanded in the 1960s.

The evidence on income changes by county indicates that the business
generated by resource extraction in itself is not enough to substantially improve
incomes for the population as a whole. Overall improvements in income levels
have appeared only in counties where income is directly augmented by the high
wages in the energy sector (thus increasing the overall average). This is one
indication that benefits have not been filtering through to other sectors of the
economy.

Table 6-5
Income Levels, Wyoming Households, 1949-1976
(current dollars)

County	Median Household Income[a]	Median Family Income		
	1976	1969	1959	1949
Campbell	15,100	11,301	6,092	2,854
Converse	13,600	8,947	5,077	2,825
Natrona	15,200	10,440	6,995	3,784
Platte	11,200	8,096	4,860	2,846
Sheridan	11,600	7,449	5,306	3,200
Laramie	14,200	9,162	6,386	3,697
Wyoming	13,500	8,943	5,877	3,482

Sources: Census of the Population, 1950, 1960 and 1970; Claire Zelinski, *Low to Moderate
Income Housing Need in the State of Wyoming,* Wyoming Department of Economic Planning and Development, Cheyenne, 1977.

[a]Income estimates for 1976 were made by the state of Wyoming and are published in the
study cited here. Because Wyoming used *household,* rather than *family,* as the basic unit the
1976 figures are not completely comparable to figures for earlier years (all obtained from
the *Census of Population*). However, the figures are still useful for examining changes over
time in the relative position of each county to the rest of the region and the state.

Income distribution. Aggregate measures of income distribution have also changed in different ways in different counties. Crudely measured interquartile variations show that during the energy-development period, from 1960 to 1977, the spread of income widened (become less equal) both in the state as a whole and for most of the case-study region (see table 6-6).[24] Campbell County, however, shows much less of an increase in inequality than do any of the other counties in the state. In fact, during the earlier stages of growth (from 1959 to 1969), there was a decrease in income inequality in Campbell County. In all the other counties, the distribution of income has grown increasingly less equal. In Sheridan, Converse, and Platte, the levels of inequality are much higher than for the state as a whole. These trends are further evidence that income benefits have not filtered through much of the region. The widening gaps in income levels are consistent with a situation where high-wage earners have moved into the region, but low-wage earners have not experienced relative improvements in their earnings.

Wages. The level of wages varies widely by county. The most significant wage effects are apparent in Campbell County, where wages comparatively high in all sectors of the economy. In other counties, some sectors of the economy continue to pay low wages. In Sheridan and Platte counties, for example, wages in mining and construction are competitive with other counties in the region, but wages in the trade and service sectors are much lower than in the rest of the region (see table 6-7).

The income distribution and wage data for Campbell County indicate that locally more filtering may be taking place from the energy sectors to other sectors of the economy although these wage gains may not accrue to the individuals who were originally employed in those sectors. The very low proportion of residents below the poverty level and the average weekly wages in this county give further indications that filtering may occur more readily in this fast-growing, isolated county. However, wage filtering offers only a partial explanation of these figures. The overall improvements in income distribution in Campbell County and the relatively higher wages in the nonbasic sectors of the economy result from the greater proportion of new, high-wage jobs, rather than improvements in earnings in traditional sectors of the economy. Filtering, as we have defined it, will occur directly through these high-wage jobs only to the extent that long-term residents receive high-wage employment. Our discussion of groups employed in growing sectors of the economy indicated that long-term residents in Campbell County appeared to have low rates of participation in the high-wage sectors of the economy.

Some econometric work that uses average weekly wages for all Wyoming counties offers evidence consistent with this interpretation. Using ordinary least squares on cross-sectional data (table 6-8), we tested the hypothesis that wage levels, by county, in each of the nonbasic sectors of the economy are a function of average wages in all basic sectors and county population size. We included a

Table 6-6
Income Distribution, Wyoming Counties, 1949–1977

County	Household (or Family) Income One Quarter of the Way Up from the Bottom of the Income Array (Q_1) (Dollars)	Household (or Family) Income One Quarter of the Way Down from the Top of the Income Array (Q_3) (Dollars)	Interquartile Variation $\dfrac{Q_3 - Q_1}{Q_3 + Q_1}$
Campbell			
1949	1,820	3,950	.37
1959	4,300	9,000	.35
1969	8,400	15,300	.29
1977	9,100	20,400	.37
Converse			
1949	1,920	4,730	.42
1959	3,280	7,060	.37
1969	5,240	12,000	.39
1977	5,500	18,000	.53
Natrona			
1949	3,080	5,780	.30
1959	5,000	8,500	.26
1969	6,950	14,440	.35
1977	7,220	20,870	.49
Platte			
1949	1,770	4,120	.40
1959	3,050	5,880	.32
1969	4,420	11,380	.44
1977	4,920	16,390	.54
Sheridan			
1949	2,080	4,720	.39
1959	3,200	7,100	.38
1969	5,000	12,000	.41
1977	4,500	15,100	.54
State of Wyoming			
1949	2,240	4,920	.37
1959	3,850	8,680	.39
1969	5,800	13,000	.38
1977	7,000	18,500	.54

Source: Census of Population, 1950, 1960, and 1970; Claire Zelinski, *Low to Moderate Income Housing Need in the State of Wyoming,* Wyoming Department of Economic Planning and Development, Cheyenne, 1977.

Table 6–7
Average Weekly Wages, 1977, in Selected Industries, Powder River Basin
(dollars)

County	Mining	Construction	Retail Trade	Services	Agriculture
Campbell	362.94	311.48	140.23	185.20[a]	
Converse	355.27	273.56	123.12	107.19[a]	
Natrona	323.62	271.24	144.34	183.85	141.07
Platte[c]	303.25	250.00	104.08	105.15[a]	
Sheridan	374.72	220.93	117.27	134.59	137.19
Laramie	328.58	243.78	128.90	140.17[b]	118.72

Source: *Wyoming Covered Employment and Wage Data by Industry and County, 1975–1977,* Research and Analysis Section, Employment Security Commission of Wyoming, Casper, 1977.

[a]Services with agriculture.

[b]Services with public administration.

[c]These figures are from a period just preceding the major boom in Platte County.

dummy variable to distinguish counties with high levels of nonbasic employment from other counties. We made this distinction based on the assumption that local economies dominated by nonbasic activities might have higher proportions of managerial workers and thus show higher average wages in these sectors compared with other counties.

For most sectors, the test showed a strong relationship between size of place and average wages in nonbasic sectors. For services (retail and wholesale), we could reject with 95 percent confidence the hypothesis that population size was unrelated to nonbasic wage levels. However, we could not reject the null hypothesis with this degree of confidence for the relationship between wages in the basic sectors and wages in most nonbasic sectors (see table 6–9).

Although these findings are not conclusive for many reasons, they are consistent with the hypothesis that wage filtering is not an important effect between basic and nonbasic sectors.[25] Other forces seem to dominate in determining wage levels. Total population size, for example, influences the mix of occupations in each sector, and thus affects wage rates. In addition, increases in population size may more than proportionately increase demand for some nonbasic occupations, thus raising wages more directly.

Cost of living. Increases in income throughout the region have been further offset by changes in the cost of living. With the exception of the urban portion of Natrona County, the entire region was a low-cost area to live, at least through the early 1960s. In recent years, however, prices have risen substantially, and costs of many items now compare unfavorably with the slower-going areas of the state (see table 6–10). The change is apparent over longer periods of time in

Table 6-8
Population and Average Weekly Wages, All Wyoming Counties, 1977

County	Population 1977	Average Weekly Wage, All Basic Sectors	Average Weekly Wage, Nonbasic Sectors					Dummy Variable[a]
			Wholesale	Retail	Finance, Insurance, Real Estate	Services	Average	
Albany	31,000	212	176	104	164	208	168	1
Big Horn	12,200	241	167	97	186	145	128	0
Campbell	27,800	330	276	140	239	185	177	0
Carbon	17,400	338	215	119	193	120	129	0
Converse	9,300	332	144	123	194	107	127	0
Crook	5,000	242	189	85	200	108	102	0
Fremont	33,200	288	193	124	169	153	144	0
Goshen	12,500	204	153	124	199	105	128	1
Hot Springs	6,100	279	210	101	153	109	113	0
Johnson	6,800	248	210	105	178	101	114	0
Laramie	64,800	254	246	129	197	140	150	1
Lincoln	9,800	310	186	98	203	94	117	0
Natrona	64,400	304	288	144	211	183	192	0
Niobrara	3,000	264	115	117	148	84	114	0
Park	19,900	273	220	111	200	125	131	0
Platte	8,500	265	148	104	181	127	119	1
Sheridan	21,400	260	197	117	207	135	137	0
Sublette	4,000	240	217	106	183	102	114	0
Sweetwater	34,800	339	257	128	198	147	151	0
Teton	7,000	188	177	110	183	111	116	1
Uinta	10,100	250	166	101	162	175	135	0
Washakie	8,200	237	197	116	182	113	130	0
Weston	6,600	268	215	107	207	95	121	0

Source: *Wyoming Covered Employment and Wage Data By Industry and County, 1975-1977*, Research and Analysis Section, Employment Security Commission of Wyoming, Casper, 1977.

[a]Dummy variable equal to 1 in all counties where secondary employment equals or exceeds 66 percent of total employment.

Table 6–9
Estimated Coefficients Relating Wages in Nonbasic Sectors to Wages in Basic
Sectors and Size of Place, Wyoming Counties, 1977

Dependent Variable	Estimated Constant (t statistic)	$\hat{B}WBAS$ (t statistic)	$\hat{B}POP$ (t statistic)	$\hat{B}DUM$ (t statistic)	R^2
Wages in wholesale	146.93 (2.41)	0.10 (0.42)	0.0017 (3.49)	−24.27 (−1.05)	.51
Wages in retail	63.76 (3.29)	0.15 (2.06)	0.0004 (2.69)	8.21 (1.12)	.49
Wages in finance, insurance, and real estate	117.86 (3.16)	0.24 (1.73)	0.00014 (0.51)	13.92 (0.99)	.23
Wages in services	134.64 (2.56)	−0.10 (−0.53)	0.0013 (3.23)	−7.49 (−0.38)	.41
Average wage for nonbasic sectors	99.83 (3.90)	0.05 (0.56)	0.0010 (5.08)	0.31 (0.03)	.69

Note: Independent variables are as follows: WBAS = county average wage, all basic sectors, 1977; POP = county population size, 1976; DUM = dummy variable, equal to 1 where non-basic employment is greater than or equal to 66 percent of total employment; otherwise equal to zero.

housing costs (see table 6–11). In 1960, median housing values in all four rural counties were below the median level of housing values in the state and in Laramie County (where Cheyenne, the state capital, is located). By 1978, a study of cost of living relative to costs in Cheyenne showed housing prices in towns of all five counties well above the price of housing in Cheyenne. These comparative cost levels modify the earning benefits attained by residents in Campbell County and make the relative positions in low-wage groups in other counties much worse. Only in Campbell County is the relative wage index for all sectors higher than the relative cost-of-living index for 1978. In Sheridan, Platte, and Converse, relative wage indices in retail services are much lower than relative cost indices (see table 6–12).[26]

The Distribution of Public Services and Costs. Patterns of expenditures and sources of public government income have changed considerably in the region during the energy-development period. (See tables 6–13 and 6–14). The strongest shifts are apparent in the resource-extraction counties (Campbell and Converse), where special growth-related expenditures have expanded while per-capita general government expenditures (adjusted for inflation)[27] have remained stable or declined (see table 6–15). Per-capita general expenditures in neighboring

Table 6-10
Comparative Costs of Living in Wyoming

City (County)	Rank (Out of 23 County Seats)	All Items	Food	Housing	Apparel and Upkeep	Transportation	Recreation and Personal Care	Medical Care
Gillette (Campbell)	3	108.43	103.88	117.94	107.10	100.03	107.40	96.38
Casper (Natrona)	5	107.29	102.56	110.35	112.79	99.74	111.43	105.96
Douglas (Converse)	6	106.40	101.10	109.18	113.06	99.87	107.23	112.51
Sheridan (Sheridan)	7	105.94	106.79	108.12	115.01	100.56	103.87	91.22
Wheatland (Platte)	10	104.35	102.15	104.80	109.97	98.95	110.66	97.44
Buffalo (Johnson)[a]	19	99.32	105.20	83.00	130.10	88.91	106.54	97.09
Lusk (Nibrara)[a]	23	93.87	99.52	74.66	118.60	99.78	104.14	97.67
Cheyenne (Laramie)	18	100.00	100.00	100.00	100.00	100.00	100.00	100.00
Lakewood, Colorado[b]		106.83	96.24	115.14	118.21	102.78	105.15	92.87

Sources: The table is from Jim Sinclair, Michael Rigsby, and Steven Streeper, "Wyoming Cost of Living Index Revised," Wyoming State Department of Administration and Fiscal Control, Research and Statistics Division, Cheyenne, 1978. The keyed notes in the table footnote are from John Rogers and Kathryn Hoyle, "Autumn 1978 Urban Family Budgets and Comparative Indexes for Selected Urban Areas," *News*, U.S. Department of Labor, Bureau of Labor Statistics, Washington, D.C., April 29, 1979.

Note: Cost-of-living index prices as of April 5, 6, and 7, 1978. Cheyenne, Laramie County = 100.

[a]These two counties represent places within the general region that have received no energy-resource-development activities.

[b]Lakewood, Colorado, was included in the Wyoming State study to provide a comparison point outside the state. Lakewood is a suburb of Denver, Colorado, with slightly higher income and somewhat higher prices than Denver. An autumn 1978 study by the Bureau of Labor Statistics comparing family budgets in urban areas showed costs in Denver to be close to the average costs for a family in the United States. Lakewood probably has slightly higher costs than the U.S. average.

Table 6–11
Trends in Housing Values, Wyoming Powder River Basin

County	Median Housing Values[a]		Relative Price of Housing, 1978[b]
	1960	1970	
Campbell	$10,800	$20,700	118
Converse	11,100	15,100	109
Natrona	14,800	17,000	110
Platte	8,200	11,000	105
Sheridan	10,500	13,700	108
Laramie	14,500	16,100	100
State of Wyoming	12,300	15,300	

[a]Owner occupied. These data are from U.S. Bureau of the Census, *Census of Housing*, 1960, 1970.

[b]This is the cost-of-living index of housing in the county seat of each county listed. The index is based on costs in Cheyenne, Laramie County (see table 6–4).

counties have declined much more sharply, but these counties needed fewer increases in special expenditures.

Total general revenues in the two energy-extraction counties have increased faster than general expenditures, although per-capita general revenues have decreased since 1967. Property-tax revenues account for almost all of the general-revenue increase in Campbell County and about half of the increase in Converse County. Converse County's remaining general revenue increases come largely from increased fees and charges for services (see tables 6–15 and 6–16).

All three nonextractive counties in the case-study region have lower revenues now than in 1967. Their local tax revenues have declined (in constant dollar terms), as have many other major sources of revenues. For example, inter-governmental revenues dropped by 80 percent in Sheridan County, by 84 percent in Platte, and by 65 percent in Natrona County between 1967 and 1977.

In the resource-extraction counties, the larger total revenues have generally been spent in a few critical areas, although not necessarily at a greater per-capita spending level. For example, Campbell County in 1977 allocated 57 percent of its general expenditures (close to $3 million) to education (largely capital outlays). This represented an increase of almost 200 percent over county spending for education in 1967, and 62 percent of the total general expenditure increase from 1967–1977. Yet these education expenditures on a per-capita basis were lower in 1977 than they had been in 1967. Other large expenditure increases in Campbell County included transportation, public safety, and natural resources (agricultural assistance). All of these services again had lower per-capita spending rates in 1977 than in 1967. Much smaller total spending increases in libraries, parks and recreation, and public health led to per-capita spending increases for these three services.

Table 6-12

Indices Showing Comparative Costs of Living, Household Incomes, and Wages in Wyoming Counties

County	Relative Cost of Living, April 1978	Relative Household Income, December 1976	Relative Wages, 1977			
			Mining	Construction	Retail	Services
Campbell	108	106	110	127	109	132
Converse	106	95	108	112	95	76
Natrona	107	107	98	111	112	131
Platte	106	78	92	102	80	75
Sheridan	105	81	111	91	90	96
Laramie	100	100	100	100	100	100

Sources: Jim Sinclair, Michael Rigsby, and Steven Streeper, "Wyoming Cost of Living Index Revised," Wyoming State Department of Administration and Fiscal Control, Research and Statistics Division, Cheyenne, 1978 (cost of living index); Claire Zelinski, *Low to Moderate Income Housing Need in the State of Wyoming*, Wyoming Department of Economic Planning and Development, Cheyenne, 1977 (household income); *Wyoming Covered Employment and Wage Data by Industry and County, 1975-1977*, Research and Analysis Section, Employment Security Commission of Wyoming, Casper, 1977 (wages).

Note: Laramie = 100.

Table 6-13
General Revenues
(constant dollars, 1967 base)

County	Total ($1,000)			Per Capita ($)		
	1967	1977	Percent Change 1967–1977	1967	1977	Percent Change 1967–1977
Campbell	2,015	5,515	174	265	197	−26
Converse	2,474	4,159	68	412	447	8
Natrona	21,369	14,389	−32	465	223	−52
Platte	2,581	787	−70	385	93	−76
Sheridan	5,666	3,509	−38	313	164	−48

Source: U.S. Bureau of the Census, *Census of County Governments*, 1967, 1977.

Expenditures are a weak proxy measure for quality of services. However, we can speculate from this data that even an economically active and growing county does not quickly generate revenues and services to meet the growing needs of the local population. In a few public-service areas, where previous expenditures were very low, Campbell County has improved the quality of service used extensively by many segments of the population. However, the majority of Campbell County's expenditure increases have gone toward

Table 6–14
Local Taxes Contributing to General Revenues

County	Total ($1,000)			Per Capita		
	1967	1977	Percent Change 1967–1977	1967	1977	Percent Change 1967–1977
Campbell	926	4,361	371	122	156	28
Converse	1,667	2,652	59	278	285	3
Natrona	9,953	6,696	−33	216	109	−50
Platte	968	487	−50	144	57	−60
Sheridan	2,129	1,030	−52	118	48	−59

Source: U.S. Bureau of the Census, *Census of County Governments,* 1967 and 1977.

Table 6–15
General Expenditures
(constant dollars, 1967 base)

County	Total ($1,000)			Per Capita		
	1967	1977	Percent Change 1967–1977	1967	1977	Percent Change 1967–1977
Campbell	2,168	5,213	140	285	186	−35
Converse	2,657	4,125	55	443	443	0
Natrona	21,701	14,012	−35	472	216	−54
Platte	2,211	857	−61	330	101	−69
Sheridan	5,808	3,313	−43	321	155	−52

Source: U.S. Bureau of the Census, *Census of County Governments,* 1967 and 1977.

Table 6–16
County Assessed Value, Wyoming Case Study Counties
(constant dollars, 1967 base)

County	Assessed Value		Percent Change 1970–1977	Per Capita Assessed Value		Percent Change 1970–1977
	1970	1977		1970	1977	
Campbell	107,575,500	196,476,700	+82	8,317	7,068	−15
Converse	45,361,300	99,462,200	+119	7,639	10,695	+40
Natrona	124,906,800	117,237,100	−6	2,437	1,820	−25
Platte	19,983,600	21,309,900	+7	3,081	2,507	−19
Sheridan	33,106,700	31,806,400	−4	1,865	1,486	−20

Source: Assessed values in current dollars are from State of Wyoming Annual Report of the State Board of Equalization, Department of Revenue and Taxation, Cheyenne, 1970 and 1977; figures are adjusted by the Consumer Price Index; per capita values are determined using the population estimates from table 6–3.

growth-generated needs—new schools, better highways, more police protection—
although at a lower per-capita level than in the pregrowth period.

The neighboring, nonextractive counties have developed very different
patterns of expenditure. For example, Sheridan County had both total and
per-capital decreases in spending in education, transportation, and public safety.
Yet despite major budget decreases, Sheridan has increased per-capita spending
for libraries, hospitals, and natural resources (all areas of spending important
to long-term residents).

The spread of costs for expenditures varies according to source of revenues.
Wyoming counties are particularly dependent on local revenue sources (compared with energy-development areas in either Montana or North Dakota). Much
of the energy-related growth began before legislation existed to pass some
development costs onto the energy companies.[28] Thus all five counties continue
to rely heavily on property-tax revenue and charges for services.

In Campbell, Natrona, Platte, and Sheridan counties, increases in property
assessments per capita have not kept up with inflation. To compensate, Campbell, Platte, and Sheridan all have increased their tax rates since 1967. Natrona
has a somewhat lower tax rate, but still maintains a county-level mill levy higher
than the state average (see tables 6–16 and 6–17). Only Converse County has had
growth in its tax base to a degree that allows major reductions in the tax rate.

These revenues and taxation trends have some interesting implications.
First, all five counties have increased their expenditures on some social amenities
(such as libraries and recreation). This occurs even in counties with no coal-
generated revenues, where total revenues have *decreased.* Thus, coal revenues
do not seem to have determined these spending increases. Second, although
revenue does not always increase in proportion to the total population increase,
counties with coal revenues certainly have been wealthier than counties without
this source of income, and they have spent the majority of their increased
revenues on growth-related services.

Table 6–17
Total Mill Levies at the County Level, Wyoming
Case-Study Counties
(mills per dollar assessed value)

County	1970	1977
Campbell	15.563	20.559
Converse	17.142	14.950
Natrona	21.490	18.500
Platte	19.060	20.500
Sheridan	18.000	20.807
State average	17.677	18.440

Source: State of Wyoming Annual Report of the State Board of Equalization Department of Revenue and Taxation, Cheyenne, 1970 and 1977.

Summary of Distribution Patterns in Northeastern Wyoming

Experiences in these Wyoming counties provide some interesting evidence regarding the distribution patterns proposed earlier. First, there is little evidence of a filtering process at work. Direct employment of local workers in the energy industry tends to be very limited, especially in early years, and little of the income generated by the new growth is gained by people in traditional sectors of the economy. Although employment opportunities in other sectors have increased, the labor force seeking work has also increased. Rapidly growing areas attract job seekers, and in addition, many secondary earners in energy-worker households are also looking for work.

Structural economic and social barriers exist that may impede filtering. Newcomers tend to be very different from long-term residents, in terms of education and training, age, family structure, and willingness to be mobile. Although this study does not statistically analyze the level of influence of each factor, it is clear that many of these characteristics are important in determining the allocation of jobs.

Some of the outcomes appear to be closely tied to the nature of boom-town growth. The speed of development makes it unlikely that local workers can obtain training to compete for new jobs or that local businesses can obtain the financing and planning assistance necessary to expand. In addition, in most places, the inflationary aspects of growth offset many of the small gains that both long-term residents and newcomers experience.

The state of Wyoming makes a concerted effort to mitigate the costs of growth-inducing industries. Wyoming's Industrial Development Information and Siting Act[29] sets up a procedure for drawing energy companies (and other firms involved in large-scale development) into the mitigation process. A variety of other acts overcome some of the planning and financing barriers faced by local government.[30] Without these programs, both the total and distribution effects of growth would be more extreme. Some communities would carry costly improvements without added revenues, passing such costs onto local taxpayers. Unlike some other western states, Wyoming does not redistribute energy-related revenues among different jurisdictions according to the level of energy impact. Thus, even with the mitigation programs, many local areas pay for the costs of growth without gaining the added revenues. Clearly, public policy is another major factor determining the distribution of growth.

A Regional Perspective on Public Policy and Energy-Resource Development

Policies and programs exist in local government, state government, and at the federal level to respond to regional and local issues raised by energy-resource development. These policies fall into several categories, including: (1) general policies regulating facility siting and operation; (2) programs to mitigate communitywide facility and service shortages; (3) programs directed toward the needs of a targeted group; and (4) programs to provide longer-term economic stability for the region. The focus of programs and policies varies considerably among the different government levels.

Local governments tend to be reactive, addressing problems as they become critical, and developing programs only as the new development makes them financially feasible. After a decade of experience with energy development, state governments have begun to anticipate some of the major regional and local concerns that arise in the course of energy-resource extraction and related activities. Wyoming and a number of other states have established policies backed by fairly comprehensive sets of programs regarding energy-development activities within the state.

In constract, the federal government has no overall program to respond to the regional effects of energy policy, despite the decisive role played by federal agencies in determining the pace and location of energy-resource development. Although a few place-specific or resource-specific programs exist, such as the Coastal Zone Management Act of 1972[31] and the Powerplant and Fuel Use Act of 1978,[32] Congress has yet to enact a comprehensive assistance program or other location-specific policies for inland energy-resource-development sites. Even the Synthetic Fuels Corporation Act (1980),[33] which provides for an extensive and direct role of the federal government in expanding the synthetic-fuels industry, contains no explicit instructions concerning the regional effects of the industry's growth.

Most programs are developed to address aggregate trends, within the national, regional, or local jurisdiction. Although few programs are developed explicitly for a particular group of people, they often tend to serve some groups more effectively than others.

Policies Regulating Plant Siting and Operations

Most federal policies toward plant siting and operations have no explicit focus on location, but cover nationwide concerns such as environmental protection and occupational safety and health. Federal-government leasing policy, however, such as Bureau of Land Management mineral leasing, clearly involves making location decisions about energy activity. For these decisions, the federal-government considerations are based on nationwide demand for the minerals in question, and the economics of the industry. The local implications of the development are considered secondarily, if at all. Federal leasing policy may benefit some local landowners by increasing property values, but it offers no means of counteracting local costs for all groups.

State-level controls over siting and operations look much more closely at local consequences of the activity. Although the state ultimately makes decisions based on what is perceived to be best for the state as a whole, local concerns, as expressed through plans and zoning ordinances, also have an important role. As in the case of the federal government, the states have not chosen to control the location, pace, or level of private development as a means of reducing negative social or economic impacts. However, state permits for energy development often require impact-mitigation programs as an accompaniment to industrial development. Required programs do not necessarily make the community better for the average person than it was before energy development, but they reduce the number of additional problems caused by development. The permits tend to emphasize planning assistance, leaving funding to a variety of different sources (from local tax revenues to federal or private industry funding). Most permits have not required energy companies to make direct expenditures on facilities.

Local communities are less able to use their regulatory powers regarding location (such as zoning) to finely tune the effects of growth or the role played by energy companies. With the exception of attempts to keep mining and energy-conversion activities at some distance from established towns and to attribute some facility costs to the energy companies, local governments have not tried to control the social or economic consequences of energy development through location controls. However, some of the zoning and subdivision ordinances may marginally reduce the costs of growth for taxpayers throughout the county.

Impact-Mitigation Programs

Impact-mitigation programs play an extremely important role in controlling local costs of growth. They have a much weaker effect on improving the quality of life of the region compared with its predevelopment levels.

Existing programs at the state and federal levels[34] concentrate primarily on planning assistance and provision of funding for expansions of basic community facilities. The majority of expenditures for community-impact assistance have gone to road, sewer, and water facilities. A major portion of the remaining expenditures have gone to education and protective services. All these programs serve needs created by the new growth. Of these, only the expenditures on education are at all likely to produce qualitative improvements in the services received compared with predevelopment levels. Much smaller amounts of money have been used to augment publicly shared amenities, such as library facilities and parks. The most direct benefits of these programs are felt by newcomers, who find housing costs cheaper and public facilities more accessible than they would have been in an unassisted town. Long-term residents, especially those who no longer have children in school, benefit only in the sense that potential negative impacts are reduced—the town is less disrupted and congested than it would have been without these programs.

Federal assistance programs are financed through congressional appropriations, spreading the costs nationwide, rather than to the locality or industry. In contrast, state governments have made direct attempts to bill energy companies for many of these costs, either through industry contributions to local facilities or through taxation on energy production. To some degree, this forces energy companies to internalize the costs of locating in the state. However, taxes are generally based on production level, which means there are no distinctions made among companies regarding actual local impacts imposed by a particular facility.

Local governments may also attempt to mitigate growth impacts on their own. Energy-related revenues at the county level in production areas frequently cover increased expenditures. However, most states have been less successful at cushioning the costs incurred by municipalities within some energy-producing counties and by neighboring counties that do not have taxing jurisdiction over the energy- production activities.[35]

Where local costs are not covered by outside revenues, long-term residents tend to bear a heavy burden for local mitigation measures. Their share of local property-tax burdens tends to be high, whereas their level of participation in the new goods and services is often lower than that of newer residents.

Targeted Programs

Few mitigation programs are targeted to specific group needs. The occasional programs operating in energy-development communities, such as housing subsidies for low-income people and senior citizens, are generally funded through existing federal programs. Although the need for these programs is often a direct result of energy development, state ordinances often explicitly exclude many targeted programs from funding by energy-impact revenues. Local government often bears the cost of these programs, with possible federal assistance. Energy companies my pay indirectly through county taxes, but this only occurs in counties actually receiving energy-related local tax revenue. Counties receiving only residential impacts, rather than primary industry location (for example, Sheridan County, Wyoming), suffer most from lack of funds and are least able to assist vulnerable populations.

Long-Term Development Programs

Few programs at any level of government consider the long-term economic viability of a region highly dependent on extractive energy industries. Attempts at economic diversification by Platte County, Wyoming, and a federal demonstration program in Mercer County, North Dakota, have in fact made these counties even more dependent on local energy production. Both counties have tried to attract new industries that use by-products of energy production. These industries may help to absorb the excess capacities left over from the construction boom. However, this type of employment does not provide an alternative for the community and the people within it twenty or thirty years in the future, if there is a substantial drop in regional energy production. In contrast, a program built on existing nonenergy economic activities (such as agriculture) would benefit some of the more vulnerable population groups now and offer greater possibilities of future stability.

Policy for Whom?

Energy-development policies and programs concerned with local consequences primarily provide a cushioning effect for the tremendous growth demands generated by the industry.[36] The major beneficiaries of this type of policy include: (1) the industry, which benefits through greater employee productivity, reduced turnover, and easier recruiting; and (2) the newcomers to the region, whose costs of living are cushioned by impact programs and whose needs (schools, job services, recreation) are met by public facilities and services. Longer-term residents often find conditions worse than before, although to the extent that new public demands are provided for the community through outside funding, the social and financial costs of growth are reduced. Some local groups (such as young families) make extensive use of a portion of the new facilities, but overall, the level of amenities provided in the community is much less of an improvement for long-term residents than for newcomers. Often, problems faced by the predevelopment population (particularly its older members) are not addressed by mitigation programs.

Most of the proposed and currently implemented policies addressing the local consequences of energy development look at problems incrementally. They are directed toward the needs of single communities at specific points in time. They do not look closely at the range of needs engendered by growth among different population groups within a wide geographic area. Nor, with the exception of a few state-level programs, do they look at long-term needs in response to growth. The limited understanding of group needs and the failure to plan for the longer-term consequences of energy-resource-dependent development may lead to a need for new policies, one generation in the future, that address problems of economic decline and depression in these regions.

Toward Some Alternative Actions

One reason public policy has been remiss in coping with distribution consequences in local development is that it is much more complicated to identify needs of specific subgroups of the population than to develop programs tied to population growth and budget figures for a geographic area. Distribution outcomes can vary considerably among groups or between two similar groups in different locations. Any specific program might work well for a group in one county and fail entirely in other areas.

Despite the complexities of the problem, several policies could be established to protect local groups from some of the more severely negative distribution outcomes:

1. The review procedures established by each state could be expanded to include identification of population subgroups within each county. The study, at a minimum, should identify the major social and economic groups in each region, define each group's role in the predevelopment social structure and economy, and identify characteristics of each group that might be vulnerable to changes induced by the energy industry.

2. Before a siting permit is granted, states could make legal and planning assistance available to vulnerable groups (including Native American tribes) so they may provide feedback on energy-industry proposals, and so they can make informed requests for more concrete assistance.

3. Impact assistance at all levels should consider the needs of these subgroups of the population. Assistance could take the form of increased expenditures on social services for displaced groups, special loans and grants for long-term residents to enable local business to compete with outside entrepreneurs, and other targeted programs relevant to a particular situation.

4. Either the companies, or the state using energy incomes, could provide relocation and retraining assistance for displaced groups.

5. Long-term planning efforts for the region must expand to consider the economic activities of people outside the energy industry. Even local groups that find windfalls in the early years of growth may be wiped out after the initial boom. Long-range plans should consider means of reducing the region's dependence on energy activities.

6. Regional, social, and economic effects should be an additional consideration in both federal and state resource-development policies. Decisions about the location, scale, and timing of development may be based in part on these effects.

In general, the costs of these programs should be covered by the industry or the federal government, as part of the cost of western energy resources and the expansion of domestic energy supplies. However, the programs need to be administered through cooperative efforts by state and local governments. Agreements reached by government agencies in the interests of specific groups will need to include long-term guarantees. For example, protective clauses in leases and permits or constitutional guarantees may be necessary to ensure that vulnerable groups will continue to receive assistance even if the minority participating in the energy industry eventually become a voting majority in the county or state.

Some of the programs proposed here can easily be added to current mitigation efforts. For example, state and local governments could certainly expand the variety of social services funded through energy tax revenues. Other programs are more problemmatic and will require careful consideration in planning and implementation. Diversification of industry in rural agricultural areas has faced many barriers in the past. Although the energy industry may help to overcome some limitations, it is also likely to create new impediments to diversified economic growth. In addition, some types of diversification could further displace local groups. Clearly, these regions would benefit from a long-range planning effort that views energy development as only one alternative activity for the local economy.

Notes

1. Leholm et al., *Profile of North Dakota's Coal Mine.*

2. Some of the long-term demographic consequences of boom growth are discussed in Rust, *No Growth.*

3. The employment multiplier (e) may be defined in several ways: one common definition is $e = \Delta T/\Delta B$; where ΔT is the change in total employment and ΔB is the change in basic employment.

4. Wyoming Department of Economic Planning and Development, "Coal and Uranium Development."

5. This problem is discussed in more detail in Cortese and Jones, "Sociological Analysis."

6. This approach is clearly described in Gilmore and Duff, *Boom Town Growth Management,* as well as in many other case studies of energy development in the 1970s.

7. These factors are discussed in much more detail in Kroll and Ivory, "Urbanization Impacts and Boomtowns."

8. See, for example, Gold, "Trespasses and Other Social Impacts."

9. The filtering pattern described here is basically an extension of the process that produces income or employment multipliers. See Thompson, *A Preface to Urban Economics,* pp. 142–143; Martin White, Western Energy Company's project manager from Colstrip, Montana, describes some benefits of the type mentioned here in "A Report on Mitigation."

10. For experience in depressed areas, see Robinson, *Backward Areas;* the suburban experience is described in D. Netzer, "Financing Suburban Development," in *Municipal Needs, Services and Financing,* ed. Beaton (New Jersey: Center for Urban Policy Research, Rutgers University, 1974).

11. U.S. Bureau of Mines, *Minerals Yearbook,* 1973; Chamber of Commerce brochures, interviews.

12. This information came from interviews with city officials; monitoring records kept by Missouri Basin Power in Platte County; and the U.S. Bureau of the Census, *Census of Governments,* 1967, 1972, and 1977.

13. Where not stated otherwise, information in this section came from field observations and interviews.

14. Wyoming Crop and Livestock Reporting Service, *Wyoming Agricultural Statistics.*

15. Wyoming Department of Administration and Fiscal Control, *Wyoming Data Handbook.*

16. U.S. Bureau of the Census, *Census of Governments,* 1967, 1972.

17. U.S. Bureau of the Census, *City and County Yearbook.*

18. Rafferty, "Socioeconomic Impact."

19. *Wyoming Data Handbook,* p. 130.

20. Mountain West Research, Inc., *Construction Worker Profile.*

21. Carter Oil Company response to questionnaire from the author, September 1979.

22. Interviews with company and county officials.

23. This trend is noted in Wyoming Employment Security Commission, *Wyoming Labor Market.* The situation affects the incomes of farm operators in other ways as well, by making it more difficult and more costly to hire additional workers in the summer months.

24. Interquartile variation is defined as Q_3-Q_1/Q_3+Q_1 where Q_1 is the household (or family) income one quarter of the way up from the bottom of the income array and Q_3 is the household income three quarters of the way up from the bottom. The measure is further described in Thompson, *Preface to Urban Economics.* As noted in table 6-6, the calculations for 1977 are based on a different source than calculations for earlier years. We may find that if 1980 census figures are used, the inequality gap has not increased as widely as implied by the 1977 figures. However, the comparative positions of counties are more likely to remain unchanged.

25. Clearly, this is a crude test, and more extensive, detailed analysis would be needed to determine filtering patterns more conclusively. The data used here, from the Employment Security Commission of Wyoming, are aggregated and incomplete. Wages in agriculture are not included in average basic wages, and wages in specific nonbasic sectors may represent quite different mixes of occupations from county to count.

26. The cost-of-living indices are drawn from the Sinclair study cited in table 6-10; relative wage indices are constructed from the average-wage data where

$$\text{Wage Index (County A, Sector A)} = \frac{\text{Average Wage (County A, Sector A)}}{\text{Average Wage (Laramie County, Sector A)}}$$

27. The analysis here is based on constant dollars. Thus, before changes are interpreted, the current-dollar figures are deflated, using the consumer price index, to 1967 dollars. The data for county revenue and expenditures patterns come from U.S. Bureau of the Census, *Census of Governments,* 1967, 1977.

28. The passage of the Wyoming Industrial Siting Act in 1975 made it possible to charge companies some of the costs of energy development.

29. *Wyoming Statutes,* Title 35, Article 12.

30. Such acts include the State Land Use Planning Act, *Wyoming Statutes* 9-19; the Joint Powers Act, *Wyoming Statutes* 9-1-129 to 9-1-136; and the Wyoming Community Development Authority, Wyoming *Statutes,* Title 9, Article 18, chapter 1.

31. This act includes PL 92-583 and amendments (PL 94-370, 1976, and PL 96-464, 1980), which offer impact assistance to coastal communities affected by a variety of energy-resource-development activities.

32. PL 94-620, Title VI, provides assistance only to areas affected by coal and uranium extraction, processing, and transportation, not including power-generating activities.

33. PL 96-294.

34. Examples include Title VI of the Powerplant and Fuel Use Act of 1978 and the wide range of Wyoming state legislation cited earlier.

35. North Dakota is an exception to this tendency. The state severance-tax legislation allocates a portion of revenues to municipalities and neighboring jurisdictions (see *North Dakota Century Code,* chapter 57-61, Coal Severance Tax and chapter 57-62, Impact Aid programs).

36. An important exception exists in some areas where mineral resources are owned by Native American tribes. For example, the Crows and Northern Cheyenne tribes have focused on policies that will tie any local energy-resource development to tribal economic-development goals.

References

Beaton, W. Patrick ed. *Municipal Needs, Services and Financing.* New Brunswick, N.J.: Center for Urban Policy Research, Rutgers University, 1974.

Cortese, Charles F., and Jones, Bernie. "The Sociological Analysis of Boom Towns." *Western Sociological Review* 8, no. 1 (1977): 76-90.

Gilmore, John, and Duff, Mary. *Boom Town Growth Management.* Boulder, Colo.: Westview Press, 1975.

Gladstone Associates. *Analysis of the Economic Base and Growth Potentials, 1976-1990, Gillette and Campbell County.* Washington, D.C., 1976.

Gold, Raymond L. "Trespasses and Other Social Impacts of Northern Plains Coal Development." Missoula, Mont.: University of Montana, Institute for Social Research, 1976.

Kroll, Cynthia and Ivory, Mary. "Urbanization Impacts and Boomtowns." In *Synthetic Liquid Fuels Development: Assessment of Critical Factors.* Vol. 3, edited by Dickson et al. Washington, D.C.: Energy Research and Development Administration, Office of Conservation, May 1977.

Leholm, Arlen Jr. Leistritz, F.L., Weiland, J. *Profile of North Dakota's Coal Mine and Electric Plant Operating Workforce.* Fargo, N. Dak.: Dept. of Agricultural Economics, North Dakota State University, 1975.

Lund, R.E. *Personal Income in Wyoming Counties, 1929-1959.* Laramie, Wyo.: University of Wyoming, 1963.

Mountain West Research, Inc. *Construction Worker Profile.* Billings, Mont.: Old West Regional Commission, 1975.

North Dakota Century Code. chapter 57-61, Coal Severance Tax, and chapter 57-62, Impact Aid program.

Rafferty, Tim. "Socioeconomic Impact Monitoring Report No. 24." Wheatland, Wyo.: Missouri Basin Power Project, July 1978.

Robinson, E.A.G. *Backward Areas in Advanced Countries.* New York: St. Martin's Press, 1969.

Rust, Edgar. *No Growth: Impacts on Metropolitan Areas.* Lexington, Mass.: Lexington Books, D.C. Heath, 1975.

Sinclair, Jim, Rigsby, Michael, and Streeper, Steven. "Wyoming Cost of Living Index Revised." Wyoming State Department of Administration and Fiscal Control, Research and Statistics Division, Cheyenee, 1978.

Thompson, Wilbur R. *A Preface to Urban Economics.* Baltimore, Md.: Johns Hopkins Press, 1968.

White, Martin. "A Report on Mitigation and Monitoring of Socio-Economic Impact of Large Scale Energy Development Projects." Paper prepared for Atomic Industrial Forum, Inc., and the Edison Electric Institute, December 1976.

Wyoming Community Development Authority. *Wyoming Statutes,* Title 9, Article 18, chapter 1.

Wyoming Crop and Livestock Reporting Service. *Wyoming Agricultural Statistics.* Cheyenne: Wyoming Department of Agriculture, 1977.

Wyoming Department of Administration and Fiscal Control. *Wyoming Data Handbook.* Cheyenne, 1977.

Wyoming Department of Economic Planning and Development. "Coal and Uranium Development of the Powder River Basin—An Impact Analysis." Cheyenne, June 1974.

Wyoming Employment Security Commission. *Wyoming Covered Employment and Wage Data by Industry and County, 1975-1977.* Casper, Wyoming, 1977.

——— . *Labor Force Trends,* vol. 15, no. 6. Casper, Wyoming, June 1978.

——— . *Wyoming Labor Market Information Review.* Casper, Wyoming, 1977.

Wyoming Industrial Development Information and Siting Act. *Wyoming Statutes,* Title 35, Article 12.

Wyoming Joint Powers Act. *Wyoming Statutes*, 9-1-129 to 9-1-136.

Wyoming State Board of Equalization (1950, 1960, 1970), and Wyoming Department of Revenue and Taxation (1975, 1977). *Annual Reports*. Cheyenne.

Wyoming State Land Use Planning Act. *Wyoming Statutes*, 9-19.

U.S. Bureau of Mines. *Mineral Yearbook*, 1950, 1960, 1965, 1970, and through 1978.

U.S. Bureau of the Census. *Census of Agriculture*, 1969, 1974.

_____ . *Census of County Governments*, 1967, 1977.

_____ . *Census of Governments*, 1967, 1972, 1977.

_____ . *Census of Housing*, 1960, 1970.

_____ . *Census of Population*, 1950, 1960, 1970.

_____ . *City and County Yearbook*, 1977.

U.S. Coastal Zone Management Act of 1972 and amendments. PL 92-583, PL 94-370, 1976, and PL 96-464, 1980.

U.S. Powerplant and Fuel Use Act of 1978. PL 95-620, Title VI.

U.S. Synthetic Fuels Corporation Act. PL 96-294, 1980.

Zelinski, Claire. *Low to Moderate Income Housing Need in the State of Wyoming*. Cheyenne: Wyoming Department of Economic Planning and Development, 1977.

7

Industrial and Regional Policy in Multiregional Modeling

Roger Bolton

Other authors in this book define and analyze many issues related to the coordination of industrial and regional policies. In this chapter I concentrate on analyzing and evaluating the usefulness of a set of tools for the analysis of such policies: multiregional modeling.

I offer a general critical review of multiregional modeling and recent research in the field. I first describe what multiregional modeling is and explore some basic conceptual issues. I then describe briefly the results of a recent survey of the field by Benjamin Chinitz and myself, in which we examined in detail several operational input-output or econometric multiregional models. We concentrated on how each of them might be used in simulating the effects on regions in the United States of various federal policies, including ones that might be characterized as industrial or regional. The details of our review are readily available elsewhere (Bolton and Chinitz, 1978; Bolton, 1980a, c), so here I present only general conclusions. Then I dwell a bit on what I think is the research frontier in the field, describe some very recent developments since our earlier review, and speculate on future developments as they bear on the congruencies and conflicts of industrial and regional policies.

What Multiregional Models Are

Most generally, the models are systems of equations with which we can forecast or simulate the effects of policies and other events on economic and demographic variables in many different regions of a national economy. The systems of equations may be input-output, or econometric, or combinations of the two. Income, employment, unemployment, population and migration, and wage rates are the most important variables; there may be significant disaggregation by industry, demographic group (age, sex, or race), or type of income. In the U.S. context, the regions range from states or groups of states down to Bureau of

Much of this chapter is based on my portion of a previously unpublished paper by Benjamin Chinitz and myself (Bolton and Chinitz, 1980), which in turn relied partly on our earlier study (Chinitz and Bolton, 1978) and an article (Bolton, 1980c). I am grateful to Ben Chinitz for his collaboration in our work on multiregional modeling during the last several years. I am also grateful to Ben Stevens, George Treyz, T.R. Lakshmanan, and Mead Over. Any errors or ambiguities are mine alone.

Economic Analysis (BEA) economic areas and Standard Metropolitan Statistical Areas (SMSAs) and even to counties.

In all but one of the operational models, national totals are exogenous, and are rigid control totals for the distribution of activity by regions: distribution is a zero-sum game. This limits their use for analysis of the policies I am considering. But that feature is not necessary in any theoretical sense, and there are more recent efforts in which national variables and regional variables are determined simultaneously. The national totals are not independent of the regional distribution and regional distribution is not a zero-sum game. There is already one operational model of this kind, and many regional scientists consider such simultaneity a desirable characteristic for the next round of models. This simultaneity between regions and the nation would be in addition to the simultaneity between one region and other regions, which is of course already present in many models, but which is a simultaneity between a region's share of a fixed national control total and other regions' shares of the same total.

What is the relationship between multiregional models and models for single regions? A multiregional model is a "complex" of single-region models, because it produces a forecast or simulation for every region in a national economy. Those who are interested in a single region have a choice. They can use a single-region model, incorporating whatever detail they want on the linkages between a region and other regions. (They can certainly stop far short of a multiregional model: even if they include links with other regions, they can be selective in their choice of other regions to allow for interaction and which variables to make endogenous.) Or they can use a multiregional model and "notice" only the results for the region they are concerned about.

In practice, very few single-region models have rich detail on the links between the region in question and other regions, and I know of none that allows the region to affect the nation as a whole. In other words, the national totals are exogenous, not endogenous. A multiregional model, on the other hand, inevitably produces a number of single regional models, all with the same level of detail. It raises more urgently the issue of whether national totals should be exogenous or endogenous to the regions.

People interested in industrial or regional policy probably need forecasts or simulations for many regions, so they need a multiregional model. This is certainly true of federal policymakers and anyone concerned with the political ramifications of industrial or regional policy. But even if they are more parochial and need results for only one region, they do have a choice between a single-region and a multiregional model. Which is better cannot be settled a priori. It depends on the costs, on the detail desired, on how important the links are between the region and various other regions, and on whether the other regions can be treated as exogenous. For a given research budget, the single-region model can be built in much finer detail. On the other hand, gaining interregional feedbacks and simultaneity is worth paying *something* for. In addition, the analysis of even a single region may be better if it can be comparative, and that requires a multiregional model. On the other hand, the greater complexity of the multiregional model may also bring greater error, especially in detailed components. There is little empirical literature on the trade-offs, and research on the subject is needed. (However, see the limited evidence on the National Regional Impact Evaluation System (NRIES) model later in the chapter.)

Some General Observations

Policy Handles

Needs for both forecasting and policy analysis have created interest in models. However, they impose somewhat different requirements. In particular, policy analysis requires that a model have policy handles—economic variables that explicitly describe economic or legal phenomena that can be manipulated by policies. A model might be good at forecasting even if it does not include such variables explicitly, because the policy instrument might not change in either the historical period or the forecast period. But policy analysis requires hypothetical manipulation of some instruments, and a model cannot simulate the effects of the policy unless the policy can be translated into changes in some variable in the model. In our review of operational models, Chinitz and I were impressed by how few of them explicitly incorporate instruments that policymakers more and more want to vary, or how few of them even allow the alternative of translating the policy into changes in other variables. The shortcomings are especially troublesome in analysis of policies targeted at particular industries or regions, which are particularly attractive in the context of dealing with selective regional growth and decline and of picking "winners" and easing the decline of "losers."

Consistency between National and Regional Models

Multiregional models produce results for all regions in a nation, so they automatically produce results for the nation as a whole. Thus they contain a national model as well as the various regional models. National variables by definition are sums of their regional counterparts (income, employment, final demands, and so on) or are weighted averages (for example, unemployment rates, wage rates, prices). It is also relevant that some national aggregates are theoretically appropriate, independent variables in the structural equations for a single region. Any national variables used in that way should be consistent with the national variables implied by the sum or average of regions.

There are three ways to insure this consistency. The most common one is to determine the national variables first, and then force sums and averages of regional variables to equal them. The result is called a top-down model, and the regional parts of the model are said to be driven by the national model. The national model determines national totals independently of the regional distribution, and regional results are constrained to equal (in sum or average) the predetermined totals. This independence may even apply to each industry separately; the national model determines national totals of output and employment in each industry and then the regional models allocate the totals to the regions (or, in the jargon of some modelers, "share out" the totals to regions).

This practice is so common that the national model which drives the regional models is often an "off-the-shelf" model built by other researchers who use it primarily for national analyses rather than regional ones. A popular choice is INFORUM, a national macromodel developed by Clopper Almon at the University of Maryland (Almon, 1974). Three commercial firms, Chase Econometrics, Data Resources, Incorporated, and Wharton Econometric Forecasting Associates, use their own national macromodels to drive their multiregional models (Chase actually uses its model and INFORUM in combination). The main requirement in an off-the-shelf model is that its industry detail matches the detail the analyst desires for regional simulations.

I also note that all the long-run economic projections for regions of the United States are top-down in nature. However, those making long-run projections often build their own simplified national model to produce the national control totals. The official Bureau of Economic Analysis projections made in 1974 (OBERS) and in 1980 (sometimes unofficially called New OBERS) are examples (BEA, 1974, 1980). The builders of the MULTIREGION econometric model (described later), developed their own model for both long-run regional projections and some kinds of policy analysis.

Top-down is nearly universal. But theoretical objections leap to mind. Might not the regional distribution of demand affect the total level of output and employment in the nation? Yes, if the amount of excess capacity in labor and capital is not the same in all regions. This seems fairly likely in the context of industrial and regional policy. In the same context, consider a policy that picks "export winners" and assists them. Some industries will be more responsive than others to such a policy. If this is the case, a policy can make a difference for the national total of real output by making a difference for the level of national exports. If that is so, then the industrial composition, and also the regional distribution of output and employment, must be determined simultaneously with the national totals because the regional consequences of such a national policy will not be uniform.

A second way to achieve consistency between the nation and regions is at the opposite end of the continuum from the pure top-down approach. It is to eschew control totals, and to determine all national variables jointly and simultaneously with regional variables. Every national variable is automatically calculated as the appropriate sum or average of the regional counterparts, and those sums or averages are entered in any equation where a national variable is an independent variable. National forecasts or simulations "fall out," as it were, at the end of the process and are not constrained by any prior information. This is a pure "bottom-up" approach. However, there are no operational models like that, and I doubt anybody will build one. One reason is that some national variables are nearly uniform for all regions, so a model is improved if a uniformity constraint is imposed on the regional models. Another reason is that some national variables are rather independent of what is happening in regions. Examples of nearly uniform variables are some monetary and financial market variables, the international exchange rate and other international financial variables, producer prices in some industries with national markets, and conceivably even wage rates for some industries or occupations that have essentially a national labor market. In an economy like the United States, the interregional variation in some variables is so small that it is best to ignore it, especially when good regional data are hard to come by anyway. Examples of independent national totals are some federal expenditure categories and perhaps some types of investment.

If a variable is uniform across regions, the best model may still be one that determines its uniform level simultaneously with other variables—regional and national—that are sensitive to regional distribution. Consider this example: total personal income in the nation is a bottom-up variable, but it is also an argument in the structural equations for interest rates, which in turn affect housing demand and business investment in the regional models. Even if interest rates are uniform across the nation, they are indirectly sensitive to the regional distribution of activity through the connection with personal income. Thus, there should be a continuous loop of interdependence from the regional models to the national variables and back to the regional models.

This leads us to a third approach, which seems most defensible. It is a hybrid model in which national and regional variables are determined simultaneously, but with prior constraints on some national variables, such as regional uniformity or even total exogeneity to regions. We can see a bit of movement in multiregional-modeling practice away from the pure top-down approach toward this hybrid approach, and it is a potentially important development in regional modeling. (It may also affect single-region models for regions large enough to influence the nation in some ways, such as California, Texas, New York, Pennsylvania, and Illinois.) It seems to have been influenced by modeling efforts in Europe; see the discussion of Courbis's REGINA model (1979a, b, 1980). It also accords with the long-standing position of Chinitz, who has urged greater emphasis on supply effects in modeling regional patterns and national growth (see, for example, Chinitz, 1966). Recall also Richardson's criticism of modelers for concentrating on what he called competitive growth, by which he meant that regional economic analysis merely allocates exogenous national growth among regions. He urged more attention to generative growth, in which developments in a region have a feedback on the aggregate growth rate (Richardson, 1973, pp. 86–88).

Recall also earlier writings in the normative theory of government public-works investment and defense procurement, which stressed that the real output effects of government expenditure depend on the regional distribution of the expenditure, because unutilized capacity and the supply elasticity of real output and employment vary from region to region (Bolton, 1966, 1971, 1977, 1979; Haveman and Krutilla, 1968).

The movement toward a hybrid approach is an improvement: regional models certainly must recognise that the allocation of resources in space affects total production and factor demand in the nation. When labor moves from a declining region to a growing one, for example, it is not usually that a fixed national output is being reallocated to a different region, rather national output may increase, because employment and productivity of labor are increased. Labor is sufficiently immobile, and wages sufficiently different in different regions, that total employment and earnings in the nation depend on *where* there are labor demand and supply. These considerations are all the more important in the context of policies examined in this book.

Now of course, against the theoretical advantages of "bottom-upness" must be set some practical limitations. Regional data are not fully satisfactory, perhaps most notably in prices of goods and services, private investment in equipment, and output by industry. The interregional variation in some variables is too small to justify the added complexity of a hybrid approach; what is "too small" is a matter of judgment. We must remember that what is theoretically desirable can introduce enormous complexity in the national part of a multiregional model. It is an open question whether modelers can tinker with the existing off-the-shelf national models to meet the requirements of the hybrid approach. Further development of the hybrid approach will require close cooperation between regional and national model builders, whereas previously the prevailing practice was for the two groups to work rather separately.

An especially interesting modeling problem is investment. For some kinds of investment the national total should be sensitive to the regional distribution of demand and of unutilized capacity. Housing and business investment in local-market industries (trade, services, and finance, in most regions) are examples. However, some other kinds of investment, especially by large firms, may be determined independently of regional factors, so that a predetermined national total is allocated by firms to regions in a top-down way. A top-down approach to investment is a practical modeling technique, and a theoretical rationale would stress that large firms are national in character and base their investment plans on national financial markets and total firm-wide profits (Crow, 1979; Lakshmanan, 1980). On the other hand, the neoclassical theory of location and optimal-factor demand leads us toward the bottom-up approach. How we settle this issue will depend on how we see the firm as an organizational unit and what theory of investment we use, as well as how we view the economy as a complex of regions. The intersection of investment modeling and the hybrid approach is one of the exciting research areas of the future.

The REGINA Model

In Courbis's description of his multiregional model of France (Courbis, 1979b), he defended bottom-up principles on several grounds: the labor-participation rate is sensitive to employment opportunities, which vary by region; there is hidden unemployment in agricultural regions, so the creation of new jobs there adds much less to national employment (and pressure on wages) than the same number of jobs in other regions; the Paris labor market dominates the national economy, so labor demand in the Paris region has a greater effect on national wage trends than the same demand elsewhere; these wage trends affect prices and profits and the scope for internal financing, and thus investment and output in the nation; technical coefficients differ from region to region; household-savings rates and the structure of consumption vary from region to region, so both total consumption and its structure depend on the regional distribution of income; housing investment and public investment depend on the exodus from rural areas and the rate of growth in urban areas.

In a simulation with his REGINA model, Courbis showed some of the effects of a spatial dstribution on the national economy (Courbis, 1979b). He assumed that policy gradually reduced the Paris region's share of manufacturing investment by two percentage points, causing the transfer of 40,000 industrial jobs to other regions. The effect in the simulation was to increase unemployment in Paris, lower the rate of growth of wages there, and, because of Paris' influence on provincial labor markets, also reduce the rate of growth of wages in those labor markets. As a result, the national inflation rate was reduced, which in turn stimulated exports and reduced imports, and increased output and reduced unemployment in the nation.

The American economy may be different, but as I have noted earlier there are reasons to believe the spatial distribution of demand affects national totals here as well. Although there is no longer much hidden unemployment in agriculture, there are great variations in excess capacity, unemployment, and "discouraged workers" from region to region. Whether an increase in demand results in an output increase or in inflation will depend on its regional distribution. The regional distribution of private and public investment has potentially important effects on product prices and financial markets. In the American context, water and energy supplies in various regions will also cause feedbacks from regional developments back to national totals in agriculture and energy industries.[1]

General Structure of Multiregional Models

Figure 7-1 shows the structure of a top-down multiregional model. Note the sharp distinction between the national model and the one-way links between the nation and each regional model. The arrows between one region and another reflect interregional trade or other links; they may be simultaneous or recursive. They are not present in all models.

Each regional model block could be shown in much more detail, distinguishing separate sectors: export industries, local industries, labor market, household income, public sector, and so on (see the detailed diagram of a regional model in Bolton, 1980b). The arrows between regions in figure 7-1 are actually multiple links between specific sectors in one region and specific sectors in others. For example, the labor market in region 1 is linked to the labor market in region 2, because an increase in labor demand in 1 may cause a decrease in supply (through migration) in 2. Or the household income sector in 1 affects the export-industry sector in 2 if residents of 1 import goods and services from 2.

Figure 7-2 shows the structure of a hybrid bottom-up model. The graphics are intended to convey the integration of national forces and regional forces in a single model and the feedbacks from regions to the national totals. (The three kinds of national variables are described by Ballard and others, 1980a.) Exogenous variables are independent of any other national variables and regions; the money supply or some federal expenditure categories or international variables are possible examples. Endogenous national variables are of two types. There are those which are not of the regional-sum type; they may be interest rates uniform over all regions or prices or wages where markets are truly national in scope. The

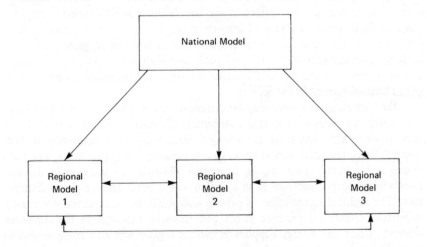

Figure 7-1. Top-Down Model

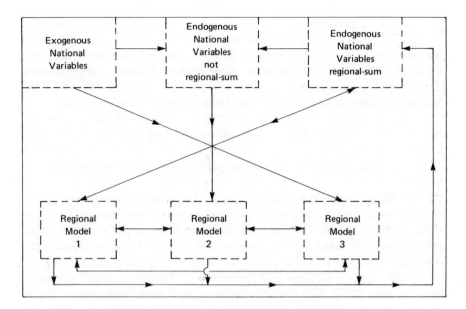

Figure 7-2. Hybrid Bottom-Up Model

second type are regional-sum (or average) variables like employment, output, and income. The regional models determine these latter national variables as shown by the feedback arrow.[2]

Results of the Review of Operational Models

The Models

In the study I briefly summarize here, Chinitz and I reviewed six operational models.[3] First are two input-output models.

1. The Income Determination Input-Output Model (IDIOM) (Dresch and Goldberg, 1973; Dresch and Updegrove, 1978). This is a Leontief "balanced" regional input-output model developed by Stephen Dresch at the National Bureau of Economic Research and now maintained by Dresch and others at the Institute for Demographic and Economic Studies (IDES) in New Haven. It is a modern version of a model originally developed by Leontief (1953) and used by him and others in 1965 to analyze the industrial and regional effects of a reduction in defense expenditures (Leontief and others, 1965). There are eighty-six industries; the regions are states; output and income are the variables. It is a pure top-down model and it is also a pure demand-allocation model, in the sense there

are no supply constraints or other supply effects: supplies of output and labor are assumed to be perfectly elastic in response to changes in demand. The model can be driven by any separate national model that has at least as much industrial detail as IDIOM itself. There is no labor market. Regional competitiveness through relative production costs and transportation costs is ignored, of course, because the shares of each region in each industry are specified exogenously.

There is no real simultaneity of determination of regional outputs and employment because a region's output and employment depend ultimately only on the industrial composition of final demand and on the regional distribution of final demand, both of which must be specified exogenously before the model is used.

IDIOM has been used to analyze the effects of a cut in defense expenditures, excise taxes on energy commodities, changes in personal-tax rates, and a public-works program, among other policies. Like any input-output model, it offers enough industrial detail to be a candidate for analysis of policies affecting the demands on different industries, but it is weak on supply-side policies.

2. The Poverty Institute (PI) Regional and Distribution Model (Golladay and Haveman, 1977). This is an adaptation of the Polenske Multiregional Input-Output (MRIO) model (Polenske, 1980) developed by Robert Haveman, Frederick Golladay, and others at the Institute for Poverty Research at the University of Wisconsin. MRIO, the core of the model, is an input-output model with constant trade coefficients linking different industries in fifty different state-regions. (Linkage between regions is accomplished by specifying that an industry i in region j always imports a fixed percentage of its requirements of input k from each other region. This, of course, introduces simultaneity. Furthermore, every industry in region j has the same import percentage of input k.) The PI version significantly extends the model by adding detailed modules on consumer demand and income distribution, so that tax and transfer policies can be analyzed. The PI version seemed to us the most relevant version of MRIO to review. It has 70 industrial sectors and aggregates MRIO's 50 states to 23 regions. The added modules, especially the income-distribution one, were remarkable achievements in the multiregional-modeling field at the time. However, the MRIO core has technical and trade coefficients based on 1963 surveys—the fact that the material is outdated is a practical shortcoming.

The model has been used at the Poverty Institute, in government agencies (chiefly in the U.S. Department of Health and Human Services), and elsewhere to analyze the effects of welfare-reform proposals, the impact of a large public-employment program, the Kemp-Roth proposal, and other policies. Like IDIOM, it is a pure top-down and pure demand-allocation model; there is no labor market.

A major research project is now under way at Boston College and the Massachusetts Institute of Technology (MIT) to build a new multiregional model, using the PI model as a starting point but updating and improving it so dramatically as to produce an almost entirely different creature. The Boston

College–MIT team plans to update MRIO coefficients, introduce more flexible consumption modules, make government and investment demand endogenous, and add detailed labor-market modules that rely on both "job competition" inflexible wage models and on more neoclassical wage-flexibility models—among other improvements!

This effort is the most ambitious and most promising research activity now under way in the multiregional-modeling field. It rests firmly on an extensive microsimulation data base in the household sector, which is essential if we are to simulate policies affecting income distribution and model the regional labor markets realistically. However, from preliminary reports it is not yet clear how the project will resolve the top-down versus bottom-up choice and what shape the national model will have.

3. Multiregional Multi-Industry Forecasting Model (Harris Model) (Harris and Hopkins, 1972; Harris, 1973, 1974, 1980). This model was developed by Professor Curtis Harris and associates at the University of Maryland and is maintained in an operational state there. It produces results for 173 BEA economic areas in one version and more than 3,000 counties in another, including output and employment in 99 industries; it also estimates population in each of 8 age-race groups, equipment investment in 69 industries, and value of construction of 28 different types. It is the most detailed of all models. It is an econometric model with a linear programming submodel to determine optimal transportation and commodity flows.

It is a top-down model using INFORUM as the separate national model. However, it includes elaborate specifications of supply behavior, regional competition, and the labor market, so it goes far beyond the two input-output models just described. The model is recursive, so the variables for a region do not enter directly into the equations for another region. But the linear programming model of commodity flows determines location rents, which affect a region's share of an industry in a subsequent period. It has been used to analyze effects of new highway and energy-facility investments, offshore oil development, and large-scale coal development in Montana, among other things.

4. MULTIREGION (Olsen and others, 1977; Olsen and Allaman, 1978; Olsen, 1980). This is an econometric model developed by Richard Olsen, David Bjornstadd, and others at Oak Ridge National Laboratory and maintained in an operational state there. It produces results for population, migration, and employment in each of the 173 BEA economic areas; employment is detailed by 37 industrial sectors. There are no output or income variables. So far the model has been used primarily in making long-run projections for regions and in analyzing the demand effects of energy developments and energy policies.

It is a pure top-down model, and can be used with a variety of national models. It is a dynamic recursive model, projecting results at five-year intervals. A region's share of the employment depends on its market potential, which is a function of employment in other regions and distance to them, as of five years previous. There is thus regional interdependence but no real simultaneity. The model is remarkable for its demographic detail and its emphasis on very-long-run changes in population and employment. There is a labor-market submodel, with endogenous labor-force participation and migration.

5. Chase Econometrics Model. This is a proprietary model operated by Chase Econometrics.[4] It consists of separate top-down models for each state, driven by a combination of the Chase macromodel and INFORUM (the first determines total output in the economy and major aggregate demand components, the second converts the demand components into industry outputs and employment). There is no simultaneity. The model forecasts employment, income, and population for each state, and employment and income for the 104 largest SMSAs. Disaggregation provides detail for twenty-one Standard Industrial Classification (SIC) industries within manufacturing, a single nonmanufacturing total, and eight categories of personal income. Work is in progress to disaggregate nonmanufacturing into several sectors.

There is a labor-market submodel, population is endogenous, and regions' shares of national manufacturing-industry shipments are related to relative business costs and the national capacity-utilization rate in manufacturing. There is thus considerable emphasis on the supply side of regional economies.

6. National-Regional Impact Evaluation System (NRIES) (Ballard, Glickman, Gustely, Wendling, 1979, 1980a, b, c, d). This hybrid bottom-up model was the most innovative model we reviewed. NRIES was developed by Kenneth Ballard and others at the Bureau of Economic Analysis in the Department of Commerce and is operational there. It produces results for each of the fifty states and the District of Columbia, and output and employment in thirteen industrial sectors. It has been used in many policy simulations, including effects of changing regional distribution of federal grants, a hypothetical expansion in the Department of Housing and Urban Development (HUD) budget, the Humphrey-Hawkins Bill, and effects of increased federal purchases from the aircraft industry. Population and migration are endogenous.

Output in each industry and region is a function of output in other regions in the same year and also of some national variables; some of the latter are determined in the "bottom-up" way, so the model is very highly simultaneous.

This is the only operational hybrid bottom-up model I know of. Only a few variables are uniform across all regions and exogenous to the regions. These include some interest rates, consumer-price indices, implicit price deflators for industry output, and a consumer-confidence index. Included in this group also are the proportions of national output that go to durables and to federal durable-goods purchases (the level of national output itself is a bottom-up or regional-sum variable). The ratio of consumption of durable goods to disposable personal income is also a national variable in equations for durable-goods output in each region.

Ballard and others provide an interesting comparison of NRIES and single-region models, one of the few such comparisons I know of. They computed the NRIES mean absolute percent errors (MAPE) statistics for twelve individual states with the MAPE statistics of the single-region models for the same twelve states. The NRIES errors were for 1963-1976 (annually) and for varying time periods in the single-region models. They found the MAPE statistics roughly comparable; NRIES errors were lower than those of the state models in a slight majority of cases. This was encouraging, first, because the NRIES is more aggregated than the other models, and second, because the national component of NRIES is largely endogenous whereas it is largely exogenous in the other models (Ballard and others, 1980a, p. 84, p. 89).

Hypothetical Federal Policies

In our review, Chinitz and I evaluated each of the models as to its suitability for analyzing a number of specified federal policies: an across-the-board cut in personal-income-tax rates; an increase in the investment-tax credit; a public-works program, targeted to certain regions; a targeted investment credit (the credit is larger for investments in some regions than in others); and a change in the level and/or regional distribution of national-defense expenditures. The fourth policy in the list is a leading example of an industrial and/or regional policy in the sense we are considering in this book. The fifth is not, but the methodology of analyzing it is somewhat similar to the methodology we would have to use in analyzing industrial or regional policies.

The common thread in industrial and regional policies is the targeting of the policy on specific industries or on specific regions, or on specific industries *in* specific regions. If industrial policy, for example, does involve picking winners for purposes of public subsidies, tariff protection, import quotas, or export promotion, we must have a model that has the potential winners as separate industries, and that has appropriate policy handles. Policy handles might be the level of production costs in the industry (so that subsidies can be translated into changes in costs), the demand for imports of competing importers, the demand for the product by foreigners, and so on.

Likewise, assume regional policy involves targeting income support to distressed people in distressed regions, but we want to avoid adverse incentives inhibiting long-run mobility and also to avoid windfall gains for nondistressed persons in distressed regions (windfalls are a classic nagging problem with "place" policies as opposed to "people" policies). In this case, the model should have fairly rich detail on the industrial and occupational composition of labor demand in a region and also detail on the labor-market adjustment process, including labor-force participation and migration decisions. Ideally, it also should have some mechanism for determining nonlabor income from regional sources, especially rents and proprietors' income, and the real income derived from the net fiscal balance of regional governments.

In particular, the labor market should be detailed enough so that the following question can be answered: in a distressed region, if some kind of federal "adjustment assistance" is not offered, what will be the time profile of unemployment and income losses for typical individuals in the region? In other words, how long would people remain unemployed, or employed at jobs with lower wages than they could earn after the adjustment assistance (which would allow them to earn more because they moved to other regions and/or were retrained)? We can measure the efficiency and distribution benefits of adjustment assistance only if we can identify the difference the assistance makes for real output and the real income of typical individuals. We cannot do that without knowing what would have happened in the absence of the policy. It is similar with costs: the costs of reduced mobility can be measured only if we have a handle on when people would have moved or gotten jobs in another industry if there had been no assistance. This is a standard problem in benefit-cost analysis: we can evaluate the policy's effects only if we can specify the "with" and the "without" situations.

The distribution of benefits and costs is crucial here. A regional labor market is not homogeneous in the sense that what happens is identical for all individuals. The average wage and the unemployment rate for the whole region conceal a great deal of variation, and do not provide full detail on the income-distribution effects of events and of policies designed to mitigate events. A multiregional model might give a reasonably good indication of what we call the regional distribution of effects and policies: it might simulate accurately the variation across regions in the average wages and unemployment rates. But something more is needed to get the intraregional distributional effects. The unemployment rate, for example, is the average number of "zeroes" in a group of workers who are getting either a *zero* (no job) or a *one* (a job) in a competitive labor market. The effects on individuals depend on their personal characteristics, on the process of labor-market adjustment (job competition or wage competition or a mixture), and on the industrial structure of the region with and without the policies. This strongly suggests the microsimulation approach to modeling distribution effects (see, for example, chapter 6). Unfortunately, data quality and data management problems make it difficult to have an accurate complicated model for regions smaller than states. But states are hardly homogeneous labor markets, which both makes modeling difficult and clouds the interpretation of the distribution results.

Conclusions of the Review

First, there is a lot of diversity in the group of models. No single theoretical approach has swept the field. One builder devotes special attention to one block or one set of linkages, another builder devotes attention to others. It is striking how we may go into lavish detail in some parts of the model, but be rather casual on other parts, or accept with little change theoretical conceptions from other sources. In a few cases, the results show very clearly the stamp of one person and the scholarly tradition from which he comes. My comment is not a criticism; each builder should exploit his comparative advantage, and there is room for competition. It does mean there are advantages if a research team is assembled from the start with the diversity of persons necessary to give more evenhanded attention to all the important aspects.

A notable example of the uneven attention I am talking about is the PI model, where there is great detail in the two modules attached to the basic MRIO model—one module to translate fiscal policies into changes in consumer demand by industry and region, and the other to translate changes in regional-industry outputs into changes in the size distribution of income. Yet the regional core of this model is the unchanged MRIO model, still used with the now-outdated interregional trade coefficients based on commodity-flows data from 1963. The authors' interest in welfare-reform policy and income distribution and their desire to use a microsimulation technique to predict consumer expenditures and household earnings led them to develop the modules, but they did nothing to modify or update the basic regional aspect of the model. As a result, some of the reported results are misleading (Bolton, 1980d).

Furthermore, the PI model can analyze only consumption effects; like other operational input-output models, investment and state and local purchases are not endogenous. Yet in a regional analysis we want those final demands to respond to local income and employment conditions. In many regions those responses may be as important as the consumption effects of a policy, even a policy that has changes in consumption as its primary goal. Finally, there is no supply side in the model and no labor market. The PI model is merely a useful example; I could use other models to multiply these illustrations many times over.

Second, the attention to the supply side (in all but the two input-output models) is gratifying. It is a welcome move away from the purely demand-oriented export base and input-output models that have dominated regional modeling. There is still ample room for improvement; modelers in general still seem dissatisfied with their progress here. In particular, there is room for improvement on the demographic side where the picture is clouded by a serious data problem for smaller regions. There is not much confidence in the intercensal population estimates and there is even some doubt about the census ones for smaller regions.

Third, there is relatively little explicit modeling of the transportation system of the regional or national economies.[5] Transportation is an industrial sector that has output, and employs labor and perhaps other inputs. But transportation as it affects sellers and buyers of other goods is usually not given much attention. In most cases there is little attention to the costs of transportation or capacity limitations on particular links, and to any "handles" for transportation policies to affect location. This seems to me an interesting commentary on a field in which the theory of spatial-allocation resources has otherwise had a great impact.[6]

Fourth, bottom-up principles have been surprisingly slow to emerge. The BEA's NRIES model is the only operational hybrid model, and it was just completed in 1978. Although there is still limited experience with NRIES, it is clear there are the usual problems with a pioneering effort.

Fifth, multiregional models are often weak in simulating effects of the economy on the public sector. Here we may distinguish between effects on the public sector in regions and effects of the public sector (I go into this at length in Bolton, 1980d). The "of" effects are the usual array of policy impacts—government expenditures, tax rates, and regulations. They are the meat and potatoes of regional policy analysis. But there are also feedbacks from the regional economy to the public sector—on tax bases and revenues and expenditure levels, and on the composition of taxes and expenditures. Many single-region models are very good at these "on" effects; witness the Alaska model of Kresge and Seiver (1980), the Massachusetts Economic Policy Model of Treyz and others (1980), and other models. But the inclusion of these effects in multiregional models is less frequent and more rudimentary.

Why does this matter? In the present context, it matters not so much in terms of the direct effects on state and local budgets, but in terms of the feedback effects of those budgets on the real incomes of individuals. When the regional economy changes, the resulting effects on tax bases and public-service demands force changes in the budget. That leads to the effects of, which the public-sector modelers usually worry about—the changes in real incomes of taxpayers, receivers of transfer payments, and consumers of public services. In many stagnant and declining regions, which industrial or regional policies may be designed to deal with, a major component of the real-income effects of events and mitigating policies comes through the rise in tax rates and the cutbacks in public services that regional governments are bound to make as they struggle to balance the budget.

Put another way, the regional government sector should be endogenous, and the feedback loop should consist of: economy → government → economy. The first arrow is the "on" effects, the second is the "of" effects; we need good models of both arrows. If we are interested in income distribution when we set industrial or regional policy, we must capture the effects of government budgets on individuals. But that means we must also capture the effects of the regional economy on the public budget in the first place, and we must also model the political decision-making process by which an initial imbalance in the budget is corrected. These are significant goals for the future.

Sixth, for policy analysis, as opposed to forecasting, there is a general problem of inadequate or absent policy handles. How serious this is depends on the model and policy. For example, the input-output models are well suited to handle demand policies that are designed to shift demand curves for goods and services; they are totally inadequate to handle supply policies that operate through tax costs or other business costs, or through subsidies to new business or public capital. On the other hand, econometric models, unlike input-output models, do not have explicit final demand components (consumption, investment, exports, government purchases, and so on) and for that reason are often hard to use in particular applications. Often the effect of a change in demand for the products of a particular industry, for example, must be accomplished by a constant-term adjustment; the constant term of the industry's output (or employment) equation is shifted by some constant that must be determined in advance by the analyst. The shift cannot simply be the amount of consumer or government expenditure on the products of the industry, because we must allow for imports from other regions and also for indirect demands. It is often not clear just how authors made the adjustments when they report simulations.

There are surprisingly few policy handles for analyzing investment. This is especially true for the effects of investment as they operate through the existence of capital stock. (Present models handle much better the demand effects of construction.) Yet now regional analysts and policymakers are especially interested in policies that will alter the regional allocation of investment (and they do not confine their interests to construction employment). They are also interested in the effects of more—or better—capital stock in particular industries, in transportation, and in the public sector—effects on business costs, access to markets, the quality of public services, and the quality of the environment.

This leads us to the seventh conclusion, which is that investment and capital stock are not well modeled in the current generation of models, a problem independent of whether we are interested in policy analysis or not. Investment and the supply effects of capital stock are inadequately specified even in models that are otherwise complicated and sophisticated. In some cases, investment is totally exogenous, and a policy analyst must do a lot of preliminary work to specify the regional distribution of the investment caused by a policy; he must do on his own much of what he wants the model to do. In other cases, investment is only implicit in equations that link a region's share of output in an industry to some national and regional variables according to a lagged adjustment process. The existence of capital stock and capacity are not often explicitly recognized, nor is the utilization of capacity. Indeed, I would say that it is in the treatment of investment that regional models fall most short of national models.[7]

Poor data? Of course. They are poor or nonexistent on the realized rate of return on capital in a region (even on price-cost margins), on factors determining the expected rate of return on new capital, and on the quantity, age, and quality of the existing capital stock. But data quality is not wholly exogenous in the metamodel that describes model-building itself. Why has the quality of data lagged? Partly because the data are inherently difficult to collect, verify, and manage, but also because two intellectual approaches have dominated regional economics. One is Keynesian demand or export-base modeling, in which the investment process has always been implicit rather than explicit. The base is linked directly to national variables; the local sector is linked directly to the base. If the base expands or contracts, in time the local sector will follow. Something must be happening to investment and capital stock in the process—capital is being added or it is wearing out and not being replaced—but our models have not been explicit about what happens and how fast it happens and how both these factors affect the new equilibrium. A naive observer would not know capital exists, nor would the naive observer of many of today's multiregional models (modern single-region models are usually better). But the problems of regional stagnation or decline and the debate on reindustrialization suggest that what served reasonably well in single-region models in the past does not suffice for multiregional models now.

The other intellectual tradition I refer to is input-output, in which investment is there, but exogenous. It implies that there is some other model(s) that can be brought into play, and also that what happens to investment is independent of what the input-output models says is happening in the regions. In practice, the user of input-output has assumed that what happened to investment was nothing—he held it constant, even while he changed many other variables and intricately traced out their effects.

This, however, leads me to the next conclusion. Despite their shortcomings, input-output models do have an advantage in distinguishing between direct, indirect, and induced demands. The distinction is important, because the vulnerability of a region to shifts in demand (for example, owing to defense or foreign-trade developments) depends not only on the total amount of employment involved, but also on whether the region is dependent in a direct, indirect, or induced sense (I discuss this in detail in Bolton, 1979).

It should be possible to retain these advantages of the input-output model while combining it with other approaches to mitigate or eliminate its gravest defects. There is already some experience with this, in single-region models and in multiregional-model designs (Bourque, Conway, and Howard, 1977; Treyz, and others, 1980, Treyz, 1980; Social Welfare Research Institute, 1981), and in one recently completed multiregional system (Treyz, Stevens, and Ehrlich, 1979, not covered in the Chinitz-Bolton review). It is also used in some national macro-models (Almon, 1974; Jorgensen, 1976). The advantages of the integration of input-output with other models are why I think the Boston College–MIT effort I described earlier is so important.

Finally, a conclusion on the empirical aspects is in order. Given our present regional data bases, there is a trade-off between data quality and small-region detail. The Harris model, for example, shows this; it offers incredible detail, but it is so complex and rests on such questionable data bases that some might reject the chance to obtain the detail. Nevertheless, it is widely used and Harris is now at work to improve the empirical base (Harris, 1980). I have already

referred to data problems on investment and capital and migration and population. Even for regions as big as states, industry outputs are not available except for economic census years; intercensal years must be estimated by the
Kendrick-Jaycox method which assumes that output moves proportionally to
some other variable (such as total wages and salaries) which is measured on an
annual basis.[8] A serious empirical problem is that long time series are not
available for small regions, so we must base empirical relationships on a cross-
section or on a very few cross-sections pooled together. As is well known, this
presents problems when we estimate true elasticities and the parameters of
dynamic adjustment processes (see further discussion of this in Bolton, 1980a,
and literature cited there).

The Research Frontier

At the time Chinitz and I did our review, Wharton Econometric Forecasting
Associates were constructing a new model, funded by the Electric Power Research Institute (see Adams and others, 1977; Fromm and others, 1980). However,
work has been suspended. The design was noteworthy because it was another
hybrid bottom-up model; if completed, it would have been the only one besides
NRIES. The Wharton group generally has been noted for its enthusiasm for
bottom-up. One early design was for a highly simultaneous model, with perhaps
twenty regions (states or groupings of states) and nine industrial sectors. Relative
costs were to be important in labor demand and in migration and labor-supply
equations.

The group had been planned to use the Wharton Annual and Industrial
Model to provide control totals for some national variables, but to use bottom-
up principles for others. The experience of blending an existing (and widely
used) off-the-shelf national macromodel with regional models, on hybrid principles, would have been extremely valuable. Ballard, for example, did not
proceed in this fashion in constructing NRIES, but built all the national equations from scratch. Just how do we blend an existing national model with
regional models in a hybrid product? No one knows, and I anticipate that
considerable experience will be needed before anyone does.

Treyz, Stevens, and Ehrlich (1979) have recently completed a multiregional
model for states, using generally the same principles in the state models as used
in the Treyz single-region model for Massachusetts (Treyz and others, 1980). It
is a purely top-down model, with no simultaneity; each state is assumed to have
the same identical Cobb Douglas production function for capital and labor and
the same input-output coefficients for materials and energy, but a different
import function estimated from transportation data. The group has not yet
reported realistic policy analyses, but a noteworthy feature is that the model will
be generally available to the public at extremely low cost through the National

Cooperative Highway Research Program (National Academy of Sciences), which funded the model.

Finally, Treyz has proposed a new design for a multiregional model, which combines some features of his single-region model for Massachusetts with very interesting and innovative suggestions for the labor-market module (Treyz, 1980). So far his design has not been implemented, but I recommend it highly. Treyz makes little distinction between local and export industries; he uses a common production and transportation-cost framework for all industries, and relies on duality and optimal behavior by firms. He uses a very neoclassical approach. A region's relative production cost matters in terms of how much of its own market it provides from its own production, as opposed to imports; no region has a completely sheltered market in any industry. The wage rate and unemployment rate help balance the labor market, as in most other models, but Treyz's complex formulation relies on some concepts not yet found in other models, such as labor-force surplus or deficit and the number of available trained workers. He also suggests separate functions for migration between every pair of states, a major departure, and he notes that the Continuous Work History Sample of the Social Security Administration could be relied on for estimates of migration functions. Treyz also calls for construction of some national variables on the bottom-up basis. Finally, his proposed design is good in terms of effects *on* the public sector and effects *of* it. Regional government spending is a function of income and demographic variables, employment conditions, and federal aid. Tax rates are automatically set at a level sufficient to raise the required revenue, but the tax structure (degree of reliance on different kinds of taxes) is an exogenous policy handle, and it affects production and living costs in the region relative to the nation. This feature of the public sector helps meet some of the criteria I mentioned earlier.

What of the Future?

First, there should be continued development of the hybrid bottom-up principle. As I see it, a major task will be the successful blending of existing national macromodels with regional models in a hybrid system. There will be some false starts and considerable experimentation in the cooperation between experts in national macromodeling and regional modeling. We will have to go beyond tinkering with national models. By now, a number of research groups have substantial experience in both kinds of models, so it is possible there will be competing proposals.

Second, much needs to be done on investment and capital. This work must be closely integrated with the development of hybrid models, because it is not yet clear how and to what degree bottom-up principles should be used in specifying investment.

Third, there should be more integration of input-output with econometric models, which would allow the advantages of both approaches to be maintained. The key to integration will presumably be to use econometric models to predict investment and other final demands and labor-market adjustments, and input-output to predict the indirect demand shifts. It is important to allow technical and trade coefficients to change gradually over time in response to technological change and maybe (ideally) to factor prices. It is crucial to make investment endogenous. Saying all that does not accomplish the needed integration, and again we will need to experiment.

Fourth, there may be more explicit modeling of transportation. In this connection, I refer the reader to an interesting recent paper by Boyce and Hewings (1980), who suggest a new approach to combined input-output and transportation and commodity-flow modeling. They suggest avoiding the extremes of least-cost optimum models, which allow no cross-hauling, and suggest positing some amount of cross-hauling in the system, and indeed having some amount of cross-hauling as a constraint on the location of new production capacity and the movement of goods. The amount of cross-hauling would be represented by Wilson's entropy measure (1970). The idea is that some amount of cross-hauling is necessary because, first, commodity production and flow data are very aggregate, and second, there is indeed some inefficient spatial allocation in the real world. When combined with input-output, this approach to transportation takes the input-output relations as additional constraints in production and transportation allocation. Unfortunately, if for various reasons we use states as the regions, very fine-drawn transportation specifications may not make much sense. It is hard to think of modeling transportation between California and Texas as point-to-point movement!

Finally, one aspect of the frontier is the organization of research teams. I have commented on the interesting biases and unevenness found in present models, and also on the need for regional and national modelers to work more closely together. The next really successful multiregional model will probably be put together by a larger group of people than before, a team of experts from many different areas—national models, regional input-output, investment, public finance, transportation, energy, demography, and microsimulation data—in addition to regional economists.

One intriguing system, which has just begun to be discussed, is the concept of specialized interchangeable modules.[9] The whole system would consist of several different modules: a national model, an input-out module for output determination, an optimal-factor-demand module to determine labor demand and investment, a population-migration-labor-supply module, and a transportation module. The team would have to integrate the modules and resolve contradictions among them, most notably in a module on the labor market. There would need to be rules to resolve differences between initial national variables from a national model and the regional sums or averages. Resolution of the differences among modules might have to be on an iterative basis.

Each module would be built by recognized experts in their respective fields. Furthermore, the whole system might conceivably be designed so that different experts' modules are interchangeable. For example, expert x and expert y might both build a labor-supply module. Expert x's might be better for some purposes (short-term cyclical analysis); y's better for other purposes (long-term growth analysis); x's might be more disaggregated; x's might have policy handles different from y's; and so on. One input-output module might be used for some analyses (for example, short-term energy forecasts), another for other analyses (long-term technical changes). As another example, several different national models might be interchanged in the system.

Such a grand system would tax coordination resources to the limit, and it would be extremely expensive. But it would offer advantages, and the marginal cost would be reduced somewhat if the various modules had independent lives of their own, rather than being limited to inclusion with others in the multiregional-model system. Whether it would be manageable, or if so, worth the cost, we cannot know now.

Notes

1. See Honea, Vogt, and Hillsman (1979), cited by Lakshmanan and Roy (1980). The ongoing major study of the High Plains region in the United States is partly motivated by the sensitivity of total U.S. production of some agricultural commodities to developments in this relatively small region.

2. Figure 7-2 combines ideas from Courbis (1980) and Ballard and others (1980a). The names of the three kinds of national variables are from the latter source.

3. This section rests heavily on Bolton (1980c).

4. Specifications of this proprietary model are not generally available to the public. Our review was based on material made available by Chase personnel and on their briefings.

5. Harris is an exception, but many object to Harris's particular specification of the linear-programming transportation submodel. See Fjeldsted and South (1979) and Harris's reply (1979).

6. One aspect of transportation cost, the truck travel time between population centers, is used in MULTIREGION to define the market potential for an industry in a region. This was done in order to capture the effects of the improved interstate-highway system on industrial location and migration during the 1950s and 1960s (Olsen and others, 1977). However, no other aspect of transportation cost is explicitly modeled.

7. Harris does model investment explicitly, but not capital stock. He enters lagged investment into location and employment equations to proxy for capital stock.

8. The NRIES model used some newly prepared time-series estimates of annual output by state, constructed to estimate these regression equations; the BEA has not yet released the series.

9. Walter Isard and others, including myself, discussed this possibility at the June 1980 meeting of the Conference on Multiregion Models at the First World Regional Science Congress in Cambridge, Massachusetts, and at the November 1980 meeting of the Regional Science Association in Milwaukee, Wisconsin.

References

Adams, F. Gerard, and Glickman, Norman, eds. *Modeling the Multiregional System.* Lexington, Mass.: Lexington Books, D.C. Heath and Company, 1980.

Adams, F. Gerard; Hill, John; and McCarthy, Michael. "A National-Multiregional Economic Model for Forecasting Electricity Consumption and Peak Load: A Proposal." Wharton Econometric Forecasting Associates, Philadelphia, 1977 (submitted to the Electric Power Research Institute).

Almon, Clopper, Jr.; Buckler, Margaret B.; Horowitz, Lawrence M.; and Reimbold, Thomas C. *1985: Interindustry Forecasts of the American Economy.* Lexington, Mass.: Lexington Books, D.C. Heath and Company, 1974.

Ballard, Kenneth; Glickman, Norman; and Wendling, Robert. "Using a Multiregional Econometric Model to Measure the Spatial Impacts of Federal Policies." In *The Impact of Federal Policies on Urban Areas.* edited by Norman Glickman. Baltimore, Md.: Johns Hopkins University Press, 1979.

Ballard, Kenneth; Gustely, Richard; and Wendling, Robert. *NRIES: Structure, Performance, and Application of a Bottom-Up Interregional Econometric Model.* Washington, D.C.: Bureau of Economic Analysis, U.S. Dept. of Commerce, 1980 (1980a).

Ballard, Kenneth, and Gustely, Richard. "NRIES: A Bottom-Up Multiregion Model of the United States Economy." Presented at NSF conference on An Assessment of the State of the Art in Regional Modeling. Harvard/MIT Joint Center for Urban Studies, Cambridge, Mass., 1980 (1980b).

Ballard, Kenneth, and Wendling, Robert. "The National-Regional Impact Evaluation System: A Spatial Model of U.S. Economic and Demographic Activity." *Journal of Regional Science* 20:2(1980): 143–158 (1980c).

Ballard, Kenneth, and Glickman, Norman; and Gustely, Richard. "A Bottom-Up Approach to Multiregional Modeling: NRIES." In Adams and Glickman, *Modeling the Multiregional* (1980d).

Bolton, Roger. "Defense Spending: Burden or Prop?" In *Defense and Disarmament,* edited by Bolton, pp. 1–53. Englewood Cliffs, N.J.: Prentice-Hall.

———. "Defense Spending and Policies for Labor-Surplus Areas." In *Essays in Regional Economics,* edited by J. Kain and J. Meyer, pp. 137–160. Cambridge, Mass.: Harvard University Press, 1971.

_____ . "The Political Economy of Defense Manpower Policy No. 4." Department of Economics, Williams College. Unpublished paper, 1977.

_____ . "The Impact of National Defense Spending in Urban Areas." In *The Impact of Federal Policies on Urban Areas,* edited by Norman Glickman. Baltimore: Johns Hopkins University Press, 1979.

_____ . "Multiregional Models in Policy Analysis: A Survey." Research Paper 30, Dept. of Economics, Williams College, Williamstown, Mass., 1980a.

_____ ' "Multiregional Models: Introduction to a Symposium." *Journal of Regional Science* 20:2(1980b): 131-142.

_____ . "Multiregional Models in Policy Analysis." In Adams and Glickman, *Modeling the Multiregional,* pp. 255-284 (1980c).

_____ . "The Public Sector in Regional Models." Extended comments presented at NSF conference on An Assessment of the State of the Art in Regional Modeling. Harvard/MIT Joint Center for Urban Studies, Cambridge, Mass., 1980d.

Bolton, Roger, and Chinitz, Benjamin. "Multiregional Modeling." Presented at meeting of American Economic Association, Denver, Colorado, 1978.

Bourque, Philip; Conway, Richard; and Howard, Charles. *The Washington Projection and Simulation Model.* Seattle: Graduate School of Business, University of Washington, 1977.

Boyce, David, and Hewings, Geoffrey. "Interregional Commodity Flow, Input-Output and Transportation Modelling: An Entropy Formulation." Paper read at Conference on Multiregion Models, First World Regional Science Congress, Cambridge, Mass., 1980.

Bureau of Economic Analysis, U.S. Dept. of Commerce. *Area Projections to 1990,* Washington: U.S. Government Printing Office, 1974.

_____ . "Regional and State Projections of Income, Employment, and Population to the Year 2000." *Survey of Current Business* 60:11(1980): 44-70.

Chinitz, Benjamin, and Bolton, Roger. "Multiregional Models in Policy Analysis." Unpublished paper, 1978.

Chinitz, Benjamin. "Appropriate Goals for Regional Economic Policy." *Urban Studies* 3:1(1966): 1-7.

Courbis, Raymond. "The REGINA Model: A Regional-National Model for French Planning." *Regional Science and Urban Economics* 9(1979): 117-139 (1979a).

_____ . "The REGINA Model: Presentation and First Contributions to Economic Policy." In *Econometric Contributions to Public Policy,* edited by Richard Stone and William Peterson, pp. 291-311. New York: St. Martin's Press, 1979 (1979b).

_____ . "Multiregional Modeling and the Interaction between Regional and National Development: A General Theoretical Framework." In Adams and Glickman, *Modeling the Multiregional,* pp. 107-130.

Crow, Robert. "Output Determination and Investment Specification in Macro-economic Models of Open Regions." *Regional Science and Urban Economics* 9:2/3 (1979).

Dresch, Stephen, and Goldberg, Robert. "IDIOM: An Inter-Industry, National-Regional Policy Evaluation Model." *Annals of Economic and Social Measurement,* July 1973.

Dresch, Stephen, and Updegrove, Daniel. "IDIOM: A Disaggregated Policy-Impact Model of the U.S. Economy." Institute for Demographic and Social Studies, New Haven, Connecticut, 1978. Mimeographed.

Golladay, Frederick, and Haveman, Robert. *The Economic Impacts of Tax-Transfer Policy: Regional and Distributional Effects.* New York: Academic Press, 1977.

Harris, Curtis. *The Urban Economies 1985.* Lexington, Mass.: Lexington Books, D.C. Heath and Company, 1973.

_____. *Regional Economic Effects of Alternative Highway Systems.* Cambridge, Mass.: Ballinger, 1974.

_____. "Reply." *Journal of Regional Science* 19:4(1979): 493–500.

_____. "New Developments and Extensions of the Multiregional Multi-Industry Forecasting Model." *Journal of Regional Science* 20:2(1980): 159–172.

Harris, Curtis, and Hopkins, Frank. *Locational Analysis.* Lexington, Mass.: Lexington Books, D.C. Heath and Company, 1972.

Haveman, Robert, and Krutilla, John. *Unemployment, Idle Capacity, and the Evaluation of Public Expenditures.* Baltimore, Md.: Johns Hopkins University Press, 1968.

Honea, R.; Vogt, David; and Hillsman, D. "A Framework for Identifying Regional Constraints to National Energy Planning." Paper read at Regional Science Association meeting, Los Angeles, 1979.

Jorgensen, Dale, ed. *Econometric Studies of U.S. Energy Policy.* Amsterdam: North-Holland, 1976.

Kresge, David, and Seiver, Daniel. "The MAP [Man in the Artic Program] Model: An Economic/Demographic Model of Alaska." Presented at NSF conference on An Assessment of the State of the Art in Regional Modeling." Harvard/MIT Joint Center for Urban Studies, Cambridge, Mass., 1980.

Lakshmanan, T.R. "A Multiregional Multi-Industry Policy Model." Paper read at the Northeast Regional Science Meetings, Amherst, Mass., 1979.

Lakshmanan, T.R., and Roy, Probir. "Relationships between National and Regional Economic Models: Alternative Perspectives." Unpublished paper, 1980.

Lakshmanan, T.R. et al. "Factor Demand and Substitution Models in a Multiregional Framework." Paper read at Conference on Multiregion Models, First World Regional Science Congress, Cambridge, Mass., 1980.

Leontief, Wassily et al. *Studies in the Structure of the American Economy.* New York: Oxford University Press, 1953.

Leontief, Wassily et al. "The Economic Impact—Industrial and Regional—of an Arms Cut." *Review of Economics and Statistics* 47 (August 1965): 217–241.

Olsen, Richard et al. *MULTIREGION: A Simulation-Forecasting Model of BEA Economic Area Population and Employment.* Oak Ridge National Laboratory, Oak Ridge, Tenn. (NTIS ORNL/RUS-25), 1977.

Olsen, Richard, and Allaman, Peter. "Comments on the Design and Implementation of Multiregional Models." Paper read at the Regional Science Association meetings, Chicago, 1978.

Olsen, Richard. Paper read at NSF conference on An Assessment of the State of the Art in Regional Modeling." Harvard/MIT Joint Center for Urban Studies, Cambridge, Mass., 1980.

Polenske, Karen. *The U.S. Multiregional Input-Output Accounts and Model.* Lexington, Mass.: Lexington Books, D.C. Heath and Company, 1980.

Richardson, Harry. *Regional Growth Theory.* London: Macmillan, 1973.

Social Welfare Research Institute, Boston College, MIT Multiregional Planning Staff, and Sistemas, Inc. "MRPIS [Multi-Regional Policy Impact System]: A Research Strategy." author, Boston, Mass., 1981.

Treyz, George. "Design of a Multiregional Policy Analysis Model." *Journal of Regional Science* 20:2(1980): 191–206.

Treyz, George et al. "An Overview of the Massachusetts Economic Policy Analysis (MEPA) Model." Paper read at the NSF conference on An Assessment of the State of the Art in Regional Modeling. Harvard/MIT Joint Center for Urban Studies, Cambridge, Mass., 1980.

Treyz, George; Stevens, Benjamin; and Ehrlich, David. "An Eclectic Core Model for State Policy Analysis and Forecasting." *Handbook 3, Regional Economic Analysis for Transportation and Planning.* National Cooperative Highway Research Program, National Academy of Sciences, Washington (preliminary version, 1979; revised version forthcoming).

Wilson, A.G. *Entropy in Urban and Regional Modeling.* London: Pion, 1970.

Index

Index

About the Contributors

Roger Bolton, at the time the chapter was written, was chairman of the Economics Department at Williams College. During the 1981–1982 academic year, he will be a visiting professor in the Economics and City and the Regional Planning Departments at the University of Pennsylvania. He has also taught at Harvard and Wellesley. Dr. Bolton has written widely in the areas of regional economics, multiregional modeling, and the regional economic impacts of federal defense expenditures.

Miles Friedman is executive director of the National Association of State Development Agencies. He was director of legislation and policy with the National Council for Urban Economic Development from 1977 to 1980 and, prior to 1977, he taught courses in state and local government at George Washington University. He has published numerous articles on economic development, urban policy, state and local government, business incentives, and public-private partnerships in local economic development.

Harvey A. Garn was director of the Urban Economic Development Program of the Urban Institute from 1968 to 1980. He left to become project director of a team developing an urban policy for Egypt. Prior to joining the institute, Mr. Garn directed the Office of Program Analysis and Economic Research at the Economic Development Administration, U.S. Department of Commerce.

Cynthia A. Kroll is a regional planner with the Association of Bay Area Governments (the Council of Governments for the nine counties of the San Francisco Bay region). From 1974 through 1980, Ms. Kroll worked at SRI International (formerly Stanford Research Institute) on varied aspects of natural-resource use and energy development in the western United States. She has also taught courses in city and regional planning at the University of California at Berkeley, where she received a masters of City Planning and is completing her doctorate.

Larry C. Ledebur is director of the Economic Development Program at the Urban Institute. Prior to joining the institute in 1978, he served as senior economist and associate director of research for the White House Conference on Balanced National Growth and Economic Development. From 1975 to 1977, Dr. Ledebur was a visiting scholar and senior research economist in the Office of Economic Research of the Economic Development Administration, U.S. Department of Commerce.

Harry W. Richardson is professor of economics at the State University of New York at Albany. He is the author of seventeen books and numerous papers, mainly in regional and urban economics. He has worked in more than a dozen developing countries in Asia, Latin America, and Africa for agencies such as the World Bank, the United Nations, and AID.

About the Editors

Michael E. Bell is a senior economist on the Economic Policy Staff in the U.S. Department of Commerce. Prior to joining the Department of Commerce in 1978, Dr. Bell served as senior economist for the Subcommittee on the City, Committee on Banking, Finance and Urban Affairs, U.S. House of Representatives; as senior economist for the District of Columbia Tax Revision Commission; and as research associate in the Taxation Section of the Advisory Commission on Intergovernmental Relations. He received the Ph.D. in economics from the State University of New York at Albany. A member of the American Economic Association and the National Tax Association, Dr. Bell is the author of a number of articles and books on a variety of state and local public finance, intergovernmental, and urban/regional issues.

Paul S. Lande is the director of the Construction Information Service, Data Resources, Inc. Dr. Lande directs work at DRI having to do with the modeling and analysis of construction activity. He came to DRI from the Economic Development Administration in the U.S. Department of Commerce. Dr. Lande received the Ph.D. in economics from the University of Southern California and has taught urban and regional economics at Ohio State University. A member of the American Economic Association and the Regional Science Association, he is the author of several publications on urban and regional economic activity.